Making
the
American
Religious
Fringe

Exotics,
Subversives,
and
Journalists,
1955–1993

Sean McCloud

Making the American Religious Fringe

THE UNIVERSITY OF

NORTH CAROLINA PRESS

Chapel Hill & London

© 2004
The University of North Carolina Press
All rights reserved
Set in Cycles
by Tseng Information Systems, Inc.
Manufactured in the
United States of America
The paper in this book meets the
guidelines for permanence and durability
of the Committee on Production Guidelines
for Book Longevity of the Council on
Library Resources.

Library of Congress
Cataloging-in-Publication Data
McCloud, Sean.
Making the American religious fringe: exotics,
subversives, and journalists, 1955–1993 / Sean
McCloud.
   p. cm.
Includes bibliographical references and index.
ISBN 0-8078-2829-7 (cloth: alk. paper)—
ISBN 0-8078-5496-4 (pbk.: alk. paper)
1. Mass media in religion—United States—
History. 2. United States—Church history—
20th century. I. Title.
BV652.97 .U6 M33   2004
070.4'492—dc22   2003016079

cloth   08 07 06 05 04   5 4 3 2 1
paper   08 07 06 05 04   5 4 3 2 1

CONTENTS

ILLUSTRATIONS

ACKNOWLEDGMENTS

I am indebted to many and pleased to acknowledge them here. First, I wish to thank Tom Tweed. As my dissertation adviser in the Religious Studies Program at the University of North Carolina at Chapel Hill, he read and helped improve many early versions of this work. But even more, Tom is my mentor, best critic, and supporter. My debt to him extends far beyond the confines of this work. I also thank my wife, Lynn Abbott-McCloud. I was the first in my family to attend college, and it was Lynn's unwavering belief in me that led to the completion of my undergraduate degree and entrance into graduate school. Simply put, without her love and support this book wouldn't exist. I also thank Peter Williams. As my master's thesis adviser and mentor in Miami University of Ohio's Comparative Religion Program, Peter set me on an academic course that prepared me well for UNC's Ph.D. program. I cherish the relationships I've had—and continue to have—with these three compassionate, intelligent, and inspiring individuals.

I want to thank the many people who read, commented on, and thus helped shape this work. In addition to Tom Tweed, David Bromley, Glenn Hinson, Laurie Maffly-Kipp, and Christian Smith served on my dissertation committee. They all asked great questions and offered useful suggestions. To have a dissertation committee of probing critics who are also kind and supportive may sound unrealistic, but it was my lucky fortune. My dissertation writing group at UNC, Thomas Pearson and Todd Butler, read and helpfully commented on multiple drafts. Diane Winston and Mark Silk served as good critical readers for my manuscript. Comments and questions from conference participants at SSSR, AAR, and Duke-Carolina Colloquium meetings proved useful, as did the lively student discussion about sections of Chapter 5 in my spring 2001 Religion and Popular Culture Seminar at the College of Charleston.

There are other individuals and institutions who deserve thanks. Elaine Maisner, my editor at UNC Press, has been incredibly supportive of this work, and I can't praise her enough. I also thank the University of North Carolina Department of Religious Studies for a Perry Family Summer Research Grant. I greatly appreciate all the work the reference librarians at UNC's Davis Library put in to get me a plethora of magazine articles. I also thank Joan Abbott for her positive words and encouragement—not to mention chess games.

Last, but definitely not least, I thank my daughter Sinéad Arianna Abbott-McCloud. Born in the same year I began writing this, Sinéad changed my life dramatically and positively. This book is dedicated to her.

Making
the
American
Religious
Fringe

Cults and fringe groups are everywhere—at least in the mass media. In a 1998 episode of *The Simpsons*, Homer, that animated working-class everyman, is brainwashed into joining a group called the "movementarians." His wife, Marge, escapes the cult's heavily guarded compound and arranges for Homer's kidnapping and successful deprogramming—he renounces his new faith for a glass of beer. In the same year an episode of *Justice Files* on the Discovery Channel featured "criminal cults." In *Maclean's* you can read about "killer cults." Or if you prefer cyberspace, you can visit an unrelated internet website with the same name. For those more geographically inclined, one edition of *Newsweek* in the late 1990s offered a map of the United States marked with groups "Living on the Religious Fringe." The *New Yorker* in April 1997 contained a back-page humor piece titled "This Just In from Our Cult Desk." Written by Christopher Buckley, it consists of seven fictitious news stories, including the following two:

INAGADDADAVIDA, Calif.—Over half the forty-eight members of the 2000 Club millennial cult who committed suicide last week by eating live gila monsters and washing them down with peach schnapps had already had their brains surgically removed, according to the Belvedere County Medical Examiner.

"It's a fairly rare procedure," he said, "but these folks seemed to know what they were doing."

WAWAII, Hawaii—The religious cult leader who urged his eighty-four followers to leap into an active volcano told authorities that he had been planning to jump in himself but remembered at the last minute that he had forgotten to pick up his dry cleaning.

Frederick Lugoff, sixty-four, known as Frodo to members of his New Vesuvians cult, was apprehended by park rangers who became suspicious after they saw dozens of people wrapped in tin-foil holding their noses and jumping into the crater. The group believed in purification by immersion in molten lava. Lugoff's lawyer said his client had been depressed recently at not being able to attract new members.[1]

Buckley's piece was published less than a month after thirty-nine people in the Heaven's Gate commune committed group suicide. In March 1997, Marshall Appelwhite and his small following became convinced that the Hale-Bopp comet's appearance signaled their time to leave the physical, earthly plane of existence. On 26 March, the group jointly "exited" their bodies, using a mixture of phenobarbital, alcohol, and plastic bags over their heads.

That the *New Yorker* could extract humor from the tragedy speaks volumes about how many journalists—and their readers—view groups that they label "fringe." In the last thirty years the word "cult," today's most common term for religious groups categorized as marginal, has lost any original sociological meaning and now conjures images of brainwashing, coercion, deception, exploitation, perversion, and fraud.[2] For many Americans, these associations are so much taken for granted that they have become doxa: socially constructed opinions, assumptions, and inclinations so ingrained they seem natural, permanent, and fixed. Unlike many interpreters of groups labeled fringe, my interest is not to attack or defend certain movements. To deny that cruel acts have been committed by some in religious groups is as shortsighted as claiming that all members of new religious movements commit atrocities. Instead, I want to examine how the contemporary negative connotations of *cult, fringe, sect,* and other such terms became accepted and applied to such a wide range of groups in the mass media. In other words, this book is not about fringe religions, but about the characteristics that many of the largest and most influential magazines attributed to groups that they labeled fringe. I trace mid- to late-twentieth-century reporting on the fringe in one form of American journalism: the magazine. And I consider a range of questions. How have magazine depictions of religious center and periphery changed since the 1950s? What specific motifs did journalists use to portray groups that they viewed as marginal and mainstream? And ultimately, why might magazine writers and editors consistently have represented the fringe in certain ways?

Argument One: From Mass Movements, Exoticism, and Subversion to Individuals, Brainwashing, and Coercion

In this book I offer two theses. The first is historical, answering what happened by attending to questions of change and continuity over time. Using a case study approach, I argue that print media depictions of the American religious fringe in the largest national magazines changed significantly from 1950s to the early 1990s. In the Cold War years, the most prominent fringe portrayals focused on working-class white and African American groups, as well as certain religions prominent in California. Periodicals like *Time*, *Newsweek*, *U.S. News and World Report*, the *Saturday Evening Post*, *Life*, and *Look* reported on the "California cults," the "Third Force in Christendom," and the Nation of Islam by using themes of mass movements, exoticism, and subversion. Significantly, and in contrast to the Cold War style of American religion reporting, members of fringe religions were seldom portrayed individually, but instead namelessly grouped as indistinguishable, often fanatical "true believers" in mass movements. Promoting a broad American cultural consensus that stood apart from "godless" communism, news and general-interest magazines occasionally portrayed marginalized religious groups as having those characteristics least suitable for sustaining representative democratic capitalism. In short, sometimes the fringe was un-American.

In the late 1960s and early 1970s, subjects and themes changed. Cold War consensus ideology yielded to a growing recognition of cultural diversity spurred by the civil rights and youth counter-culture movements. At the same time, magazine coverage ambivalently framed the gurus, Asian new religions, occult spirituality, and Evangelical Jesus movements that attracted white middle- and upper-middle-class youth. Eventually, coverage would also feature the grievances of a growing "anticult movement" made up of parents who wanted to remove their adult children from these groups. By the mid-1970s, journalistic images of the fringe had darkened. Magazines like *Newsweek, McCall's,* and *Reader's Digest* promoted an image of a growing cult menace by highlighting the dangers that dictatorial leaders of fringe groups posed to the unsuspecting "mainstream" through brainwashing and coercion. The mass suicide in Jonestown in 1978 seemed to confirm the negative stereotypes and led to homogeneous portrayals in a variety of magazines. By 1993 this "cult menace" motif had become so thoroughly inscribed in many magazine narratives that it dominated news stories about the fifty-one-day standoff in Waco between the Branch Davidians and the Bureau of Alcohol, Tobacco and Firearms (ATF).

Despite these changes over time, at least two continuities existed. First, throughout the thirty-nine-year period of study, the largest news and general-interest magazines consistently described groups and individuals as "fringe" if they demonstrated high levels of religious zeal, dogma, and emotion. Labeling certain religious practices and beliefs marginal, writers and editors in the largest news and general-interest magazines broached longstanding debates in American religious history about emotional versus rational religion, exotic versus familiar spirituality, and normal versus abnormal levels of piety.[3] Journalists acted as "heresiographers," identifying false or inauthentic religion and thus symbolically establishing boundaries between a mainstream religious center and a suspect periphery.[4]

The second continuity involves the power of images and words to uphold or subvert social hierarchies. I argue that the largest news and general-interest magazines often labeled religious groups mainstream or fringe in ways that symbolically reproduced and legitimized inequalities of race and class in postwar America. Relegating certain groups, activities, and beliefs to the religious margins, journalists concomitantly banished certain classes and racial groups to America's social periphery. In other words, writers and editors in periodicals like *Time, Newsweek,* and *Life* frequently offered, under the guise of objective reporting, a spiritual apologetics for the dominant social order. Overall, and in several ways, magazines like *Time, Newsweek, Life, U.S. News and World Report, Esquire, Reader's Digest,* and the *Saturday Evening Post* assumed a normative American mainstream that was white, upper middle and middle class, male, and religiously liberal or nonaffiliated. In presupposing this, they sometimes distinguished religious fringe from mainstream by class and race as much as by theology or the size of a movement. Perhaps unsurprisingly, these periodicals generalized and normalized the perspectives and concerns of the very groups from which surveys tell us the vast majority of their journalists and readers came.[5]

But journalists did not always speak with one voice. The national print media is best viewed as an arena of symbolic production where magazines categorize groups as mainstream or marginal, orthodox or heterodox, religious or nonreligious in ways that accord with the social locations of their producers. The American religious fringe is a constructed and contested category that is constantly in flux, reflecting certain interests, concerns, and power positions. For example, magazines that placed theological considerations before economic, political, or racial ones—like *Christianity Today*, written by and for conservative Evangelicals, or *America*, a Jesuit periodical—sometimes offered categorizations of mainstream and fringe that questioned the overwhelmingly homogeneous portrayals found in *U.S. News and World Report*, *Time*, *Life*, *Newsweek*, *Reader's Digest*, and *Esquire*. Likewise, magazines geared toward African Americans, like *Jet*, held different assumptions and concerns and thus depicted the Nation of Islam very differently from *U.S. News and World Report* or *Time*. In addition, small religious groups like the International Society of Krishna Consciousness (also known as Hare Krishnas) and the Nation of Islam published their own periodicals and pamphlets. These also offered alternatives to the dominant fringe representations. Like the black newspapers in the communications scholar Ronald Jacobs's study of urban unrest coverage, these media sites—created by groups labeled fringe—offered "a place for counteracting the effects of (in this case representational) hegemony, by constructing alternative narratives" about themselves and the so-called mainstream religions.[6] At the same time, however, I will demonstrate that many alternative representations failed to challenge the broader categories and characterizations that the largest magazines had established. Often, rather than question the mainstream and marginal categories themselves, journalists writing "from the fringe" strove only to improve or reverse their religious, racial, or economic group's status within the existent classifications.

Argument Two: Societal Change, Identity Construction, and the Journalistic Habitus

While my first thesis traces what happened to American religious fringe coverage over time, my second addresses the more speculative question of why it took such routes. In other words, why did magazine portrayals of the fringe change over time and why did certain continuities in coverage remain? I propose two complementary explanations, one historical and one sociological. First, I suggest that changes in fringe depictions coincided with larger changes in society, culture, and the magazine industry. Socially, the 1950s to the 1990s saw increasing racial, ethnic, and religious diversity. The United States simultaneously witnessed an ideological move from a Cold War consensus culture to one in which pluralism and difference became a significant, and widely accepted, part of public discourse. The media scholar A. J. van Zuilen notes that the magazine industry reflected this shift. General-interest magazines like *Life*, *Look*, and the *Saturday Evening Post*, which strove to speak to and for all Americans, either declined or disappeared by the early 1970s. During the same period, special-interest consumer magazines, made to appeal to niche markets divided by race, gender, age, profession, and hobby interests, came to dominate the industry.[7] In the following chapters, I hope to show that American religious fringe coverage reflected these social, cultural, and industry changes in various ways.

My second argument is sociological, and I posit it to partly account for the similarities and differences in coverage over time and across various types of periodicals. I argue that the American religious fringe functioned for journalists as a "negative reference group" in a process of identity construction. Here I am indebted to and influenced by the work of the sociologist Christian Smith, who reminds us of the basic sociological principles that "social groups know who they are in large measure by knowing who they are not," and "almost invariably, social comparison favors the categories that comprise people's own identities"[8] As a negative reference group, the cultic margins helped to define what writers and editors either desired or perceived themselves, their readers, and American culture as a whole to be. Religious fringe groups served this function by acting as, in Smith's words, "models for what they do not believe, what they do not want to become, and how they do not want to act."[9]

This book is not primarily about those who work in magazine production rooms, nor is it about what goes on in those places. It focuses on the articles produced. At the same time, suggesting that fringe depictions were part of a process of identity construction begs the question of *whose* identity was being defined, especially in the largest and most influential periodicals. In other words, who were the agents and what were the processes that created such representations? As noted earlier, the largest news and general-interest magazines promoted differentiations between mainstream and fringe that symbolically reproduced and legitimized power disparities of class and race. Specifically, magazines like *Time*, *Life*, and *Newsweek* constructed categories of center and periphery that favored certain groups over others. At the same time, and especially before the 1970s, these magazines frequently relegated to the margins religious movements that attracted minority and working-class Americans. In doing this, they attributed certain stereotypical characteristics to varied groups. Journalists imagined the religious mainstream as moderate, tolerant, ecumenical, rational, and implicitly white middle class and upper middle class. They usually depicted the American religious fringe as just the opposite—fanatical, bigoted, parochial, emotional, and implicitly ethnic and lower class. These characterizations served to symbolically legitimize social, racial, and class differences as natural and inevitable.

I argue that these depictions can *partly* be explained by examining the socioeconomics, broader demographics, and professional practices of journalists. Behind the continuities in the portrayals there existed a similarity of social locations. Many (but of course not all) of the largest news and general-interest magazine writers and editors shared approximate dispositions, conscious opinions, professional obligations, and unconscious assumptions. They shared, to borrow a term from the social theorist Pierre Bourdieu, a journalistic "habitus."

Bourdieu defines *habitus* as "a system of lasting, transposable dispositions which, integrating past experiences, functions at every moment as a matrix of perceptions, appreciations, and actions."[10] The habitus, similar to Marxist class consciousness, is "the product of history," formed by the "structures constitutive of a particular type of environment (e.g. the material conditions of existence characteristic of a class condition)."[11] But unlike Marx's concept, which implies conscious strategizing, the habitus is mostly doxa, unconscious actions and presuppositions. In other words, and in terms of this study, writers and editors often did not consciously scheme to impute negative characteristics to the American religious fringe and associate it with subordinate classes of people. Rather, as the media scholar Robert Lichter and his colleagues have proposed, it was "not a matter of conscious bias but rather of the necessarily partial perspectives through which social reality is filtered."[12]

There were, of course, exceptions. Some writers, editors, and publishers carried out explicit agendas through their magazines. Henry Luce and Time Inc. provide an excellent example. The son of missionary parents, Luce created *Time*, *Life*, *Fortune*, and the "March of Time" movie newsreels not just to offer audiences abbreviated news, but to promote Luce's views on domestic and international policy. *Time*, founded by Luce and his business partner Briton Hadden in 1921, was designed to be a "magazine devoted to summarizing progress," as well as to reporting the events of the day with a particular point of view.[13] Along with *Life*, founded in 1936, *Time* reflected Luce's politics and beliefs until his death in 1967. Luce's periodicals attacked President Franklin Roosevelt and the New Deal. They promoted American expansionism and decried isolationism. After World War II, they called for a domestic American cultural consensus and international military intervention to help contain communism at home and abroad. In the early 1960s they supported the Vietnam War. While Luce's biographer James Baughman notes that most of the news media backed the Vietnam War at the outset, he argues that *Time* in particular acted "as a virtual extension of the administration," even to the extent of withholding stories that would have revealed how President Lyndon Johnson's administration was lying to the public.[14] "'I am a Protestant, a Republican, and a free enterpriser,'" Baughman quoted Luce in the 1950s. "'I am biased in favor of God, Eisenhower, and the stockholders of Time Inc.—and if anybody who objects doesn't know this by now, why the hell are they still spending 35 cents for the magazine?'"[15]

So undoubtedly, some American religious fringe stories were consciously contrived to promote certain agendas. But many more were not. Instead, writers and editors unwittingly framed stories in ways that reflected their backgrounds, interests, experiences, profession, and worldview—in a word, their habitus. Throughout the period of study, journalists in the largest magazines were overwhelmingly members of gender, racial, educational, and income groups that held the majority of social, political, and cultural power. The media scholar Robert Lichter and his colleagues found that in 1979–80 journalists at the largest national news magazines —as well as in newspaper and television—were 95 percent white, 79 percent male, 68 percent northeastern, and 42 percent urban. Ninety-three percent were college graduates and most (78 percent) reported an individual income over $30,000 in 1979. Fifty-four percent called themselves politically liberal, 17 percent conservative. Interestingly, 50 percent reported having no religion, 20 percent were Protestant, 14 percent Jewish, and 8 1/2 percent Catholic.[16] In a more narrow study of several media institutions, the media scholar Herbert Gans came up with similar demographics (with the exception of religious affiliation—apparently he didn't ask) for the years 1965–69, 1975, and 1978. In terms of content, he concluded that magazines tended "to universalize upper-middle class practices as if they were shared by all Americans."[17] Combined, these studies examine selected journalists from 1965 to 1980. While I have no demographical information for 1955 to 1964, given what we know about the professionalization of magazine journalism after World War II, demographics were likely similar. In terms of gender and race, journalists were likely even less diverse in this earlier period.

Bourdieu suggests that the different categories and classifications used by social groups to organize their worlds tend to symbolically reproduce—in his term, homologize—existent class relations.[18] Bourdieu is a reductionist who asserts that material interests provide the basis of all competing human concerns and classification schemes. For Bourdieu, "classification struggle is a fundamental dimension of class struggle."[19] He argues that "different classes and class fractions are engaged in a specifically symbolic struggle to impose the definitions of the social world most in conformity with their interests . . . The (object at) stake is the monopoly of legitimate symbolic violence—that is to say, the power to impose (and even indeed to inculcate) instruments of knowledge and expression of social reality (taxonomies), which are arbitrary (but unrecognized as such). The field of symbolic production is a microcosm of the struggle between the classes."[20] In terms of my study, this could explain why relatively elite, privileged, white magazine journalists, in constructing insider and outsider identities, would relegate working-class and black groups to the fringe. But Bourdieu's assertion could also problematically imply that class was the only factor determining all journalistic constructions of the American religious fringe.

Class was an important element in fomenting religious fringe representations, particularly in the largest magazines. But it was not the only factor involved. For example, outside the largest periodicals and in Roman Catholic and Evangelical reporting, theology was frequently most significant in determining who was labeled fringe. In this case, the classification strategies of the religious periodical reporter were determined more by religious interests than material ones. Even in the largest newsmagazines like *Time* and *Newsweek*, where class stereotypes were often explicit, other variables such as race, region, and theology sometimes held equal or greater importance in determining what was fringe. And there is no evidence to show that these variables were always influenced by and subordinated to class concerns. California cults coverage in the 1950s and 1960s, for example, lumped wealthy new religions like the Self Realization Fellowship together with relatively working-class denominations like the Four-Square Gospel Church. In this case, the shared geographic location of the movements diminished the significance of any obvious class differences.

In the largest magazines' portrayals of the religious fringe, class was often a primary tool of distinction. But it wasn't the only one. Given this caveat, the notion of a journalistic habitus can still be useful in providing interpretations of religion coverage. One need not fully accept the materialist, reductionist basis of Bourdieuian theory to see that "elective affinities" certainly existed between journalists' social locations and the stories they produced. If one conceives of class as more than a status grounded in material circumstances, but also a category of identity rhetorically and symbolically made and unmade through representation, one sees that it served *some* journalists as a prominent implement, like race, politics, theology, and region, that distinguished between insiders and outsiders in American culture. Further, in analyzing competing (dominant and latent) constructions of mainstream and margins in print media, Bourdieu's theories help to explain how and why different magazines struggled to promote certain conceptions of the world that theologically, socially, and symbolically reflected and supported various perceptions, interests, and desires.

Methods

My theoretical orientation is shaped by ongoing discussions in the study of American religions. The field, under the influence of such scholars as Thomas Tweed, Robert Orsi, and others, has moved away from consensus views of American culture to one that focuses more on the contacts and contestations between different religious and cultural groups.[21] My approach sees no unified "American culture and values" out there, but argues that different groups within society often seek to promote their own values and cultures as the most natural and acceptable for all.[22] This separates me from studies of the media and religion like Mark Silk's *Unsecular Media*, which presents a consensus view of culture by arguing that there are cultural norms, based in Christian topoi, that all Americans agree upon, and that journalists use when writing religion news. Whereas Silk argues that news media "approach religion with values and presuppositions that the American public widely shares," I stress that there are actually *multiple*, sometimes overlapping American publics that hold a variety of complex, divergent, and often contradictory views.[23]

I am also informed by ongoing discussions about the purpose and goals of religious studies. I agree with the religion and cultural studies scholar Susan Mizruchi, who suggests that the study of religion should be "an exercise in disruptive classification, interrogating earlier modes of classification regarding religion and culture while at the same time developing categories for capturing what has been mystified (as opposed to specified in contemporary theory) and unified (as opposed to fractured or fragmented in historical practice)."[24] This work strives to be an exercise in disruptive classification by unveiling the power relations and unquestioned assumptions underlying normative categories like mainstream and fringe. In recent years, several scholars have noted the tendency of American religious historians to situate particular groups as central or peripheral to the story of religion in America.[25] Robert Baird's division of Evangelical and non-Evangelical denominations in 1844, William Warren Sweet's differentiation between the "great Protestant churches" and the "unhealthy offspring" of revivals in 1930, and Sydney Ahlstrom's presumption in 1972 of a grand Puritan epoch all exemplify past historians' assumptions that classifications of mainstream and fringe were fixed and unproblematic.[26] But the use of center and periphery language in American religion scholarship, more often used to describe mainstream versus fringe practices, and beliefs versus unequal power relations, has always obscured more than it has revealed. By interrogating such classifications in national print media, I hope to contribute to the growing scholarship in American religion that eschews using such simplistic categories and instead makes them the object of study.

Finally, in dealing with magazine images and words, this work is informed by the growing interdisciplinary scholarship, particularly in the field of cultural studies, on representation. Representations directly shape our everyday, embodied experiences and perceptions. The media scholar Stuart Hall writes that "in part, we give things meaning by how we represent them—the words we use about them, the stories we tell about them, the images of them we produce, the emotions we associate with them, the ways we classify and conceptualize them, the values we place on them."[27] Representations both shape and mirror social relations. They can be liberating, even revolutionary. Representations can symbolically subvert social hierarchies. But perhaps more often, they do the opposite. The power to represent is entwined with social, economic, and political power. Representations can take the form of stereotypes that uphold unequal power relations and even foment violence. Representations of marginalized groups in the United States have sanctioned not only dismissive humor pieces in the *New Yorker* but pipe bombs in Laotian Buddhist temples, riots outside Catholic convents, vandalism to southern black churches and midwestern Muslim temples, and—as I argue in Chapter 5—the government assault in 1993 on a Texas sectarian commune of the Branch Davidians.

Sources

Most scholarship on religious fringe representations focuses on groups that journalists label cults. The majority of this work fails to clearly define the object of study, and instead often uses broad terms such as "media" and "mass media" as if they were a monolithic and undifferentiated whole.[28] More systematic studies examine newspapers or a small selection of national newsweeklies.[29] Most focus on coverage of only one group or a predetermined cluster of groups.[30] Few are longitudinal, and only one study that I am familiar with examines in detail any form of mass media coverage before 1972.[31] In this work, I analyze one specific media form over an extended period of time—including the seventeen years prior to 1972.

My primary sources are magazines distributed nationwide and indexed in *The Reader's Guide to Periodical Literature*.[32] Most had large circulations during the period under study, distributing between one and eight million copies an issue, though some special-interest magazines—especially religious ones like *Christian Century*, *Christianity Today*, and *Catholic World*—had distributions between 20,000 and 155,000.[33] I divide my sources into three categories. The first, and the one I highlight, is newsmagazines. These had some of the largest circulations and include *Time*, *Newsweek*, and *U.S. News and World Report*. The second type is general interest magazines. These included news, but their topical reach extended to fiction, human interest, and other subjects. *Life, Look, Reader's Digest,* and *Saturday Evening Post* fall under this category. The third category of periodicals appealed to special interests. These include journals of politics and opinion (*National Review* and *The Nation*), gender-specific magazines (*Esquire, McCall's,* and *Ladies Home Journal*), age-specific ones (*Seventeen,* and *Senior Scholastic*), those directed at African Americans (*Jet* and *Ebony*), and several religious periodicals, including two that were Protestant (the conservative Evangelical *Christianity Today* and the liberal ecumenical *Christian Century*), two that were Catholic (*Catholic World* and *America*), and one that was largely Jewish (*Commentary*).

I found my sources by using the *Reader's Guide to Periodical Literature* and later by turning the magazine pages to find additional, unindexed articles. I examined numerous stories on specific groups, from Methodists to Mormons, Baptists to Anglicans. I also looked for terms that lumped theologically disparate groups together. Articles with "cults" and "sects" in their titles caught my attention. I found that the terms "offbeat" and "fringe" served similar functions. To my surprise, extended coverage of single groups that were labeled sects, cults, or fringe proved insubstantial until the early 1970s. One exception was the Nation of Islam or, as the news media called them, Black Muslims. From 1959 to 1965 over sixty articles appeared on that group, making them the most covered "fringe movement" until the mass suicide of the Peoples Temple in November 1978. Because journalists reported so much on the Nation of Islam, Chapter 2 focuses on depictions of it.

I collected well over 500 articles from the period 1955–93, a relatively small number for thirty-nine years. To give some perspective, consider an estimated 390 articles on Catholicism listed in the *Reader's Guide to Periodical Literature* between 1961 and 1962 alone. Fifty-eight of these appeared in nonreligious magazines. I read for content, tone, editorial point of view, choice of images and captions, and narrative frame. I considered journalists' word choices particularly important, heeding Hartley's and Montgomery's reminder that "particular selections in vocabulary are thus part of particular modes of representation doing particular kinds of ideological work."[34] I realize that my own latent assumptions and situatedness, just like those of the journalists whose stories I write about, inevitably govern my authorship. As a scholar of American religion with a rural, nonreligious, working-class background, my narratives and conclusions are as situated as those of journalists. So while I tried to be fair, it seems rather disingenuous to merely suggest that I did my best to let the primary sources guide my case study choices. I agree with the assertion of the feminist philosopher of science Donna Harraway that "translation is always interpretive, critical, and partial," but I also agree with her suggestion that the "only way to find a larger vision is to be somewhere in particular."[35] As the religious historian Thomas Tweed suggests, "it is precisely because we stand in a particular location that we are able to see, to know, and to narrate."[36] I conceived this work from a particular social location. The conclusions I reach seem fairly convincing from this site. Of course, readers will decide whether they are persuasive from other social locations.

Caveats

I have identified my main arguments, sources, and approach. But I also must offer several caveats. First, one can find religious fringe depictions in newspapers and comics, on websites and television—even on t-shirts. A study of these other media would likely yield somewhat different conclusions. For example, the sociologist David Bromley suggests that coverage of "cults" has historically been more negative in local than in national newspapers.[37] It is also unclear how denominational journals might compare to national mass-market magazines. But these questions are beyond the current study's focus. The "mass media" is large and diverse in both technological form and representational content. This study considers primarily one, albeit a large and influential, mass media site. Although I do discuss other forms of media, for the most part I focus on periodicals and resist the temptation to generalize beyond them.

Readers also might ask why, given its conspicuous presence, television is not my primary source. As early as 1959, forty-four million American homes had television sets.[38] By the mid-1960s, most Americans owned televisions and watched them six to seven hours a day.[39] Robert Lichter and his colleagues have noted that "the development of a national media network did not really come to fruition until the late 1950s and early 1960s." "This," they argue, "was due, in part, to the emergence of television."[40]

Despite the obvious importance of television, I use print sources for several reasons. First, although television became the most popular medium in the period under study, most magazines did not decline in circulation until the early to mid-seventies. Some, like *Time* and *Newsweek*, have not declined at all.[41] Lichter and his colleagues even argue that "paradoxically, the advent of television increased the influence of a few East Coast newspapers and magazines."[42] Television did not make magazines uninfluential: it became another, complementary medium. Second, with some reservations, I agree with Herbert Gans that the similarities between electronic and print news media are often more decisive than their differences.[43] On the other hand—and perhaps most important —magazines, because of their style and format, contained more lengthy and sustained religious fringe discourse than television or any other media form. Interestingly, national magazines, television news, and even mass-market paperbacks frequently entered into symbiotic relationships when representing the American religious fringe. In my research, I found that television newscasts about the Nation of Islam inspired interest from the print media, and articles in newsmagazines about "cult deprogrammers" inspired interest from the television news. Popular books like Eric Hoffer's *The True Believer* also found their way into 1950s and 1960s representations. Because of this relationship among media forms, television news stories and popular books do appear in this study, even if I do center on magazines.

Granting me the right to focus on magazines, some readers might still question the value of analyzing together such varied types. After all, newsmagazines in some ways have more in common with newspapers than with general-interest magazines, and religious journals obviously differ in style and content from those devoted to other special interests. I suggest in response that only by examining various stripes of religious, news, general-interest, and special-interest magazines side by side, commenting on the same topics during the same period (sometimes even the same week), can one begin to see how theological, social, political, racial, and economic concerns partly dictated how certain religious groups were covered.

A second caveat concerns agency in the production of fringe representations. As noted earlier, this study is about the words and images produced in newsrooms, not the newsrooms themselves. At the same time, who produced the images and words—and how and why they did—are important questions. In examining primary documents, some historians analyze information about individual authors in an attempt to understand the personal motives that underlay creation of the documents. In examining fringe representations in news and general-interest magazines, and despite examples like that of [founder Henry] Luce and Time Inc., I often found the psychological motivations of individual journalists less important than their general social locations and professional practices.[44] I agree with the media scholar Wendy Kozol, who argues that the institutional structure of mass media means that authorship is *always* multiple rather than individual. Writing about *Life* magazine, Kozol argues that "to speak only of an individual producer, whether [Henry] Luce, the editors, or the photographers . . . underestimates the commercial structures and social conditions that affected production."[45] In their study of *National Geographic*, Catherine Lutz and Jane Collins similarly suggest that in editing and production rooms, "producing pictures, captions, and layout is a social and creative act in which negotiation and unacknowledged struggle result in the ultimate artifact, rather than a single plan deliberately followed through."[46] Given these considerations, I suggest that the journalistic habitus proves a useful interpretive tool. While it would be erroneous to claim that all journalists in a given magazine had the same demographics, it is not shocking that people from similar social locations did favor certain ways of framing stories.

A third caveat recognizes that this work focuses on stories primarily about movements that journalists considered fringe. Because of this, I say less about coverage of groups that they considered "mainstream." There are no chapters on Methodists, Baptists, or Episcopalians, even though these groups sometimes received more attention in newsmagazines than those featured here. In my research, I found that "non-fringe" religion news in magazines like *Time* ranged from the quirky (YMCAs in Israel and the theology of Charles Schulz's comic strip *Peanuts*) to the doctrinal (Anglicans debating the proper age at which to baptize members) to the dull (reports on annual denominational conventions).[47] But more important, my analysis of this coverage supported—rather than challenged—my arguments. Regardless of the topic or featured group, religion articles in the largest news and general-interest magazines consistently viewed as fringe high levels of exoticism, dogma, and emotion. Longitudinal studies of newsmagazine coverage of Methodists, Episcopalians, and other once-named "mainline" denominations would be valuable additions to scholarship.[48] But this is beyond the present study's scope.

A fourth caveat reminds readers that I examine depictions of the American religious fringe in national mass-market magazines, not reader responses to them. Identifying the interpretive patterns of magazine articles is one task; gauging the response of readers is quite another. As with the photographers for *Life* in the 1950s studied by Wendy Kozol, magazine reporting about the religious periphery "sought to win consent for a preferred reading through discursive strategies that constrained the range of options" that readers had.[49] In other words, writers and editors framed stories and accompanying photos in ways that suggested which topics were most important and who the "heroes" and "villains" of the news were. On the other hand, Kozol argues, "photographs are polysemic texts, that is, they are open to different interpretations and can be read in a variety of ways . . . although representations are abundantly meaningful, those meanings are neither unified or stable, nor are they read the same way by all audiences."[50] My textual sources, like Kozol's photographs, are polysemic: though writers framed them in ways that suggested a particular reading, readers might choose to authorize alternative ones. For example, a series in *Christian Century* in 1957 by Marcus Bach covered the Unity church, Baha'i faith, Jehovah's Witnesses, and Psychiana, a mail-order religion founded by Frank Robinson in 1929. Many readers responded with letters asking how they could get in touch with the groups.[51] Dismayed, the managing editor, Theodore Gill, vehemently responded with an essay condemning all four movements as heretical.[52] As in that instance, what writers and editors want to communicate may not be what readers choose to receive. While it is hard to gauge how individual readers respond to journalistic accounts, the media undoubtedly influence audience perceptions.[53] Stuart Hall argues that "the mass media are more and more responsible (a) for providing the basis on which groups and classes construct an 'image' of the lives, meanings, practices and values of other groups and classes; (b) for providing the images, representations and ideas around which the social totality, composed of all these separate and fragmented pieces, can be coherently grasped as a 'whole.'"[54] Similarly, though more in terms of initiating action, Bourdieu asserts that "the very fact of reporting, of putting on record as a reporter, always implies a social construction of reality that can mobilize (or demobilize) individuals or groups."[55] I agree with both Hall and Bourdieu in accepting that national periodicals have established connections between certain characteristics and the religious margins that audiences have accepted. For example, the contemporary association of the terms "cult" and "brainwashing" has been partly constructed and inculcated by American mass media. Since at least the late 1970s, as readers might guess, polls show that many Americans hold suspicious and even negative views of religious groups they consider marginal. For example, a Gallup poll in 1989 asserted that 62 percent of Americans would not want religious sects or cults as neighbors, twice as high as the second-most disliked and almost equally press-beaten category, fundamentalists.[56] A poll conducted by *USA Today* three days after the Branch Davidian standoff ended in flames found that 93 percent of respondents blamed the tragic outcome on the group's leader, David Koresh.[57] To this day, however, there has been no substantive evidence proving how the fire began, though assertions have ranged broadly from Davidian mass suicide to FBI malfeasance. Although I would never claim that representations by the mass media caused these unfavorable public responses, they certainly contributed by promoting negative, unnuanced images of the groups in question.

In explaining the national print media's role aiding in readers' constructions of the American religious fringe, I find Stuart Hall's concept of "articulation" useful. Hall defines articulation as "the form of the connection that can make a unity of two different elements . . . a linkage which is not necessary, determined, absolute, and essential for all time."[58] A "point of articulation," to use Gilbert Rodman's expanded phrase, is a social site where unrelated phenomena may become linked such that their mutual association appears inherent and natural.[59] The sociologists James Richardson and Barend van Driel have noted that print media coverage of cults disproportionately focuses on crime and conflict, calling it the "stream of controversies" approach.[60] In such stories, brainwashing and coercion are often associated with the groups. As I noted earlier, "cult" is the most common contemporary moniker that journalists use to denote groups they consider marginal. In an extension of this process of articulation, then, brainwashing and coercion become associated with a wide range of groups labeled fringe. In this book, I focus on points of articulation—California cults, the Third Force, the Nation of Islam, Asian Gurus, the Jesus movement, the Occult, and the "Cult Menace"—that connected various motifs and themes to the American religious fringe.

Organization

This book consists of five chapters, grouped into two sections. The first section, titled "Monitoring the Marginal Masses: Exoticism, Zealotry, and Subversion during the Cold War, 1955–1965," contains two chapters. The first looks at how journalists of the period 1955–65 characterized some religious groups in American society as central and others as peripheral. I discuss the conception in the 1950s of what Will Herberg has called the "triple melting pot" of mainline Protestants, Catholics, and Jews. I then analyze two fringe categorizations that connected a variety of theologically disparate movements. The "Third Force in Christendom," a term first proposed by the liberal ecumenist Henry Van Dusen in 1955, linked a diverse group of working-class denominations, ranging from Pentecostals to Jehovah's Witnesses. Similarly, journalists used "California cults" to connect and exoticize miscellaneous groups based in California. Chapter 1 makes two points. First, a classist, Cold War discourse ran through many newsmagazines' articles on the Third Force and California cults. This latent discourse reflected ambivalence toward "lowbrow" culture and the working classes, associating them with fanaticism, mass hysteria, and dangerous religious zeal. Second, religious fringe classifications were contested. For example, Evangelical and Catholic periodicals proposed alternatives to the Third Force classification that centered their own faiths, while marginalizing liberal Protestants.

In the second chapter, I argue that the largest news and general-interest magazines viewed the Nation of Islam as a lower-class group with subversive tendencies—like all working-class mass movements in their view. But race, of course, played the major role in magazine depictions. Here, during the volatile civil rights era, were blacks who refused both the adjective and the noun in the classification "American Negro." They identified themselves as Muslims, which for them also signaled non-American, and they shunned the word "Negro," favoring "black." For white print media journalists, the Nation of Islam was a movement of "others" four times removed: by class, race, national self-identity, and religious affiliation. In this chapter, I identify three themes that dominated the group's coverage, chronicle alternative representations, and suggest why print media reporting on the Muslims abruptly changed in 1965.

The second section, "Reconstructing an American Religious Fringe, 1966–1993," traces the gradual emergence of recurring "cult menace" motifs in the national print media and carries the study into the 1990s. Chapter 3 charts the beginning of a decisive shift in journalists' representations. In the late 1960s and early 1970s Asian religions, the Jesus movement, and the all-inclusive "occult" appeared in the pages of the largest periodicals as harmless, even banal, curiosities. By 1975, however, journalists consistently depicted these same movements as imminent dangers and generalized certain negative incidents beyond particular groups to "cults" in general. I suggest that a number of elements, including the anti-cult movement, combined to account for this change. Another important factor was that many of these religions attracted white middle-class youth—part of the group whose social location was idealized in the largest magazines.

In Chapter 4 I examine the appearance of brainwashing, deprogramming, and cult apostate accounts. I argue that changes in the business of journalism, as well as a propensity to accept simplistic brainwashing theories, led magazines of all stripes to increasingly portray the fringe as dangerously deviant. I end the chapter with coverage of the mass suicide at Jonestown in 1978, a point of articulation that decisively welded dangerous cult images to the American religious fringe. Chapter 5 brings the study of fringe representations up to 1993, ending with print coverage of the standoff between the Branch Davidians and the ATF that ended with a smoldering commune and over eighty Davidians and several federal agents dead.

PART I

Monitoring
the Marginal
Masses

Exoticism,
Zealotry, and
Subversion
during the
Cold War,
1955–1965

chapter one

EXOTICISM AND
THE DANGERS OF
RELIGIOUS ZEAL

DIFFERENTIATING

FRINGE FROM

MAINSTREAM,

1955–1965

In 1958 *Life* published a pictorial and essay on the "Third Force in Christendom." The editors described it as a movement of "gospel-singing, doomsday-preaching sects" that stood apart from Roman Catholicism and "historic Protestantism."[1] *Life* included a table titled "U.S. Third Force Groups," listing various Pentecostal denominations, the Seventh-Day Adventists, Independent Fundamental Churches of America, Jehovah's Witnesses, Churches of Christ, and Church of the Nazarene, among others.[2] In the essay, Henry Van Dusen, the president of the Union Theological Seminary who invented the term "Third Force" three years earlier in *Christian Century*, asserted that most Third Force sects were Protestant offshoots. But he added that Brazilian Spiritism, "a strange amalgam that mixes Catholic belief with elements of Voodooism, primitive animism, and extreme emotion," was a Third Force group with Catholic roots.[3] "No one," he concluded, "can tell whether the Third Force will persist into the long future as a separate and mighty branch of Christianity, or whether it will ultimately be reabsorbed into classic Protestantism."[4] But more and more, he asserted, "there is a growing, serious recognition of its true dimensions and probable permanence."[5]

Two years earlier, *Newsweek* had published "The Way of the Cults." The story focused on the numerous "sects in the Los Angeles area which can best—or most conservatively—be described as odd-looking to almost anybody who does not live in southern California."[6] The unnamed authors dubbed California the "cult center of the United States" and offered several explanations. "One theory," *Newsweek* wrote, "is that cults attract the elderly, and so does California."[7] Other reasons included the ease with which religions could gain legal status in the state, the Los Angeles area's responsiveness to the colorful, and the particularly deep emotional needs and gullibility of its citizens.[8] The writers briefly described several groups, including the Self-Realization Fellowship, the Theosophical Society, the Vedanta Society, and Aimee Semple McPherson's Pentecostal Four-Square Gospel Church. "Some of these movements may strike the viewer-from-afar as positively odd," *Newsweek* concluded, "yet Los Angeles has proven that oddity, as some may call it, can attract wide and devoted followings."[9]

These two articles are typical of the coverage of groups labeled fringe, offbeat, and marginal in the 1950s and early 1960s. For example, it was not unusual for *Life* to use someone like Van Dusen, a liberal Presbyterian ecumenist, for editorial commentary. As other scholars have noted, postwar news and general-interest magazines focused on "personalities," whether actors, politicians, or mainline Protestant leaders.[10] Henry Luce's *Time* and *Life*, in addition to competitors like *Newsweek* and *Look*, all quoted ecumenical Protestant and Catholic leaders throughout the period. In addition, magazines owned by Luce, in promoting an American religious and cultural consensus, occasionally produced editorials supporting ecumenical efforts.[11] The story in *Newsweek* on "California cults" is also representative. Articles in the largest news and general-interest magazines frequently exoticized, rather than demonized, the American religious fringe and frequently looked west to California for religious oddities. Both the *Newsweek* and *Life* articles are also representative in that writers and editors deemphasized theological differences and lumped disparate groups together under various fringe classifications, "Third Force" and "California cults" being the most prominent. Simultaneously, they left the mainstream undefined, at most designating it with status-rich terms like "historic Protestantism" and "traditional churches."

These and similar articles constitute a "discursive formation."

Stuart Hall defines this as "a cluster (or formation) of ideas, images, and practices, which provide ways of talking about, forms of knowledge and conduct associated with, a particular topic, social activity or institutional site in society. These discursive formations, as they are known, define what is and is not appropriate in our formulation of, and our practices in relation to, a particular subject or site of social activity; what knowledge is considered useful, relevant and 'true' in that context; and what sort of persons or 'subjects' embody its characteristics."[12]

I call the discursive formation constituted and addressed by the articles under study "the American religious fringe"—that changing set of characteristics attributed to groups variously labeled "cults" and "sects," and described as "offbeat" and with similar terms meaning marginal or peripheral.[13] This chapter examines some of the primary traits that magazine articles ascribed to the fringe during the heightened Cold War years 1955–65. Specifically, the largest news and general-interest periodicals consistently used two somewhat contradictory themes to depict groups that they considered marginal or offbeat. First, like *Newsweek*'s article and Van Dusen's description of Spiritism, they tended to portray the religious periphery as exotic—weird, colorful, and mysterious—yet mostly harmless. Second, and more ambivalently, writers and editors depicted fringe movements as zealous, emotional, and dogmatic. Magazine writers suggested that high levels of commitment, enthusiasm, and exoticism were excessive, even "unhealthy." Though exoticism and zealotry might initially seem unconnected, magazine portrayals tied them together in ways that coincided with Cold War discourses about communist containment. Specifically, articles symbolically "contained" religious zealotry and spiritual exoticism to certain classes of people and a particular region of the country, just as American containment policy sought to restrict and contain the spread of communism at home and abroad.

Studying how writers and editors in the largest national news and general-interest magazines differentiated mainstream from marginal in this period reveals several things. First, common print media religious classifications reflected four major tensions that permeated U.S. society in the 1950s. These, according to the religious historian Robert Ellwood, were the binary oppositions of the mass versus the individual, the exotic versus the domestic, communism versus capitalism, and alternative living arrangements versus the traditional nuclear family.[14] Either explicitly or implicitly, articles consistently associated the religious fringe with mass (lowbrow) culture, exoticism, alternative living arrangements, and occasionally, communism. In promoting a broad American cultural consensus that stood apart from "godless" communism, news and general-interest magazine portrayals occasionally characterized marginalized religious groups as having those characteristics least suitable for sustaining representative democratic capitalism.

Second, and more broadly, writers differentiated mainstream from fringe in ways that symbolically replicated and legitimated social power relations.[15] For example, nearly all the Third Force sects that *Life* named were working-class denominations. At the same time, the magazine used a white, upper-middle-class, ecumenical church leader—someone whom most journalists identified as mainstream—to comment authoritatively on the Third Force. In general, magazines like *Time, Newsweek, Life,* and *Look* assumed a normative mainstream that was white, upper middle and middle class, male, and religiously liberal. In doing this, they sometimes distinguished religious fringe and mainstream by class and race as much as by theology.

Expanding the Center, Imagining Consensus:
The 1950s Religious Revival and the Triple Melting Pot

Before and shortly after World War II, journalists, politicians, and pundits frequently presumed the predominance of a mainline, theologically moderate "Protestant Establishment," to use E. Digby Baltzell's term, that held political, social, and economic power. Further, and more problematically, they often saw this group as the standard in defining "normal" and "mainstream" religious activities and beliefs.[16] But writers and editors during and after the war turned to a slightly broader conception of the center. In the 1950s a religious "revival," spurred by a postwar baby boom, suburbanization, and the growth of a homogenizing national mass media, coincided with increasingly pluralistic conceptions of the American religious mainstream. The historian James Hudnut-Beumler notes that the religious revival witnessed an unprecedented increase in church affiliation, church building, and religious tithing.[17] When American GIs returned home from World War II, many married, moved to the suburbs, and had children. Hundreds of thousands of postwar Americans read *The Power of Positive Thinking* (1952) by the Protestant pastor Norman Vincent Peale. Many also watched the Roman Catholic Bishop Fulton Sheen's television show *Life Is Worth Living* and read Rabbi Joshua Liebman's *Peace of Mind*, both as "nondenominational" in their messages as Peale's bestseller. They also built and attended churches, cathedrals, and synagogues. It was the period in American history when "under God" was added to the Pledge of Allegiance (1954) and the official U.S. motto became "In God We Trust" (1956). President Dwight D. Eisenhower could likewise assert that "our government makes no sense unless it is founded in a deeply religious faith—and I don't care what it is," and receive little to no media criticism over church-state separation.[18] It was during this time that journalistic conceptions of the religious mainstream started to coincide with the title and premise of the sociologist Will Herberg's bestseller, *Protestant Catholic Jew* (1955). Herberg asserted that "being a Protestant, a Catholic, or a Jew is understood as the specific way, and increasingly perhaps the only way, of being American and locating oneself within American society."[19]

Granted, Herberg's book was less a celebration of the pluralistic (and, he argued, overly generic and homogenized) revival of religion than a jeremiad against it.[20] In asserting his point, Herberg obviously exaggerated the period's religious unity and tolerance. Ellwood, for example, accurately notes that Protestant-Catholic relations in the 1950s were particularly icy at times. Among other things, he notes that the liberal Protestant weekly *Christian Century* frequently published articles critical of Catholicism.[21] The religious historian David Morgan concurs, noting that in one article in *Life* in 1947, Paul Hutchinson, editor of *Christian Century*, went as far as to declare the similarities of Catholicism and communism, asserting that "save in the purposes for which they exist, there is little difference between the international of the Kremlin and of the Vatican."[22] Likewise, Mark Hulsether argues that the more liberal *Christianity and Crisis* also entered the 1950s perceiving "Catholicism as a third great totalitarian threat alongside Communism and Nazism."[23] These attitudes went beyond the printed page. As Martin Marty notes, even at the end of the 1950s, some Protestant leaders like Peale and some Protestant organizations like the National Association of Evangelicals initiated or joined movements to prevent John F. Kennedy from attaining the presidency, fearing the influence of his Roman Catholic background.[24]

Still, national magazines adopted and promoted Herberg's "triple melting pot" concept of the American religious mainstream. This embrace was to be expected given the ideological commitments of publishers like Henry Luce and many of his competitors, who vigorously promoted American expansionism, anticommunism, and notions of an American cultural consensus during the 1950s and early 1960s. In identifying and opposing the Cold War communist enemy, many politicians, pundits, and magazine publishers sought to assert a unified front in all aspects of American culture, including religion. Luce's publications, but also *Look* and *Newsweek*, viewed the triple melting pot faiths of Protestant, Catholic, and Jew as theologically affirming what Herberg called "the 'spiritual ideals' and 'moral values' of the American Way of Life."[25] This "American Way of Life," which Herberg considered a religion unto itself, was characterized by democracy, pragmatism, manifest destiny, and individualism. As an ideal, it was contrasted with its opposite: undemocratic, anti-individualistic, godless communism.

Given the desire for a strong cultural consensus to oppose the communist other, magazines predictably stressed the "Americanness" of the religious mainstream. *Look* provides a good example. As noted by the media scholar Mark Silk, the periodical's cover story on Jewish Americans in 1955 suggested, like Herberg, that a Jewish identity was inherently also an American identity.[26] The pictures included in the article also strove to show the members of a family in Flint, Michigan, as typical Americans, portraying them working, attending religious services, wrapping presents, and playing football.[27] Some scholars suggest that postwar journalistic inclusiveness sometimes even went beyond "Protestant-

Catholic-Jew." For example, Silk argues that the Church of Jesus Christ of Latter Day Saints (the Mormons)—the same new religion on which the U.S. government declared war in the mid-nineteenth century—"was fully brought into the fold of national media acceptability" by 1958.[28]

Just as the desire for cultural consensus led magazines to embrace the triple melting pot, it could also result in criticism of religious prejudice and divisiveness. Again, *Look* provides a good example. In 1956 the magazine published "Why Do Our Religions Fight Each Other?: A Leading Catholic Author Warns That Religious Intolerance, Hatred, and Bigotry Imperil Our Democratic Way of Life." In this article the Catholic ecumenist John O'Brien, head of the Commission of the National Conference of Christians and Jews, suggested that religious prejudice could actually cause physical and mental illness. "Fear and anxiety over fancied dangers from people of a different faith," he wrote, "tend to beget ulcers, neuroses, and phobias of various kinds."[29] In contrast to the unhealthy divisiveness of religious prejudice, O'Brien promoted American cultural consensus. In a section very much in line with the Cold War desire to promote a unified front against communism, O'Brien suggested that "Americans like to see members of different faiths live together in a spirit of understanding, friendship, and good will. Differences in creeds should not mar the civic and social relations of neighbors. In matters of religious belief, Protestants, Catholics, and Jews may be as distinct and different as the fingers of an outstretched hand, but in all that makes for the economic, social and moral betterment of a community and the unity and strength of our nation, they should be as united as the fingers of a clenched fist."[30]

Identifying the Fringe by Regionalizing It:
California Cults and Exoticism

While news and general-interest magazines like *Look* seemed to embrace the notion of the triple melting pot, and while some articles positively framed Mormons, journalistic conceptions of the center rarely ventured beyond the more liberal, ecumenical branches and figureheads of Protestantism, Catholicism, and Judaism, let alone outside these traditions. On the contrary, the pluralistic, consensus-driven notion of the religious mainstream actually led journalists to draw the boundaries between center and periphery even more sharply. That some Americans in the 1950s and 1960s implicitly and explicitly differentiated mainstream and fringe religions is not surprising. Throughout American history, clerics, journalists, politicians, and historians have labeled certain religious movements as central or peripheral to national or religious purposes. Take, for example, the antebellum debates over the compatibility of Roman Catholicism with American ideals. Nativists like Samuel Morse asserted that Catholic immigrants, because of their allegiance to the pope, posed an imminent threat to American democracy. On the other side of the debate stood Catholics like Orestes Brownson, a convert who suggested that Catholicism was the religion actually *best* suited for the United States.[31] In a country where the Constitution prohibits a state-sanctioned church, classifications of insider and outsider, orthodox and heretical, have often acted as a strategic substitute for socially and politically legitimating some groups and delegitimizing others. As might be expected, many interpreters historically have focused on identifying and describing the fringe, while assuming a mainstream that often included their own religious group. Over the past four centuries not just Catholics but Shakers, Mormons, Jehovah's Witnesses, and others have been labeled heretical, cultic, and un-American. Scholars note that all these groups have been subject to similar macabre and frequently unsubstantiated tales that linked them with licentiousness, kidnaping, conspiracy, and even murder.[32]

Philip Jenkins suggests that these "cult scares," and the recurring tales of atrocities committed by fringe groups, are "endemic" in American history. For example, he suggests that the World War II period saw a "great anti-cult scare" focusing variously on Nazi sympathizers, African American new religions, Jehovah's Witnesses, polygamist Mormons, and Holiness-Pentecostals.[33] The crucial factor fomenting this war-era scare, Jenkins argues, was a fear of subversion.[34] With the exception of Nation of Islam coverage, which I detail in Chapter 2, journalistic fringe representations in the late 1950s and early 1960s were overtly less alarmist.

I agree with Jenkins's suggestion that the 1950s may be one of those "bizarre and quite rare decades in which the nation is not exercised over alleged cult atrocities of whatever kind."[35] In contrast to the fear-inducing cult exposés of previous and later decades, the period's articles often portrayed the American religious fringe as exotic and even comical. No doubt because of a shared concern with overt display of emotion, religious fringe coverage structurally resembled postwar journalistic treatments of popular teenage trends like rock-and-roll. James Gilbert, who has examined reactions to teenage culture in the 1950s, writes that magazines' "typical ingredients of contemporary reactions to adolescence" included "curiosity and fear, set against a background of reassuring noises."[36] Journalists used the same ingredients to exoticize the religious periphery.

One common Cold War trope was to identify the religious fringe with a specific region, to actually locate it on a map. Even though many of California's so-called fringe religious groups were well established outside the state, journalists in the largest periodicals, who were overwhelmingly based in the Northeast, consistently associated California with exotic cults. Several articles appeared between 1955 and 1965 connecting California and fringe religions. For example, the subtitle of Louie Robinson's 1963 *Ebony* article, "The Kingdom of King Narcisse," read: "California Breeds Another Bizarre but Colorful Sect."[37]

Consider the coverage given to the Wisdom, Knowledge, Faith, and Love Fountain of the World (WKFL). This eclectic movement established a small commune in the Santa Susana Mountains of Ventura County, California, in the 1950s. One issue of *Look* in 1959 featured a four-page pictorial of the group entitled "California's Offbeat Religions: 'We Love You.'"[38] The photo essay featured eight pictures by Cal Bernstein and accompanying text by Chandler Brossard. The presentation of the group evoked the mystery, sexuality, and "offbeatness" traditionally associated with the exotic. The first photograph showed members standing in the dark holding lit candles, clothed in long black and white robes, staring solemnly at the camera. In succeeding shots members hugged, a novitiate received a blood test, and a member held two children. The final page showed three photographs of "Bishop Mary," a somewhat scantily clad "former actress." She is pictured performing an improvisational dance to classical music. "Like Bishop Mary," one caption read, "all Fountain members are 'creativity-conscious.'"[39] After the initial, ominous candle-lit image, the communalist WKFL was portrayed as colorfully offbeat. The pictures made the group seem more theatrical than serious, and hardly dangerous.

This is striking, because the group was steeped in controversy and violence. Krishna Venta, founder of the group, was killed in 1958 when two male followers angered by his open sexual relations with female members retaliated by blowing him up with twenty sticks of dynamite. These apostates from WKFL accused Venta of "illicit sexual relations with female cultists, including girls under the legal age of consent."[40] These accusations were confirmed by other members. But national magazine coverage, both before and after Venta's death, played down these seamy details. A few articles, like the feature in *Look*, which appeared only eight months after Venta's death, failed to even mention the specific accusations. Brossard only noted that "Venta was dynamited to bits in his office last year by two members who felt he was guilty of malpractices."[41]

Some articles did detail accusations against Venta, but their tone often was more satirical than critical. For example, the California novelist Robert Carson, writing in *Holiday* in 1965, noted that "WKFL is the invention of a bearded man, known variously as Francis Pencovic, Frank Christopher, Frank Jensen, Jesus Christ, and Krishna Venta."[42] Carson told how Venta had revealed to his followers that he had risen from a tomb and wandered the earth until settling in California. "Sad to say," Carson continued, "he managed to acquire a police record in the twentieth century, did time for issuing bad checks, and was sent to a mental hospital for a while."[43] Carson then noted that "he is no longer with us," because two followers blew him up with dynamite. "They objected to certain of his shortcomings," Carson explained, "including his free manners with the ladies of the congregation and his trips to Las Vegas for gambling."[44] Carson ended his article by noting that Venta's mother had prophesied her son's return by 1960 and that five years later the group still waited for him. "They are waiting in

Members of the WKFL holding candles, in Look, *1958.*
(Library of Congress)

Box Canyon," he concluded, "busy and devoted and possibly be-mused, but somehow impressive and loveable."[45]

Joel Foreman argues that what was perceived as shocking and troubling in the 1950s might seem tame today.[46] In terms of Krishna Venta's gambling and adultery, the opposite seemed to hold. The seamy details of sexual impropriety and misuse of funds by a "cult" leader would almost certainly have been the focus of any magazine story during the 1930s and 1940s—as well as the late 1970s through the 1990s. In the 1950s and early 1960s, however, these details were occasionally ignored and deemphasized when they did not fit the "harmless exotic" trope that journalists occasionally used to frame stories about the California religious fringe.

Writers frequently associated the whole state with the exotic and unusual. Brossard's pictorial in *Look* appeared in an issue de-voted to California. In it writers described the state's intellectu-als and local television, in addition to its religions, as "offbeat."[47] Similarly, Robert Carson suggested in his article in *Holiday*, titled "Eccentricity under the Sun," that "the state of California, most populous in the nation, seems to have more than its share of ec-centrics."[48] Given this view, writers still seemed to favor reporting on the state's specifically religious oddities. Carson devoted the majority of his piece, for example, to religions and "health cults." Writing in 1965, he suggested that "religion in California would ap-pear to have seen better days." But he was not criticizing California cults. Instead, he satirically lamented that "only a few oddments remain from the great days" of (southern) California's congested cultic past.[49]

Labeling the exotic is a crucial step in identifying its oppo-site, the domestic—that constituted as "normal" and "everyday." During the 1950s and early 1960s the boundaries between exotic and domestic and between mainstream and fringe religions were in flux. Depicting certain religious groups—or more accurately, the characteristics of certain groups—as marginal established new boundaries around a changing, vaguely defined conception of "mainstream." This occurred during a time when Henry Luce's publications, as well as Cold War politicians, sought to assert an American cultural consensus.

In addition to what one might term the "Californiafication" of the fringe, journalists less explicitly demarcated it by class. Many groups that writers and editors labeled cultic, sectarian, offbeat, or fringe were working class. Journalists portrayed most of these working-class denominations as highly committed and enthusiastic. But writers also viewed the groups guardedly, implying that too much religious zeal could be unhealthy.

The Dangers of Religious Zeal:
Neurotic Religion and Cold War Containment

On 12 April 1965, *Time*'s "Religion" section included an article entitled "Faith: Healthy v. Neurotic." "Religious belief," the unnamed writers stated, "may also be a cover-up for deep anxiety and a cause of neurosis."[50] The story reported some of the findings from the annual meeting of the Academy of Religion and Mental Health. The magazine, like all of Henry Luce's publications, was known in the postwar period for editorializing within its news coverage. In this story, however, the writers and editors let their choice of quotations stand without comment. "Both clergymen and doctors agreed," *Time* wrote, "that authoritarian religion can be a major source of neurosis."[51] One doctor suggested that some "symptoms of unhealthy faith" that often show up among new members of "dogmatic churches" were "'an irrational intensity of belief' in the new doctrine, greater concern for form and theology than for ethical and moral principles, hatred of [others'] beliefs, intolerance of deviation, and a desire for martyrdom."[52]

Neurotic religion not only harmed lay people in "legalistically-structured religions," but the clergy as well: "Clergymen with emotional problems, both pastors and doctors agreed, usually come from homes with a weak father and a domineering mother."[53] *Time* concluded the article by quoting Samuel Miller, dean of the Harvard Divinity School. Miller suggested that the measure of a healthy faith was "its ability to remain in relation to the threatening aspects of reality without succumbing to fear, shame, anxiety or hostility. An unhealthy religion runs away, becomes obsessed with a part in order to avoid the whole. The body is denied for the soul's sake; the future becomes so fascinating that it blots out the present; all truth is limited to the Bible. A healthy religion unites existence, and unhealthy ones divide it."[54]

As for identifying specific "neurotic" denominations, *Time* remained silent. The magazine did report that two of the conference papers focused on Catholic laity and United Presbyterian clergy. Yet the assertions that adherents of neurotic religion focused on the future (millennialism), believed that all truth was limited to the Bible (Biblical literalism), and displayed an "irrational intensity of faith" (charismatic enthusiasm) suggested that *Time*, like Miller, classified conservative and charismatic Christian groups as unhealthy and liberal, ecumenical ones as sound. Without mentioning any specifically, the magazine condemned the Fundamentalists, Pentecostals, Jehovah's Witnesses, and other working-class groups that Henry Van Dusen called "Third Force" as neurotic.

The article in *Time* shares features with one published in *Look* in 1956 by the Catholic ecumenist John O'Brien. Both argue that certain types of religious faith, especially those demanding high levels of commitment and belief in the falsity of others' religions, can lead to physical and mental illness. Though O'Brien's was more explicit, both articles suggested the need for ecumenical consensus. But more striking, I argue, is how both articles suggested the need to *contain* religious enthusiasm, emotion, zeal, and dogma for the sake of bodily health. I suggest that this rhetoric of containment mirrors the larger political discourse in the 1950s and early 1960s of containing communism as an external and internal threat. The ideology of containment, first articulated in 1946–47 by George F. Kennan, a foreign policy specialist with expertise in the Soviet Union, suggested that communism would not pose a threat if it could be contained to certain parts of the globe and marginalized in the American domestic sphere.[55]

Historians argue that containment ideology went beyond foreign and domestic policy concerns. Elaine Tyler May, for example, notes that the concept of "domestic containment" meant much more than negating communist influence within the United States itself. She suggests that the term "aptly describes the way in which public policy, personal behavior, and even political values were focused on the home."[56] In addition to family and home, containment metaphors focused on American culture as a whole. Andrew Ross argues that Cold War writers consistently linked communism, as well as "social, cultural, and political difference" in general, to germs and disease.[57] While germ metaphors evoke a threat to an individual's body, Ross suggests that containment discourse in the 1950s also revealed a fear of threats to the American social body. For some journalists and critics, this threat came from practices and ideas dubbed "mass," "popular," and "lowbrow."[58] In the 1950s and early 1960s, these terms referred to everything from rock-and-roll and comic books to particular styles of religion.

Religious fringe depictions reproduced Cold War containment discourse. Articles demonstrated a concern to protect the individual and social body from unhealthy dogmas and fanatical zeal. They also explicitly distinguished a hierarchy of culture and betrayed an uneasy disdain toward "popular" and "lowbrow" religion. Writers in the 1950s and 1960s used these terms to describe the primarily working-class "Third Force" denominations. For example, one issue of *Life* in 1955 included an essay entitled "Have We a 'New' Religion?" by Paul Hutchinson, a Methodist, former journalist, and editor of the *Christian Century*. The bulk of Hutchinson's essay challenged the religious revival of the 1950s, particularly the positive-thinking, therapeutic "middle-brow cult of reassurance" espoused by figures like Norman Vincent Peale, Rabbi Joshua Liebman, and Bishop Fulton Sheen. After identifying the movement, Hutchinson bemoaned it for its "too-simple, too-magical solution for all man's problems."[59] In his introduction, Hutchinson also reported that the religious revival of the 1950s was affecting highbrow and lowbrow religionists as well. While not the focus of the article, Hutchinson's comments on lowbrow religion reveal important Cold War assumptions. "Among the low-brows," he wrote, "perennial religious interest is at present showing in so-called ecstatic sects, which specialize in faith-healing, speaking in unknown tongues, spiritualistic seances, or even practices as outlandish as snake-handling."[60] Hutchinson then proceeded to associate "lowbrow religion" with "low-brow culture." "But perhaps the most accessible evidence of religion's appeal to our low-brow instincts," Hutchinson continued, "is its capture of the jukebox."[61] He explained that "this started a few years ago when several radio programs won national popularity with hillbilly singing of the 'Grand Ole Opry' variety. Most of these songs moaned about 'mother, home and heaven.' Nashville, Tenn. took up the business of recording these mountaineer chants, or publishing them in sheet form, and soon was seriously competing in sales with Broadway's Tin Pan Alley."[62]

Hutchinson's association of lowbrow religion and lowbrow culture—in this case country music—presumed a certain class of "lowbrow" Americans attracted to such diversions. He was not alone in distinguishing people and their interests along such lines. A popular 1949 essay by Russell Lynes in *Harper's*, later turned into a pictorial classification chart in *Life*, was titled "Highbrow, Lowbrow, and Middlebrow." The historian Michael Kammen suggests that many took the satirical essay seriously because they saw it as conveying "sufficient common sense and sociological 'truth' to be regarded intently by anyone so disposed."[63] The terms were so common in twentieth-century parlance that Henry Luce, in discussing the potential of the pictorial format employed in *Life*, suggested that photographs were a "common denominator with lowbrows."[64]

In implying the existence of such categories of culture and people, Hutchinson and others called upon a familiar understanding of culture and human taste developed in the late nineteenth century. As noted by Lawrence Levine, the terms "highbrow" and "lowbrow" were originally "derived from the phrenological terms 'highbrowed' and 'lowbrowed,' which were prominently featured in the nineteenth century practice of determining racial types and intelligence by measuring cranial shapes and capacities."[65] In phrenology, a "highbrow" was associated with high intelligence and reasoning skills, a "lowbrow" with a naturally low intelligence and little capacity for reasoning. In the nineteenth century, phrenology often served as a pseudo-scientific justification for white, Anglo-Saxon supremacy, "proving" the inferiority of lowbrow groups like Italians, Jews, Eastern Europeans, and Africans. Whether or not he was conscious of its etymology, Hutchinson's use of "lowbrow" was certainly consistent with its historical meaning.

While Hutchinson's article clearly revealed his disdain for "lowbrow" culture, most journalists were more ambivalent. Many writers and editors—as well as the liberal Protestant sources that they consulted for commentary—viewed the practices and enthusiasm associated with groups that they labeled "lowbrow," "popular," or "Third Force" with a mixture of attraction and repulsion. That was clear in Henry Van Dusen's essay in *Life* on the Third Force. At times Van Dusen lauded the Third Force, suggesting that it could serve as an example for mainstream Christianity. He asserted that some of its component sects resembled the earliest followers of Christ, and that "Catholics and Protestants can all learn much of Christian value from them."[66] On the other hand, Van Dusen carefully chronicled what he saw as the movement's shortcomings. Simultaneously recalling the article in *Time* on unhealthy religions and Hutchinson's critique of middlebrow religion, he asserted that its "limited intellectual outlook" was "blithely indifferent to scientific and historic advances," and that its Christian message was simplistic and incomplete. "Its spirit," he lamented, "is all too often narrow, bigoted, and intolerant."[67] In his original 1955 *Christian Century* essay, on which the *Life* piece was based, Van Dusen asserted that the ecumenical imperative was to "draw" the Third Force "into the larger community of Christ's followers," suggesting that missionizing might temper the Third Force's enthusiasm and dogma, thus helping it conform with more "mainstream" Christianity.[68]

Stories on faith healing provided another clear example of journalistic ambivalence. In an article titled "The Healing Ministry," *Time* covered the 1958 national meeting of the Presbyterian Church, U.S.A. A special committee, *Time* reported, had "noted in a preliminary report that 'there is the danger in the tense emotional atmosphere of large healing missions of a concentration on the individual healer rather than on God as the source of wholeness.'" Nevertheless, the committee suggested that "the subject of faith healing should be carefully studied." The magazine's lack of usual end-of-the-article editorializing and commentary leads one to believe that the committee's conclusions suited the periodical's editors.[69]

Richard Carter, in a 1958 article in *Coronet* on Pentecostalism titled "That Old-Time Religion Comes Back," showed similar mixed feelings toward a Third Force group. Carter's associations between the poor and religious zealotry mirrored Paul Hutchinson. Evoking the "outlandish" lowbrow practices noted by Hutchinson, Carter asserted that Pentecostalism, to achieve remarkable growth, "has had to live down the antics of early evangelists who sought attention by swallowing alleged poison or permitting themselves to be bitten by supposedly poisonous snakes; and it had to rid itself of adventurers who sometimes succeeded in transforming its wildly emotional services into unspeakable orgies."[70] Attempting to explain Pentecostalism's explosive growth among the poorer classes, Carter asserted that its tremendous appeal arose from faith-healing practices.[71] "Other religious groups," Carter suggested, "continue to regard the unbridled emotional worship of the Pentecostals as hysteria, extremism, and fanaticism."[72] He went on to note, however, that criticism was rarely voiced publicly. "'After all,'" he quoted an unnamed theologian, "'no matter what you say about the Pentecostals, they are filling a need among people.'"[73]

Though Carter did not refer to Pentecostalism as "lowbrow," he did note that "potential converts seldom live in the better neighborhoods, seldom hold the better jobs and are unlikely to be especially well-educated."[74] To stress these demographic facts, Carter related a story of one "lady evangelist" at an "Eastern" church who gave a sermon titled "The Sin That Makes Our Lord Nauseated: The Sin That Makes Jesus Christ Want to Vomit." "A detached observer," Carter asserted, "might have criticized the evangelist's grammar, her pronunciation, some of the assertions which she offered in guise of fact." But such an observer, he suggested, would have been missing the evangelist's ability to set "the congregation ablaze with love of God."[75] Carter implied that her sermon—as journalists described Third Force groups generally—was morally and intellectually weak, but emotionally powerful. He wrote that "as in the great majority of Pentecostal messages, no heed was given to worldly matters, politics, economics, social responsibilities. Indeed all that mattered was the voice, rising and falling in pitch and volume, maintaining the hot rhythm, lashing the emotions."[76]

Groups that were labeled Third Force, like Pentecostals and

Jehovah's Witnesses, were not the only groups that journalists represented as overly emotional and intellectually weak. The exoticized "California cults" also received attention. This is significant because it shows that even groups that attracted middle- and upper-class adherents, as some California groups did, could sometimes be charged with zealotry. Eugene Fleming's "California Cults and Crackpots," published in *Cosmopolitan* in 1959, showed little equivocation in its negative portrayal of religious zeal's dangers. Fleming's story frame was heavy on repulsion and light on attraction. "Lured by the sun and easy living," the subheading read, "swamis, svengalis, and just plain oddballs have gravitated westward since 1900." "Today," it continued, "not all bearded prophets are phonies, but there are countless fakes and the loyalty of their followers is amazing."[77]

After this telling introduction, Fleming proceeded to discuss some of California's more colorful religious groups—including Venta's WKFL. Fleming suggested several reasons why California emerged as a cultic haven. Like most journalists, he listed California's moderate climate. He then offered explanations that betrayed his own age and gender biases. California attracts old widows and so do cults, he postulated. In addition, young women are attracted to cults because they "are easy prey for the charms and glamour most spiritual spellbinders exude."[78] Also telling is Fleming's list of California cultists' traits. Fleming asserted that California's cultists were "pure and simple, with emphasis on the latter." "Among their numbers," he continued, "are the rootless, the naive, the fanatical and, in one case, the murderous—the 'true believers' of every bent, including the crooked."[79]

The True Believer was the title of an influential book published in 1951 by Eric Hoffer, a longshoreman turned lay sociologist. Hoffer gave the label "true believer" to the zealous individual who joined a mass movement.[80] Appearing soon after the defeat of fascist Germany and the related expansion of communism in eastern Europe, Hoffer's book struck a chord with many Americans during the Cold War and sold well. His biographer James Baker notes that Hoffer and the book received favorable press reviews as well as praise from figures like President Dwight D. Eisenhower and the historian Arthur Schlesinger Jr.[81] Hoffer asserted that the fanaticism motivating true believers of any mass movement—religious, fascistic, or communistic—"may be viewed and treated as one."[82] "Though they seem at opposite poles," Hoffer wrote, "fanatics of all kinds are actually crowded together at one end."[83] Moderates and fanatics, he asserted, are the true opposites. "And it is easier," he added, "for a fanatic Communist to be converted to fascism, chauvinism or Catholicism than to become a sober liberal."[84] And who became true believers? Hoffer's list included the poor, minorities, the uncreative, the inordinately selfish, misfits, the overly ambitious, criminals, the bored, and sinners.[85]

Few journalists writing about the religious fringe directly cited Hoffer, but many undoubtedly knew his popular and widely reviewed work. A number of books on "cults," like Richard Mathison's *Faiths, Cults, and Sects of America* and the Evangelical writer Walter Martin's *Kingdom of the Cults*, used *The True Believer* to describe those attracted to fringe religions.[86] Baker argues that Hoffer gave "true believer" its "universal meaning and usage," and even when writers and editors used terms like "fanatic," some undoubtedly meant it to be synonymous with Hoffer's term.[87] But such articulations went further. Journalists' depictions of the Third Force and California cults consistently associated them with the "lowbrow" and the "popular," contemporary terms that evoked mass culture and mass movements. And such movements were the havens of the fanatical. Andrew Ross persuasively argues that "'mass' is one of the key terms that governs the official distinction between American/unAmerican, or inside/outside."[88] Journalists associated "fringe" with "mass," and thus viewed it suspiciously.

The association, or more accurately the articulation, between the lowbrow, mass culture and the religious margins was part of a larger journalistic strategy demarcating the fringe as "other." Searching for a cultural consensus in an increasingly pluralistic Cold War society, the press often depicted the religious fringe as containing those characteristics least suitable to sustaining a unified front against communism. Journalists exoticized the periphery, sometimes regionalized it (to California), and frequently relegated it to the poor and working classes. They made it potentially un-American by associating it with Hofferian "true believers" and mass movements. At the same time, though, writers and editors domesticated the fringe, tempering it as a potential threat. Journal-istic fringe representations achieved this containment by relegat-ing sectarian and cult membership to the realm of taste. Taste, Ross writes, "legitimizes social inequalities because it presents social differences between people as if they were differences of nature."[89] In this case, journalists' depictions implied that by nature, the poor and working classes were attracted to overly emotional, zealous, lowbrow religions. Likewise, California cults naturally attracted crackpots of all classes, those unstable "true believers" ripe to join any dogmatic mass movement. As troubling as religious zealotry may have seemed, it was totally understandable—and containable —when naturalized to specific groups of people.

American religious fringe discourse connected exoticism, emo-tionalism, dogmatism, true believers, the working classes, low-brow culture, and southern California. This discursive formation contained the periphery, symbolically suppressing it as a Cold War threat. Simultaneously, this new conception of the margins also stabilized the shifting boundaries of the religious mainstream. No longer limited to a Protestant Establishment, the "mainstream" now meant things not associated with the fringe: the moderate, the tolerant, and the ecumenical. Implicitly, the center also signaled middle and upper middle class and white—the social location of most journalists and the liberal ecumenicists they consulted.

Alternative Representations:
Evangelicals and Catholics Depict the Fringe

National magazine stories depicting California cults and Third Force groups as exotic and zealous were not the only representa-tions of the American religious fringe. Some portrayals were more idiosyncratic. Marcus Bach's books and his articles in *Christian Century*, for example, suggested that the quests of "strange sects and curious cults" and "traditional churches" were "remarkably alike."[90] A professor of religion at the University of Iowa from 1942 to 1972, Bach was also a founder of the Foundation for Spiritual Understanding and a public lecturer on "interfaith understand-ing." His theological assertion that "all roads that lead to God are good," and that most religions lead to God, was unusual for its time and far surpassed mainline Protestant ecumenicism in its celebration of "offbeat religions."[91] While Bach's perennialist writings stand out, religious periodicals like the Evangelical *Christianity Today* and the Catholic *Commonweal* and *Catholic World* offered fringe representations that claimed to speak for larger faith communities. And their depictions sometimes diverged widely from those in national news and general-interest magazines.

For example, an issue of *Christianity Today* in 1960 included Thomas Zimmerman's "Where Is the 'Third Force' Going?" Zimmerman, general superintendent of the Pentecostal Assemblies of God and president of the National Association of Evangelicals, directly countered the Third Force classification proposed by Henry Van Dusen and promoted by *Life*, *Newsweek*, and *Christian Century*. That classification was faulty, he asserted, because the groups were theologically "varied and in many cases diametrically-opposed."[92] "To illustrate," Zimmerman continued, "the theological beliefs of the seventeen churches mentioned in a *Life* Magazine article in June, 1958, vary all the way from the deviant position of the cult to beliefs closely resembling those held by historic Christian churches."[93]

Alternatively, Zimmerman suggested that the seventeen churches mentioned in *Life* could be sorted into three separate categories: Holiness churches associated with the National Holiness Association, Pentecostal churches affiliated with the Pentecostal Fellowship of North America, and "others," which he described as "a segment independent of any association and varying widely, in some cases even bordering on the status of cults."[94] He continued that "churches found in the first two divisions are strongly represented in the National Association of Evangelicals. Seven out of 13 denominations, comprising a large percentage of the churches, have clearly cast their lot with the evangelical side of Christendom in contradistinction to ecumenical inclusivism."[95]

In suggesting alternative classifications, Zimmerman achieved two things. First, he carefully separated denominations associated with his own movement, the National Association of Evangelicals, from "others" that he defined as cultic. Second, Zimmerman distinguished his own "evangelical side of Christendom" from Van Dusen's "ecumenical inclusivism." Later in the article, Zimmerman criticized depictions of the "so-called Third Force" as fanatical and fringe. "'Is it not tragic,'" he quoted Edward L. R. Elson, President Eisenhower's National Presbyterian minister, "'that to be Spirit-filled is associated with fanaticism?'"[96] Rather than fanatical, Zimmerman suggested, Evangelical enthusiasm followed the practice of the original Christians. Theologically, Zimmerman argued, this made Third Force Evangelicals mainstream and central to Christianity. "One writer," Zimmerman wrote, "recently spoke of Christians who accept these (Evangelical) beliefs as 'fringe,' and 'centrifugal' types, but biblically speaking they are actually centripetal, pulling men back to Jesus Christ and back to the center of early Church theology rather than away from it."[97] For Zimmerman, "cults" and "ecumenical inclusivists" lurked on the fringe, not Evangelicals.

Zimmerman's critique of Van Dusen's Third Force classification revealed that Evangelicals drew different boundaries around the religious center and periphery. While larger news and general-interest magazines identified the fringe by levels of religious commitment, emotional display, geographical location, and socioeconomic status, Evangelical writings located the margins theologically. Most closely associated the religious fringe with the term "cult." In his work, *The Rise of the Cults* (1955), Walter Martin presented the classic Evangelical definition of the term. "By cultism," he wrote, "we mean the adherence to doctrines which are pointedly contradictory to orthodox Christianity and which yet claim the distinction of either tracing their origin to orthodox sources or of being in essential harmony with those sources."[98] If anyone was unclear as to what Martin meant by "orthodox Christianity," Russell Spittler's definition in *Cults and Isms* (1962) removed all ambiguity. "A cult then," he asserted, "is any group that claims to be Christian but falls short of an evangelical definition of Christianity."[99]

Evangelicals classified a variety of religious movements as cults. Mormons, Jehovah's Witnesses, and Christian Scientists were perennial favorites. But Evangelical writers didn't always agree on exactly what was and was not a cult. For example, one interesting debate in Evangelical literature of the 1950s and 1960s surrounded whether Seventh-Day Adventism was a cult or just an Evangelical group with some "problematic" beliefs.[100] Some writers, like Russell Spittler, even included Roman Catholics and Liberal and Neo-Orthodox Protestants in their cult books.[101] In the Evangelical classic *Chaos of the Cults*, Jan Karel Van Baalen decried Protestant modernism and dismissed religious ecumenism.[102] Defining the fringe theologically, Evangelicals partly reversed the classifications of center and periphery found in *Life*, *Newsweek*, *Time*, and other national magazines.[103] The liberal, ecumenical piety that those periodicals placed at the center became, in Evangelical taxonomies, the centrifugal forces pulling people away from the Evangelical, orthodox, Christian core.

In the characteristics that they attributed to the religious periphery, Evangelical magazines both contrasted and coincided with news and general-interest magazines. Unlike the authors of national magazine discourse on the Third Force and California cults, Evangelicals did not see the cultic fringe as exotic or zealous. For Evangelical writers in the 1950s and 1960s, cults deserved marginalization because they led people astray with false and heretical doctrines, not because they were "odd" or overly emotional. But like Van Dusen in his essay on the Third Force, Evangelicals saw cults offering lessons as well as challenges. Both stemmed from cults' apparent growth as a result of successful missionizing.

In the late 1950s and 1960s, Evangelical writers worried about a "cult explosion." "At the dawn of the twentieth century," Gordon Lewis wrote in 1966, "the cults were indistinguishable as a tiny atom, but exploding like atomic bombs the cults have mushroomed upon the American religious horizon."[104] The popular Evangelist Billy Graham further suggested that the profusion of cults was a "real challenge" worldwide.[105] Similarly, *Christianity Today* quoted Philip Edgcumbe Hughes, chairman of the International Reformed Congress, who warned about "cultic hordes."[106] Commenting on the "veritable tidal wave of strange cults that is now swirling alarmingly across the world," Hughes urged that "this satanic assault" be "repelled" by "the trumpet call of the genuine Gospel."[107]

But interpreters often used these defensive call-ups against the "cultic hordes" to suggest that Evangelicals could learn from the successes of the groups. For example, the 19 December 1960 issue of *Christianity Today* focused on "Christianity and the Modern Cults." In the first article, "The American Scene: Are Cults Outpacing Our Churches?" Harold Lindsell, dean of Fuller Seminary, suggested that the growth of cults had been somewhat exaggerated.[108] On the other hand, he asserted, cults showed a vitality that "listless" churches lacked. Lindsell suggested that cults were outpacing churches in three ways: publishing, person-to-person missionizing, and the use of radio and television to proselytize.[109] "When such activities are compared with the communication activities of the Protestant denominations," Lindsell argued, "it soon becomes apparent that the cults, for their size, are manifesting an aggressive zeal and enjoying an outreach far beyond anything being done by the denominations."[110] In a concluding essay, "Challenge of Cults," the editors of *Christianity Today* laid out the implications of Lindsell's argument. "The Church of Jesus Christ," they suggested, "has nothing to fear from the zeal and competition of the cults." On the other hand, they added, "she has much to fear from her own apathy and lethargy in this vital area of missionary concern."[111] For Evangelicals, there was little danger in emotion and zealotry. The real danger lay in too little religious zeal and emotion.

Magazines like *Life*, *Time*, and *Newsweek* frequently depended on liberal Protestants for authoritative commentary, and anti-Catholic sentiments occasionally appeared. For example, Henry Van Dusen's original essay in *Christian Century* in 1955 asserted that Third Force sects "constitute both a challenge and an embarrassment, but principally a challenge, and an embarrassment mainly because of their effective if incomplete representation of authentic Christianity."[112] In comparison, he suggested that Roman Catholicism constituted an "embarrassment and a challenge, with embarrassment predominating and the 'challenge' arising primarily because it misrepresents Christian faith."[113] A report in *Newsweek* on Van Dusen's essay reprinted his comments about Catholicism verbatim, and without editorial comment.[114]

But Catholics did not passively accept these journalistic snipes. *Newsweek* printed three letters responding to Van Dusen's piece. One, from Anthony Iezzi of Greensburg, Pennsylvania, criticized Van Dusen from a Catholic perspective. He wrote that "if Van Dusen carries the essence of Protestantism to its logical conclu-

sions, he will find that there can be no 'traditional' Protestantism. If Luther's break can be justified, then so can every individual
break, since in reality, with private interpretation, there are as
many sects as there are literate Protestants, each giving private
judgment to Christian revelation. Take away an absolute norm and
license is thereby granted to an indefinite score of relatives." [115]

Journalists in Catholic periodicals agreed with Iezzi that Protestantism was inherently sectarian. Writers in the *Catholic World*
and *Commonweal* similarly used subjects like California cults and
enthusiastic sectarianism to criticize Protestantism. In 1955 *Catholic World* published an article on California cults titled "The Land
of Itching Ears." The magazine's blurb on the author, Diana Serra
Cary, described her as a southern California resident, "herself a
member of many of the various sects and cults . . . while en route
to the true Church which she entered in 1946." [116] Cary's article
resembled news and general-interest stories in at least one way:
it represented California cults as exotic. She compared southern California, for example, to a carnival midway populated by
"shabby crystal gazers," "turbaned charlatans," "court astrologers,"
"every exotic specie of mystery religion," and various "strange Oriental seedlings." [117]

But Cary departed from the standard Cold War California cult
narrative when she suggested reasons for the cults' successes. For
Carey, it had nothing to do with California's temperate weather. Instead, she forcefully asserted that Protestantism was to blame. For
example, in a passage that loosely connected Protestantism and
communism, Carey described the California cultists as a "tragic
band of neo-pagan wanderers, lost in a no-man's land between
Orthodox Protestantism, which they feel has been slain by the
gods of Science, and the doctrines of the Communist material-
ists, which they feel spells national and political suicide." [118] Rather
than unstable "true believers," Carey saw cultists as lost souls
"reared amidst the artistic barrenness of Protestantism, and hun-
gry for the color and pageantry of a ritualistic worship rich in
symbols." [119]

Carey proposed that all cultists, like her, were really looking
for Roman Catholicism. The widespread appeal of "new Hindu

missionaries," she asserted, "lies in precisely this accent on universality, which may be in fact a sign of the great homesickness of Christians for the idea of a One True Church."[120] Indeed, she suggested, cult membership for some "has been only a prologue to their serious conversion to the Catholic Church."[121] Carey ultimately called on southern California's Catholic Church to "reach out" to cultists. "We as Catholics in possession of the full revealed truth of God," she argued, "must be aware of the dangers presented to ourselves and to poor, gullible pagans by such doctrines."[122]

While Carey used the California cults to condemn Protestantism, the editor of *Commonweal*, John Cogley, looked to "enthusiastic sectarians" to do the same. Although it names no specific groups, Cogley's editorial, "The Enthusiasts" (1957), parallels larger periodicals' Third Force stories: Cogley accused "sectarians" of being too inspiration-driven, doctrinally dogmatic, and theologically simplistic. He wrote that " 'Sectarians' are inevitably off-balance—their focal doctrine is not kept within proportion. It explains everything, far too much in fact. They find so much in it that they usually tend toward simplistic solutions and antagonize more conventional scholars and thinkers. That does not bother them in the least, for they are almost always anti-theological, putting much more stress on the Holy Spirit than on bookish knowledge. Actually they often regard the disapproval of ecclesiastical or academic worthies as a sign of God's favor."[123]

The problem with sectarians, Cogley argued, was their lack of institutional authority and discipline. Cogley conceded that organization "does seem to dampen 'enthusiasm.' "[124] "Still," he continued, "the argument for the visible Church that moves me is that human nature makes such an institution necessary: no one man can privately maintain a balance between the dazzling mosaics of Christian values."[125] The "visible Church" best suited for sectarians, Cogley suggested, was Roman Catholic. "Despite its stern discipline," Cogley argued, "the Catholic Church does provide for the inspiration and enthusiasm found in sect-like 'movements.' "[126] For Cogley, Roman Catholicism was the solution to enthusiastic sectarianism. He more indirectly hinted what Anthony Iezzi explicitly proposed: that Protestantism, with a focus on personal piety and private biblical interpretation, inevitably prompted sectarianism.

Evangelical writers used theological criteria to reverse classifications of mainstream and fringe. The mainstream, for them, included those groups that followed the orthodox tenets of Christianity. In this case orthodox, of course, meant Evangelical and Protestant. On this new map, Evangelicals relegated liberal and ecumenical Protestants, Catholics, and "cults" to the fringe and placed themselves in the middle. Similarly, Catholic writers tightened the boundaries of the center, exiling all of Protestantism to the sectarian periphery while keeping themselves safely inside. Both Evangelical and Catholic writers attacked Van Dusen's fringe categories. In doing so, they exposed the distinctions between center and periphery promoted in the larger news and general-interest magazines to be as situated as their own. In this respect, Evangelical and Catholic writers played the role of Pierre Bourdieu's "prophets," who subversively perform "the desacralization of the sacred (i.e., of "naturalized arbitrariness) and the sacralization of sacrilege (i.e., of revolutionary transgression)."[127] In other words, prophets, by offering alternative religious "goods," expose unquestioned classifications like those between sacred and profane and between orthodox and heterodox to be arbitrary and situated in human power relations. At the same time, however, neither Evangelicals nor Catholics questioned the validity of center-periphery classifications in general. Rather than subvert the taxonomy, both groups merely worked within it to optimize their own position.[128]

Even if Evangelical and Catholic periodicals dissented in some ways, larger news and general-interest magazines continued to portray the American religious fringe as exotic and zealous. They associated the fringe with "true believers," those volatile fanatics prone to join fascistic, communistic, and dogmatic mass movements. By implication, they also connected the religious periphery to the social margins: the working-class, the poor, the uneducated, the elderly, and the criminal. Journalists thereby contained the boundaries of the fringe demographically and, at least symbolically, stemmed its spread to the larger American social body.

Constructions of the American religious fringe in magazines like *Life, Time, Newsweek,* and *Look* in the 1950s and 1960s were also notable for what they omitted. Brainwashing, a staple of cult exposés after the mid-1970s, never appeared. This was not because the term was unfamiliar. "Brainwashing" entered the national vocabulary in 1953 during the Korean War, when American officials suggested that Chinese communists had brainwashed twenty American prisoners of war.[129] Shortly thereafter, brainwashing motifs surfaced in American popular culture. For example, the popular motion picture *The Manchurian Candidate* (1962) starred Frank Sinatra as a U.S. soldier captured and brainwashed by Korean and Chinese communists to return home and assassinate a presidential candidate. The film was based on the popular novel by Richard Condon from 1959. In addition to Condon's book was Gore Vidal's *Messiah* (1954), an especially interesting example because its story revolves around the growth and expansion of a California cult founded by a former mortician. In the narrative, a high-ranking former member of the cult related how its missionaries had been trained in brainwashing methods.[130] In the realm of popular nonfiction, Malcolm X, in his 1964 autobiography, published in 1964, repeated the standard Nation of Islam assertion that whites had "brainwashed . . . black people to fasten [their] gaze upon a blond-haired, blue-eyed Jesus" and live in oppression waiting for "some dreamy heaven-in-the-hereafter, when we're *dead*, while this white man has his milk and honey in the streets paved with golden dollars right here on this earth!"[131] Brainwashing terminology even appeared in one of the period's Evangelical books on cults. In his Evangelical bestseller *Kingdom of the Cults* (1965), Walter Martin asserted that cultists became "brainwashed" by their religion's authority system.[132] The term was even used in congressional hearings in the 1950s by opponents of popular culture, who accused movies, comics, and music of brainwashing American youth.[133]

Given all this, the absence of brainwashing from depictions of the religious fringe appears all the more striking. But the term never entered journalists' depictions because it didn't fit within the standard "religious fringe" story frame. While brainwashing conjured images of an innocent victim psychologically coerced into changing his allegiances, journalists' depictions of the periphery evoked mass movements of true believers naturally drawn to exotic cults and dogmatic sects. Even when apostates accused their former groups of indiscretions, as happened in the Wisdom, Faith, Knowledge, and Love Commune, journalists downplayed and even ignored the accusations because they didn't fit the accepted discourse. According to Wendy Kozol, postwar journalists covered news items like the civil rights movement and the Cold War by focusing on how these events affected particular individuals and families.[134] In this manner, writers and editors hoped to bring the story "home" to readers by putting a human face on abstract and complex issues. Journalistic representations of the American religious fringe achieved the opposite. They dehumanized the periphery by keeping discourse at the level of mass movements rather than individuals. Journalists depicted the fringe as wholly other—religiously, ideologically, and demographically.

Another motif missing in larger news and general-interest magazines was subversion. Fears of subversion permeated much Cold War rhetoric, metaphor, and symbolism. Even though stories on California cults and Third Force sects in the 1950s and 1960s associated the fringe with fanatical true believers, journalists seldom ever explicitly suggested that these groups posed actual subversive threats. But coverage of the Nation of Islam, known to postwar journalists as the Black Muslims, proved the major exception. Representations of this openly anti-American, anti-white, anti-Christian, all-black religious group revealed fears that only remained latent in Third Force and California cult stories.

chapter two

RACE, CLASS,

AND THE

SUBVERSIVE

COLD WAR OTHER

DEPICTING THE

NATION OF ISLAM,

1959–1965

In 1959, *U.S. News and World Report* published a feature article entitled "'Black Supremacy' Cult in U.S.: How Much of a Threat?" The article was about the Nation of Islam, commonly referred to in the Cold War American media as the Black Muslims. Answering this question, the anonymous writers asserted that the group had no apparent communist or foreign connections, but that they could still pose a "foreign-like" threat to the nation. "In time of war," they concluded, "the Muslims could present a major problem: they are taught they owe allegiance only to the flag of Islam."[1] For reasons of "civic safety" and "national security," *U.S. News* reassured its readers, federal and local authorities—and presumably the newsmagazine itself—would continue to keep "close tabs on the strength and influence of this "'Black Supremacy' movement."[2]

The historian Tom Englehardt suggests that "a nightmarish search for enemy-ness became the defining, even obsessive domestic act of the Cold War years."[3] But communism, he argues, proved a "bedeviling" foe to pinpoint because "it was never fully identified with or contained within any single ethnic or racial community."[4] For white journalists, however, the all-black Nation of Islam was an easily recognizable Cold War enemy. While the working-class, "true believer" status of predominantly white Third Force sects had journalists musing over the potential dangers of religious zeal, the racial makeup of the lower-class Nation had them fearing imminent revolt.

Fears about the Black Muslims were almost always articulated in the language of possibilities. Police chiefs told journalists that the group could cause problems in inner cities. Journalists told readers the movement might be a wartime threat because it could potentially be used by communists, Arabs, or some unidentified foreign enemies. At the heart of stories about the Nation of Islam was distancing and ambiguity: because *we* don't know what *they* are capable of, *we* fear *them*.

One reason for this fear may seem obvious: the Nation *rhetorically* nurtured a subversive identity. Academic studies by the sociologist C. Eric Lincoln, E. U. Essien-Udom, and others suggest that the group never openly advocated violence against whites.[5] But its members were separatists who taught that all Caucasians were devils. They shunned the word "Negro" as a negative European classification in favor of *Black*. Though no researchers ever found communist or foreign conspiratorial political connections, the Muslims taught that the United States stood for "slavery, hell, and death" and would soon be destroyed by Allah.[6] In calling themselves "Muslims" and using the Islamic flag, they symbolically rejected their U.S. citizenship. Here, during the volatile civil rights era, in the midst of the Cold War, were working-class blacks who, as the commentator Harold Isaacs suggested, called "on the Negro American to cease being both 'Negro' and 'American.'"[7] They also urged African Americans to cease being Christians. Although they invoked biblical scriptures in public speeches and writings, the Nation of Islam denounced Christianity as a tool of white oppression, a religion concocted to "brainwash" blacks and keep them enslaved to the "pale devils." For Cold War journalists and many of their readers, the Nation of Islam rhetorically attacked much of what they held dear.

Studying magazine depictions of the Nation of Islam can reveal several things. An examination of the motifs used to portray the group unmasks implicit conceptions of the foreign, the black working class, and authentic religion. Even more broadly, analyzing representational changes over time—and the cessation of media attention—unveils the erratic nature of the images. The Nation of Islam did not become any more or less dangerous, subversive, or threatening in 1965 than they were in 1959—or 1939 for that matter. But print media depictions of the group *did* change when journalists, politicians, and readers concerns shifted to inner-city riots, the Vietnam war, and, as detailed in the next chapter, the youth counterculture.

The Birth of the Nation

The Lost-Found Nation of Islam in the West, commonly referred to by journalists as the Black Muslims, began in 1930. W. D. Fard, a peddler thought by followers to be of Arabic origin, appeared in Detroit's black neighborhoods and soon began holding regular lectures in sympathizers' homes. Labeled "the Prophet" by his followers, Fard asserted that he was sent to teach Islam, the "true religion of all black peoples," to American blacks. When Fard mysteriously disappeared in 1934, Elijah Muhammad, referred to by members as "the Messenger," took over the bulk of his following. Muhammad was born Elijah Poole in Sandersville, Georgia, in 1897. Part of the "Great Migration" of African Americans out of the Jim Crow South into the urban, industrial cities of the North after World War I, he moved his family to Detroit in 1923. In fall 1931, Poole first visited one of Fard's services. By 1932 he had become Fard's "Supreme Minister."[8] After Fard's disappearance, Muhammad elevated the vanished prophet to an incarnation of Allah. But he did much more. Just as Paul is called the "founder of Christianity" by some scholars for his work in institutionalizing and expanding the Jesus movement, it was Muhammad who made the Nation of Islam into a successful national organization. He routinized its rituals, solidified its beliefs, and served as its figurehead until his death in 1975.[9] Though not its initial "prophet," he was certainly its main architect.

The theology and moral codes delivered by Fard and elaborated by Muhammad suggested that "the Black Man by nature is divine," the "Original Man" created by Allah.[10] Caucasians, on the other hand, were literally "blue-eyed devils," a human hybridization created by a rebellious black scientist named Yakub.[11] According to Nation of Islam eschatology, Allah allowed the white devils to rule the earth. The devils then invented Christianity as a tool to enslave blacks. But according to the Nation of Islam, the white devils' control of the earth was almost over. In his classic study of the group, the sociologist C. Eric Lincoln elaborated that "these devils were given six thousand years to rule. The allotted span of their rule ended in 1914, and their 'years of grace' will last no longer than is necessary for the chosen of Allah to be resurrected from the mental death imposed on them by whites. This resurrection is the task of Muhammad himself, Messenger of Allah and spiritual leader of the Lost-Found Nation in the West. The period of Grace was to last seventy years."[12]

Members of the Nation in the early 1960s believed they were living in an apocalyptic period. Allah soon would annihilate all whites and rightfully restore power to the world's black peoples. To facilitate this end-time scenario, members of the Nation proselytized blacks to give up the "white man's religion" and take up Islam. They urged blacks, among other things, to pray five times a day toward Mecca and abstain from pork, cornbread, tobacco, alcohol, and premarital sex. The movement touted black economic self-sufficiency and even urged the U.S. government to allot "two or three states" for the creation of a separatist, all-black nation.[13] With its racialized theology and separatist politics, the Nation of Islam stood in stark contrast to the civil rights movement, led by integrationists like Martin Luther King Jr.

One thing it did share with King and the civil rights movement, however, was extensive attention from J. Edgar Hoover's FBI. From the mid-1950s on, the agency closely monitored the movement and amassed thousands of pages on Elijah Muhammad and his most famous convert, Malcolm X. Ever vigilant and, as history and the Freedom of Information Act have demonstrated, often overly vigilant and dishonest in how it searched for and treated alleged Cold War enemies, the bureau saw the Nation as a potential threat. One memorandum from the FBI's Chicago office to Hoover in 1953 asserted that "the fanaticism of the MCI [Muslim Cult of Islam] members appears to be of such an extreme degree as to render possible an outbreak of violence by cult members, which might be similar in nature to the recently attempted assassination of members of the House of representatives by Puerto Rican Nationalists."[14] As noted by Muhammad's biographer Claude Clegg, the FBI not only monitored the Nation but also occasionally leaked "semi-factual and false information" to newspapers.[15] These sorts of "half-truths" sometimes made their way into magazines, reproducing a government-created image of the Nation of Islam as a subversive Cold War threat that operated behind a falsified religious front.

The Nation of Islam as Subversive Threat, 1959–1963

On 9 January 1963, the Joint Legislative Committee on Un-American Activities of Louisiana published *Activities of "The Nation of Islam" or the Muslim Cult of Islam in Louisiana.* The document recorded a state hearing on 27 November 1962 concerning Nation of Islam activities in Monroe, Louisiana. "The Committee finds," read part of the conclusion, "as a matter of fact, that the function and operation of the Nation of Islam is a cruel sham and deceit, based upon gross ignorance and superstition, using the guise or protective coloring of 'religion' to give credence and dignity to a vicious program of calculated disloyalty, sedition, subversion and racial hatred, directed to all levels of government in this state and Nation and at the white race in particular."[16] The committee concluded that "the influence of the Communist conspiracy in the Nation of Islam appears to be significant and dangerous. . . . Through the Nation of Islam, the Communists see hope for producing their desired goals of progressive disillusionment, dissatisfaction, disaffection and disloyalty."[17]

The Louisiana committee's report is obviously a state government document and not a magazine article. But it illustrates the striking similarity between the perceptions of national and local government and law enforcement officials on the one hand and those of the largest news and general-interest magazines on the other, in that it mirrors three major themes that dominated print media representations of the Nation in the early 1960s. First, although magazine reporters rarely charged that the Nation was directly linked to an international communist conspiracy, they frequently pondered the group's possible foreign connections. Reflecting Cold War concerns with protecting internal purity and consensus from foreign insurgence, interpreters associated the Nation of Islam with the "foreign." Second, when the Louisiana Legislative Committee on Un-American Activities wrote that the Nation of Islam was "based upon gross ignorance and superstition," it revealed implicit views, mirrored in most magazine articles, on the mentality of those attracted to the group. In depicting the Nation of Islam as a lower-class black movement with subversive tendencies, journalists relied on common stereotypes of African Americans and the poor as overly emotional, unintelligent, and prone to fanaticism. Third, magazine stories, like the Louisiana legislators who considered the Muslims a "cruel sham and deceit," frequently questioned the group's religious authenticity. Many Cold War writers and editors operated with implicit definitions of religion, and the Nation of Islam seldom fit their preconceptions.

In light of the shared ideological commitments between the news media and the political establishment suggested by Stuart Hall, Wendy Kozol, and others, and given that these shared commitments were heightened during the Cold War, one would have expected media and government depictions of the Nation of Islam to be similar. Stuart Hall suggests that the mass media can frequently act as a social control mechanism, limiting the range of possible discourse on given topics in ways that support the social order. Hall argues that the media "tend, systematically, to draw on a very limited ideological or explanatory repertoire; and that repertoire . . . will have the overall tendency of making things 'mean' within the sphere of the dominant ideology."[18] Wendy Kozol, in her study of *Life*, similarly argues that the magazine's photojournalism—and indeed one could argue all of Henry Luce's periodicals of the Cold War era—"presented a vision of private life that met the needs and served the interests of dominant political and economic sectors."[19] In monitoring and portraying the Nation of Islam, national news and general-interest magazines frequently acted as a symbolic, and literal, tool of social control.

Elijah Muhammad and the Nation had been well publicized in several other black-owned newspapers for years. The *Pittsburgh Courier* carried a column by Elijah Muhammad from 1956 to 1959, in addition to frequent stories about the group. The *Los Angeles Herald Dispatch* and the *New Amsterdam News* reported on and featured editorials by Muhammad as well.[20] But the Nation first garnered white media attention in 1959 on *Newsbeat*, a show airing on the CBS affiliate WNTA-TV in New York. The African American journalist Louis Lomax proposed a story on the group to the program's anchors, Mike Wallace and Ted Yates. Neither had ever heard of the Nation of Islam, but they agreed to produce the program. The result was *The Hate That Hate Produced*, a five-part series, later shown as a one-hour documentary, which aired from 10 to 17 July.[21] The story featured footage of Muslim rallies, showed the group's male drill squad (the Fruit of Islam) practicing fighting techniques, and included interviews with Elijah Muhammad and Malcolm X. In his discussion with Louis Lomax, Malcolm X set forth Nation of Islam theology and eschatology. He asserted that the white man was "by nature" evil. He also predicted that the next ten years would witness an "insurrection" resulting in "plenty of bloodshed."[22] The movement's racialized theology and Malcolm X's eloquent enumeration of it unnerved many white and black viewers. It enticed others. Within a month after the broadcasts, according to C. Eric Lincoln, the Nation of Islam had doubled its membership to almost 60,000.[23]

In the following months and years, the print media took up the Nation of Islam as a subject. Articles frequently hinted at foreign connections to intensify the representation of the group as "others." This was especially apparent in the fervently conservative, anti-communist magazine *American Opinion* in January 1963. An anonymous author, using the palindromic pseudonym "Revilo P. Oliver," reviewed two scholarly books on the Nation of Islam: C. Eric Lincoln's *Black Muslims in America* and E. U. Essien-Udom's *Black Nationalism*. Although his essay spanned sixteen pages, Oliver spent little space actually reviewing the works. Oliver instead focused on the possible connections between the Nation of Islam and an "International Communist Conspiracy." "If we regard the Black Muslims as an isolated movement promoted by racketeers or fanatics," he wrote, "they seem almost incredible, worthy of a vaudeville show." But, Oliver continued, "If we regard them as a crypto-Communist operation, the most grotesque aspects of their activity become intelligible."[24]

No evidence, Oliver admitted, had revealed a Muslim-communist connection. "And it is possible," he warned, "that no investigation . . . could obtain positive evidence of such a relationship."[25] Nonetheless, for Oliver certain factors made the allegiance undeniable. First, the "shrewdness" and "strategy" with which Elijah Muhammad conducted his "operations" obviously could not "have emanated from [Muhammad's] own mind."[26] Oliver left it up to his readers' racial prejudices to understand this argument. Second, he continued, the group "conforms perfectly to the standard pattern that the Conspiracy uses to excite race war throughout the world."[27] Third, Oliver suggested that according to an unnamed "authoritative source," the Muslims were funded by the emergent "New York Consulate of Guinea" and supported by "orthodox" Muslims of the Middle East—both of whom Oliver connected to the Kremlin.[28] At the very least, Oliver asserted, the Nation had already served vital subversive purposes. "They are already," he argued, "being used to make such vicious, and probably more dangerous, agitators as Martin Luther King seem 'moderate' by contrast, although their pretenses to be 'Christians' is scarcely more plausible than Elijah's pretense that he is a Mohammedan."[29]

One might dismiss Oliver's *American Opinion* article as extremist, reflecting the editorial policy of a virulently anti-communist, racist magazine. While that might be true, *American Opinion* was not alone in pondering the movement's foreign connections. Larger news, general-interest, and religious periodicals also took up the subject. As noted, *U.S. News and World Report* in its issue dated 9 November 1959 suggested that the "black supremacy cult" could pose a foreign-like threat to the nation. In contrast to Oliver, however, *U.S. News* found no direct foreign support for the Nation of Islam. The magazine rejected a declaration by Thurgood Marshall, counsel to the NAACP and future Supreme Court justice, that the Nation of Islam was financed by "some Arab group."[30] Furthermore, readers were reassured, "true Moslems" in both the United States and abroad "disown the so-called Temple of Islam."[31] Still, in noting unelaborated details like the mention that the "Muslim cult" made "much of Arab trappings," the article tied the group to symbolic notions of "foreignness."[32]

No governmental, academic, or journalistic investigation ever discovered subversive connections between the Nation of Islam and any foreign nation. But there were interactions between the Nation and some foreign leaders. Malcolm X, for example, met with the Cuban communist leader and American Cold War enemy Fidel Castro. In his study of the group, C. Eric Lincoln also noted that the Nation did "accept important encouragement and advice from Egyptian Nationals." Both Malcolm X and Elijah Muhammad were also received "warmly" in their visits to the United Arab Republic, and Muhammad corresponded with President Gamal Abdel Nasser of Egypt.[33] While Lincoln discovered no conspiratorial or monetary links, he found it "possible" that the interests in the group shown by "some Moslem leaders" may have been more political than religious. However, he gave no supporting evidence for this conjecture.[34]

Magazines consistently articulated conceptions of foreignness to the Nation of Islam, but I argue that it was only partly due to these international contacts. Connecting "foreignness" to the Nation was part of a larger strategy that Cold War journalists used to portray the group as "wholly other." The binary opposition between home and foreign was just one of several distinguishing "Black Muslim" from "American." And in stories about the Nation, the foreign other connected to the group could be communist, Middle Eastern, or any number of internationals considered subversive. Sometimes the Nation's foreignness lay in potential future communist associations. One example is John LaFarge's review in 1961 of Lincoln's *Black Muslims in America*. LaFarge, writing for the Jesuit periodical *America*, noted that Lincoln drew no connections between the Nation and communism. Though LaFarge did not contest this, he implied that a connection might yet evolve: "it is evident that such an organized hate movement can be skillfully used to further Communist schemes of disruption and World Conquest."[35]

In other articles, associations between the Muslims and foreignness lay less in possibilities than in analogy and comparison. In a 1963 exposé in the *Saturday Evening Post*, Alfred Balk and Alex Haley said nothing about current or potential foreign alliances. But they did ask if the Nation of Islam was, "as one columnist described them, 'the Mau Mau of the American Negro World,' and therefore a dangerous threat to our society?"[36] This reference to the Kenyan anti-colonialists was meant to conjure bloody images of violent uprisings and social disorder. Balk and Haley also conjured a foreign enemy of America's recent past by likening Nation of Islam rallies to those of Hitler's Nazi Party in prewar Germany.[37] Without explicitly mentioning it, the writers, by referring to such groups, connected the Nation of Islam to the "true believers" of Eric Hoffer's work on mass movements. " 'One thing everyone should understand,' " they quoted a police chief from Chicago, " 'is that Elijah "Muhammad" Poole is not just a run-of-the mill rabble rouser, nor is his organization just an innocuous regional sect. This man is creating a mass movement on the national scale.' "[38]

The chief's assertion that Muhammad was "creating a mass movement on a national scale" was far more than descriptive. As noted in Chapter 1, Andrew Ross argues that " 'mass' is one of the key terms that governs the official distinction between American/un-American, or inside/outside."[39] In identifying the Nation of Islam as a mass movement—a term sometimes associated in the 1950s and early 1960s with potential violence, subversion, criminality, and the lower class—journalists further marked the group as an un-American other.

Journalists viewed the Nation of Islam as a mass movement that was subject, like all other mass movements, to subversive tendencies. In his book review, LaFarge concluded that the Muslims were one example of "new mass movement specters" that "will arise to plague us" if Christian teachings were not applied to race relations "in the heart and suburbs of our big cities."[40] While not calling for Christian teachings, national newsweeklies joined LaFarge in fearing the disruptive potential of this "mass movement specter." Faced with evidence that the Nation had not been involved in any planned violence, an article in *Time* in 1959 used the common convention of quoting unnamed police officials to suggest concern. "Thus far," *Time* wrote, "the Moslems have been strictly law-abiding—a fact that worries some cops more than minor outbreaks of violence. 'It's getting worse everyday, says a Los Angeles police official, 'and I only wish I knew what it's going to take to light the fuse.' "[41] The magazine left readers to guess at what it was that might be getting worse.

In 1962, in an article titled "The Muslim Message: All White Men Devils, All Negroes Divine," *Newsweek* used similar conventions. The magazine initially noted that the Black Muslims profess nonviolence and "will fight only if attacked." "Nevertheless," *Newsweek* continued, "police worry over the fringe of new comers and hangers-on who, set off by some spark in the Muslim message, might decide to help Allah along."[42] In a 1961 article in the *Nation*, Herbert Krosney exemplified the journalistic view of the Muslims succinctly when he wrote, "they are angry and unafraid to use violence. They will make news."[43]

Admittedly, the Nation of Islam was involved in some violent incidents. During the Fard period, a member named Robert Harris reportedly sacrificed his roommate. Though this was probably an isolated incident involving two disturbed individuals, some authorities suggested that the group promoted human sacrifice.[44] In 1935 Muslims rioted in a Chicago courtroom, killing one police officer.[45] In the 1950s and 1960s, most violence involving Black Muslims resulted from police attacks on the group. In the late 1950s, New York police were found guilty by an all-white jury of severely beating a member of the Nation, who was awarded $75,000 in damages.[46] In a more ambiguous incident in April 1962, the Los Angeles Police killed one Muslim and injured seven others when officers stopped to question two street peddlers and ended up storming into a Nation of Islam temple. Though the details of the case were disputed, Nation of Islam members apparently tried to remove the police from the temple and a gunfight ensued. In addition to the casualties among Nation of Islam members, a police officer was shot. The Nation insisted that the police had initiated violence by entering the temple, and it was never proved that any member of the group was responsible for wounding the officer.[47] But media concern over the Nation of Islam far exceeded the occasional skirmishes they were involved in — especially when compared to the sparse coverage given to the Ku Klux Klan during their violent resurgence (noted later in this chapter).

Fears about the Nation of Islam were partly fueled by demographics that implicitly signaled volatility to many writers and editors. Lincoln's study of the group revealed that members were overwhelmingly between seventeen and thirty-five years of age, male, lower class, and—of course—African American.[48] As noted in Chapter 1, these demographics fit with Eric Hoffer's description of potential "true believers," those unstable fanatics who form the bulk of mass movements. Hoffer asserted that among others, the poor and minorities were particularly "susceptible" to the lure of mass movements.[49] Many journalists accurately reported that the group had made a number of converts in prisons, and "criminals" were another group that Hoffer identified as "true believer" candidates.[50] One story in *Time* in 1961, "Recruits behind Bars," took this information and linked the Nation of Islam to criminality in two ways. First, it suggested, the "Muslim movement behind prison walls . . . has become 'steadily stronger and more troublesome.'"[51] "While their leaders, protected by shaved-head honor guards, are preaching cold hatred to growing crowds in principal U.S. cities," *Time* portentously warned, "lesser Muslim agents are at work in many a U.S. prison, spreading fanatical doctrines and recruiting new brethren among Negro prisoners."[52] Note the striking parallel here between journalists' use in the 1950s and early 1960s of the word "agents" to refer to both the Nation of Islam and communists. Second, the magazine noted that some of the Muslim leadership itself had criminal records. It reported that Elijah Muhammad, inaccurately described as "high priest of the Muslims, served three years for draft-dodging in World War Two."[53] They also related that Malcolm X, "leader of Harlem's Muslims, is a former pimp who has been arrested three times."[54]

"Recruits behind Bars" suggested that "since most prisons have a large Negro population, prisons are a natural breeding ground for the hate group."[55] *Time* followed this assertion with a statement by C. Eric Lincoln, who asserted, "The prisons are made to order for Muhammad. Nine times out of ten, the potential convert was arrested by a white policeman, sentenced by a white judge, directed by a white prison guard under a white warden. The prison chaplain was white, and he knew when he got out that he could not go to a white church for help. The Negro church was not interested, but there was Elijah waiting."[56]

Time ostensibly used this quote to lend credence to its assertion that prisons were the Muslims' "natural breeding ground." It attempted to justify the statement by quoting a scholar—Lincoln was a sociologist so the assertion appeared academically sound. The magazine also tried to neutralize the statement racially: Lincoln was black so therefore it presumably couldn't be racist. Interestingly, however, Lincoln's apt description potentially subverted the dominant story frame of "Recruits behind Bars" as much as it supported it. While *Time* linked the Nation of Islam to criminality and danger, Lincoln's quote suggested that inequities in the American social system could be responsible for black prisoners' interests in the group. Lincoln's statement could be read as a critique of the white-dominated justice system, the racism of many white churches, and the apathy of many black denominations. So while the writers and editors at *Time* initially seemed to have framed the story to suggest that the Nation of Islam was a mass movement of thugs, Lincoln's quotation made the article polysemic, a narrative susceptible to multiple, even contradictory, interpretations.

When articles focused on prisoners' attraction to the Nation of Islam and the disreputable past of some of its figureheads, they had demographic profiles and police records to support them. But when they described how the group attracted disproportionate numbers of lower-class African Americans, stories in the largest news and general-interest magazines tended to rely on stereotypical assumptions that poor blacks were overly emotional and ignorant. For example, in an article in *Esquire* in 1961 titled "The Angriest Negroes," the African American writer William Worthy ignored the relatively formal and orderly style of Nation of Islam meetings to assert that the group's beliefs, speeches, and services evoked a "sort of emotionalism" that "of course, appeals mainly to the poor, the uneducated, and the unintelligent."[57] Worthy's list of potential members reads like a list out of Hoffer's influential *The True Believer*. The Muslims, Worthy declared, were "quasi-illiterate Negroes equipped with no special skills," "simple people" who were "one generation away from voodoo."[58] These assertions mirror those elaborated by Police Chief Kelly of Monroe, Louisiana, during the Un-American Activities trial described above. In his statement, Kelly said that he first encountered the Black Muslims after hearing reports of people in the "colored" section of

Monroe being "hoodooed." "Of course," Kelly stated, "knowing the people as we do in that particular area, they can easily be led astray in this type of situation."[59]

Worthy, an educated, middle-class African American journalist, and Kelly, a southern white police officer, both used a common Cold War discourse that associated the lower classes and minorities with ignorance, emotionalism, and susceptibility to fraudulent and fanatical mass movements. Focusing on Muslim strength in inner cities—an iconic American space historically used to invoke exoticism and danger—journalists spatially represented the group's otherness.[60] In story after story, this association between the group and the inner city also entailed an association with violence. Journalists warned that fiery Nation of Islam rhetoric could spur rioting among potential true believers living in "intercity trouble spots."[61] For example, in *Reader's Digest* Alex Haley quoted a police commissioner from New York as having said that "in emotionally intense minority communities, a Muslim interpretation of 'defend yourself,' backed by the well-trained 'Fruit of Islam,' could easily ignite a riot."[62]

For many writers, lower-class urban blacks appeared prone to violence because of their unsophisticated nature and overt emotionalism. The Nation of Islam had a following, C. Eric Lincoln wrote in *Christian Century* in 1965, because "tens of thousands" of blacks "simply have not reached the level of sophistication which would enable them to understand the value and dignity of nonviolent resistance."[63] Notably, Lincoln also suggested that many white southerners—particularly those in authority who fought desegregation with police dogs, water hoses, and assorted terrorist actions—were also highly unsophisticated. Lincoln's nuances, however, do not diminish his usage of lower-class stereotypes. The assertions that the Nation of Islam attracted the feeble-minded poor—made by journalists as well as academics—reveal classist assumptions that crossed racial lines. Lincoln, Haley, and Worthy were all black writers. When looking at the Nation of Islam, one wonders if they saw a working-class black mass movement threatening insurrection. One wonders also if journalists' warnings about inner-city riots may have cloaked deeper fears that such disturbances might move out of the ghettoes and into middle-class neighborhoods.

Journalists, the Nation of Islam, and "True Religion"

In his article in *Esquire*, William Worthy reported, "Federal investigations of the organization conclude that the Muslims are a paramilitary society operating on the fringes of the law and utilizing religious fervor to implement a program of secular hatred."[64] Despite Worthy's use of the FBI's ambiguous language, the federal government treated the Nation of Islam as a religion. It granted the group tax-exempt status and, after some hedging, allowed prison converts to practice the faith in federal prisons.[65] The national print media, however, did not follow suit. Throughout the 1960s, coverage continuously questioned whether there was anything "religious" about the Muslims at all.

Once again, the largest news and general-interest magazines paralleled the views expressed in the report of the Louisiana legislative committee. As noted earlier, the committee concluded that "the function and operation of the Nation of Islam is a cruel sham and deceit, based upon gross ignorance and superstition, using the guise of religion to give credence and dignity to a vicious program of calculated disloyalty, sedition, subversion, and racial hatred."[66] Nearly two years before the committee's report, *Newsweek* had similarly asserted that "unlike others, which have openly political aims, the Muslims operate behind a thin religious front."[67] After acknowledging that the group actually did adhere to some Islamic requirements, the unnamed writers at *Newsweek* reported: "Historic Islam agrees with many of these requirements, but it is quite opposed to racial discrimination; it is probably Elijah's vitriolic hatred of white people ('two-legged rattlesnakes') that brands him most clearly as a religious phony."[68] Like *Newsweek*, other magazines distinguished the "Black Muslims" from "true Islam." While William Worthy in *Esquire* described the group as a "peculiar mixture of orthodox Mohammedanism and the personal prejudices of Elijah Muhammad," *Time* noted that the "U.S.'s 100,000 true Moslems" were outraged over the group's use of the term Islam.[69] Indeed, while some Middle Eastern Islamic leaders accepted the group as a Muslim sect, several spokesmen for Muslim groups based in the United States asked journalists to not confuse them with the Nation of Islam, and sometimes mounted publicity attacks against it. Interestingly, however, most magazine articles failed to ever quote specific American Islamic spokesmen, relying on unattributed assertions credited to "true Moslems."

Journalists of all stripes seemingly agreed that the Nation of Islam's status as a religion was in question. Usually this appeared as two separable assertions that writers inherently connected. First, they denied that the Nation practiced a type of Islam. Second, they denied that it was religious at all. In the liberal *Reporter*, for example, Nat Hentoff implied that if the Nation of Islam wasn't part of "true Islam," it likely wasn't religious. "Although Mr. Muhammad and his spokesmen claim to lead what is primarily a religious movement," he wrote, "there is considerable doubt about the degree of its involvement with Mohammedanism as such."[70] William Buckley's more conservative *National Review* dubbed the group a "pseudo-religion."[71] Writing in *Ebony*, Hans J. Massaquoi concurred, calling the Nation of Islam a "quasi-religion."[72]

Most contemporary religion scholars would define the Nation of Islam as a new religious movement, a recently founded religion with some practices and beliefs that distinguish it from existing, longer-established religions.[73] The postwar Nation of Islam combined elements of Islam and Christianity with the new ideas and practices of W. D. Fard and Elijah Muhammad. Most journalists, however, held implicit definitions of religion that disregarded categories like "new religion" and "alternative religion." The Nation of Islam's beliefs, practices, and history contrasted sharply with journalists' definitions. First, the Nation merged social fields —the political and religious—that most journalists thought incompatible. By merging what were perceived as two separate categories, the Nation of Islam appeared to be, in the words of the religion scholar Bruce Lincoln, a "taxonomic anomaly": "Thus, (1) an anomaly is any entity that defies the rules of an operative taxonomy or (2) an anomaly is any entity, the existence of which an operative taxonomy is incapable of acknowledging."[74] As seen in some of the passages above, both media and government writers suggested that the group was a paramilitary or nationalist organization making cunning use of the guise of religion to pursue political goals. To uphold their established, doxic categories, journalists and many government officials fit the group narrowly into the political field and labeled it a religious fraud. Interestingly, the majority of articles in *Time* and *Newsweek* on the group appeared in the "races" section rather than the "religion" section.

By sharply demarcating the boundaries between politics and religion, the articles unwittingly promoted a journalistic tendency to see religion as, in the words of the cultural studies scholar Talal Asad, "an autonomous essence," "a transhistorical and transcultural phenomenon."[75] By positing religion as an autonomous field —untouched by politics, economics, and race relations—journalists removed it from its material, historical base and situated it onto one of essentialized, universalized morals and mores. This strategy allowed articles on the Nation of Islam to evoke, without any explicit, partisan theologizing, notions of religious authenticity and religious fraud.

In addition to the Nation of Islam's problematic merging of religion, politics, and race, the movement did not match journalists' implicit, moral definitions of religion. The "American news media," the religion scholar and journalist Mark Silk argues, "presupposes that religion is a good thing."[76] Silk suggests that the news media define "good" (i.e. "true") religion "via negativa," by identifying what it is not: intolerant, hypocritical, and false.[77] Needless to say, the Nation of Islam's aggressive rhetoric, elaborate, racialized theology, and doomsday eschatology contrasted sharply with journalists' conceptions of religion as tolerant and socially benign. One description in *Newsweek* of a Nation of Islam meeting illustrates this. "Two Negroes," it read, "plodded up and down in the golden August sunlight outside Kiel Auditorium in St. Louis, carrying placards that said, 'The Bible Say Love Your Fellow Man—We Believe the Bible' and 'Our Religion is Built in Love, Not Hate.' But they were barely noticed by the lines of Negroes filing into the city-owned hall in their Sunday-best suits and flowered-print dresses. The crowd had come—some out of belief and some out of curiosity—to hear a religious message of another sort: the bitter nationalist litany of the Black Muslims."[78]

It is important to note that not every writer labeled the Nation of Islam a religious fraud. One rare exception was Albert Southwick, writing in the ecumenical, Protestant *Christian Century*. "Whether the Black Muslims are an authentic part of Islam," he wrote in 1963, "is a matter of debate." But, he continued, "the Black Muslims do read the Koran and observe Muslims fasts and prayers." Southwick also noted that after Malcolm X's conversion, his "life was changed so that he no longer indulged in his old vices of drinking, smoking, whoring, stealing, and violence."[79] Assuming that religion positively improved one's life, Southwick suggested that Malcolm X's dramatic prison conversion served as proof that the movement might indeed be religious. It is interesting to note that Southwick, like his "secular" journalist counterparts in newsmagazines, used moral criteria to suggest that one could distinguish authentic from inauthentic religion by its effects on converts. Though he came to a different conclusion, Southwick's means of judgment were the same.

Jonathan Z. Smith suggests that "the most common form of classifying religions, found both in native categories and in scholarly literature, is dualistic and can be reduced, regardless of what differentium is applied, to 'theirs' and 'ours.'"[80] The juxtaposition by *Newsweek* of Christian brotherly love and Muslim nationalist hatred asserted just such a differentiation. As noted above, many articles implicitly proposed a dichotomy between "true religion" and "false religion." Recall the assertion in *Newsweek*: "it is probably Elijah's vitriolic hatred of white people . . . that brands him most clearly as a religious phony."[81] The article in *Newsweek*, representative of most general-interest and newsmagazine coverage in general, presumed that any movement espousing racial intolerance could not, by its very nature, be religious.

Journalists' definitions of authentic religion were morally based: true religion preached universal brotherhood and benefited societies. False ones, like the Nation of Islam, did the opposite. Though ostensibly "secular," journalists' musings over the Nation of Islam were often far from it. Writers and editors overwhelmingly portrayed the Nation as a religious fraud. In doing so, they unwittingly unveiled an implicit moral theology that distinguished the orthodox from the heterodox, true religion from false.

John Hartley and Martin Montgomery argue that "media journalism often operates with a manichean view of the world: events are constructed in terms of binary oppositions, a primary opposition being 'US' and 'THEM,' 'HOME' and 'FOREIGN.'"[82] In representing the Nation of Islam, journalists used just such an opposition. Writers applied one explicit dichotomy (American/foreign) and a slate of more implicit ones (white/black, middle-class/poor, rational/irrational, true religion/false religion). Articles strategically combined these simplistic binary oppositions with the group's own incendiary rhetoric to create a journalistic discourse portraying the members of the Nation as threatening, subversive others, ultimate Cold War enemies who stood for the opposite of everything "American." While this discourse resembled other Cold War narratives of "enemyness," and while the Nation of Islam itself nurtured an oppositional identity, representations of the group were particularly racialized and classist—so much so that portrayals of the Nation of Islam "naturalized" class and race differences. In other words, these depictions furtively suggested that certain characteristics attributed to lower-class blacks were permanent and fixed.[83] By "nature," these journalistic representations implied, working-class blacks were ignorant, easily "hoodooed," given to emotionalism, and susceptible to the pull of sinister mass movements. In depicting the Nation of Islam, journalists exercised their "symbolic power" to categorize races, social classes, and even religion in ways that supported existent social inequalities.[84]

The Nation of Islam as Social Mirror: Social Criticism and the Limits of Representational Contestation

Portrayals of the "Black Muslims" as dangerous, subversive others were not the sole representations in print media of the early 1960s. First, the Nation of Islam published its own newspapers and magazines—therein offering a markedly different self-portrait. Second, alternative representations occasionally appeared in national magazines, either in letters to the editor or in anomalous articles. For the most part, however, the motif of the Nation of Islam as subversive other hegemonically dominated coverage. By hegemony, I refer to the state in which particular discourses, representations, assumptions, and ideologies dominate a particular field or medium in society (in this case, print media depictions of the Nation). Stuart Hall argues that a hegemonic discourse "commands widespread consent and appears natural and inevitable."[85] Indeed, Cold War journalists used the "subversive other" motif to such an extent that they came to view it as the only possible way to frame a story on the group.

The most fertile source for alternatives to this popular frame was the Nation of Islam itself. The group issued its own magazines, newspapers, and long-playing records, and produced its own radio shows. C. Eric Lincoln estimates that *Muhammad Speaks*, its newspaper, had a circulation in 1961 of 600,000. If this number is correct, *Muhammad Speaks* would have been the most widely distributed black paper in the United States.[86] Nation of Islam theology inverted commonplace assumptions and classifications—instead of love, Christianity stood for hate and enslavement; black, not white, was the pure and original. Nation of Islam journalism also reversed stereotypes. One good example of this can be seen in an issue of *Muhammad Speaks* from the early 1960s, described in an editorial by James O'Gara in the Catholic periodical *Commonweal*. One article, bearing the headline "Holy Bible student Confesses Slaying Three in Negro Family," described a "white Bible student who last year was accused of murdering three members of a Negro's family in order to abduct their beautiful, 16-year-old girl."[87] This story reversed several common stereotypes. First, the writers noted that the killer was not only Christian but a Bible student. More notably, the writers reversed the racist stereotype of savagely sexual black males lusting after white women, a legend-like narrative historically employed by white racists. In *Muhammad Speaks*, it was a *white* Bible student who lusted after a *black* teenage girl. His uncontrollable, irrational, animal desires—those very characteristics sometimes attributed to poor, uneducated members of the Nation of Islam—eventually caused him to commit murder.

In creating this kind of inversion, the Nation engaged in what I call "narrative détournement." The popular culture scholar Greil Marcus defines détournement, a term used by the French Situationist International, as "the theft of aesthetic artifacts from their contexts and their diversion into contexts of one's own devise."[88] "Détournement," Marcus elaborates, "was a politics of subversive quotation, of cutting the vocal cords of every empowered speaker, social symbols yanked through the looking glass, misappropriated words and pictures diverted into familiar scripts and blowing them up."[89] In the 1950s and 1960s, the French Situationists criticized consumer capitalism from a neo-Marxian and anarchist perspective. They proposed and enacted détournement of commercial art and advertising as a strategy to demystify the endless cycle of production and consumption that they viewed as enslaving people. Rather than advertising, Nation of Islam journalists and spokesmen used stereotypical news narratives and popular racial assumptions and twisted them until they became the opposite of their original form, a parody, a "communication containing its own criticism."[90] Newsweek and Time connected the Nation of Islam to criminality. But Malcolm X, the group's most vocal spokesman, used "détournement" of such narratives by suggesting that he was a Christian during his years as a street hustler and that it wasn't until his conversion that he changed.[91] Thus, criminality was tied to Christianity, not to the Nation of Islam. Malcolm X also used the term "brainwashing" to describe Christianity's enslaving effect on blacks. As noted in Chapter 1, this predated by over ten years journalists' use of the term to describe the practices of new religious movements.[92]

Alternative depictions occasionally appeared in national magazines as well. These, however, were rare. A couple came in the form of letters to the editor, criticizing magazine stories as biased. In 1963, for example, Jerry Mahrer wrote to the Nation to criticize Herbert Krosney's article "The Negro Racists." "I continue," he wrote, "to be amazed (and perhaps I shouldn't be) by the bad press and by the false and half-true statements to which black nationalism is subjected. I am not a Black Muslim (I am not even black, for that matter), but I feel that one should attempt to understand the movement in its entirety before condemning it with the infamous label of 'racism.'"[93]

In another letter, a black ex-convict, Clarence Cooper Jr., responded at length to William Worthy's article in Esquire, "The Angriest Negroes." He suggested that Worthy was amiss in failing to detail Nation of Islam beliefs. Cooper questioned the implicit definitions that many journalists used in depicting the group. Referring to one of Elijah Muhammad's writings, Cooper wrote, "Despite the fairy tale quality of the information contained in Devine

Wisdom, there is an element of revelation that screams for black brothers' recognition."[94] In contrast to news and general-interest articles, Cooper extensively outlined the intricate cosmology of the group. Cooper concluded that "though much of what I have written may seem preposterous, the high-flying fantasy of a fanatic group that must dig its roots in somewhere, it has as much basis as Christianity, here in a land where the black man has never known the white man to be anything other than a devil."[95] In asserting that Nation of Islam theology had as much, or as little, historical and experiential basis as many Christian claims, Cooper directly countered the preferred journalistic reading of the group as irreligious and based on little more than Elijah Muhammad's personal prejudices.

On four occasions from 1959 to 1963, one mass-market and three special-interest magazines published articles that offered alternative depictions of the "Black Muslims." In September 1959, *Jet* featured Marc Crawford's "The Truth about the Black Muslims." While virtually unknown to many whites, *Jet* was a popular African American magazine that achieved national recognition in 1955 for publishing a photograph of Emmett Till's horribly mutilated corpse at an open casket funeral. While visiting relatives in Money, Mississippi, Till, a fourteen-year-old Chicagoan, was murdered by two whites angered over his "crime" of speaking to a white woman. While the title of Crawford's article suggests the shocking exposé style that most journalists used to cover the group, "The Truth about the Black Muslims" countered several national magazine depictions. Crawford asserted that the white press, chagrined that the Muslims had denied them access to one of their meetings, "branded them hate-mongers of the worst kind."[96] In August 1959, *Time* suggestively reported that Elijah Muhammad had been arrested in 1934 for contributing to the delinquency of a minor, leaving the reader to imagine what had happened.[97] In the following months and years, *Newsweek, Life,* and *Esquire* reported the arrest in similar, undetailed fashion. Crawford, however, noted that Muhammad was arrested for refusing to send his daughter to a Detroit public school, not for any sexual or otherwise criminal misconduct.[98] In addition to Crawford's text, the accompanying pictures and captions were more positive than any found in the largest newsweeklies. When captioning pictures of the leadership or educational institutions, the largest magazines frequently put quotation marks around words like "minister" or the name of the group's school, the "University of Islam." Like *Time* and *U.S. News*, *Jet* showed pictures of Muslim children learning in their private school. Unlike those magazines, *Jet* did not question its legitimacy by placing "school" in quotes. *Jet*'s caption read, "Starting Arabic in third grade at Chicago school, accredited to ninth grade, Muslim children attend school 50 weeks a year."[99] Negative connotations were also absent in the caption under pictures of a Muslim restaurant and grocery. "Restaurant observes dietary laws, permits no smoking inside," it read, adding that the "grocery store is well-stocked, staffed, prices are reasonable."[100]

The piece was not unwaveringly favorable toward the Nation of Islam. Referring to them as "close-mouthed, clannish and suspicious," Crawford clearly seemed uncomfortable in his perception that Muhammad's followers would "follow him to the death."[101] Calling Muhammad a "master psychologist" and suggesting some of the brainwashing motifs that would be used in coverage of "cults" in the late 1970s, Crawford suggested that Muhammad offered "identification, definition and belonging to all those who seek it, and in return gets a loyalty, obedience and discipline which staggers the imagination."[102] Despite these reservations, Crawford's "The Truth about the Black Muslims" offers a representation in many ways wholly at odds with those in the larger news and general-interest magazines.

In 1962 the Jewish journal of opinion *Commentary* similarly avoided the shock language and subversive threat rhetoric in most larger periodicals. In "Integration and the Negro Mood," Harold R. Isaacs placed the Nation of Islam within the larger spectrum of black civil rights activists. "The Muslims," he wrote, "represent the most extreme form of wanting out, out of America, out of the white world altogether."[103] While Isaacs did follow other journalists in asserting that the Nation attracted the "desperate poor" looking to "appease their despair," he did not rely on all the other tropes that writers used to portray the group as a social menace.[104] Like Cooper, Isaacs suggested that the movement's message resonated with some black Americans. Muhammad's "passionately violent indictment of the white world carries the ring of truth to almost any listening Negro," Isaacs wrote.

Another article that expressed a more complicated view of the Nation of Islam, this time appearing in a large mass-market magazine, was an exposé in *Life* in 1963, photographed by the famous African American photographer Gordon Parks. Like *Jet*, *Life* sent a mixed message with its photos and text. Unlike in *Jet*, however, the subversive motif played a large role in framing the photo essay and accompanying texts. For example, pictures of the Fruit of Islam, a security force for the group with training in judo, evoked the typical image of dangerous subversives. On the other hand, one page featured two photos of a Nation of Islam family praying and smiling—reminiscent of the domestic tranquility photos for which *Life* was known in the postwar years.[105]

Parks's accompanying essay similarly expressed ambivalence. Presenting a view somewhat unusual for a magazine that was still under Henry Luce's editorial eye, Parks stated that he sympathized with the Muslims in their criticism of American racism. "I have had faith in America for as long as I remember," he suggested, "But I have also been angry—even bitter. It is now time for America to justify this belief I have in her, to show me I have not believed in vain. I want my children and their children to keep this faith flowing through their veins. But in all honesty I cannot ask of them love for a country incapable of returning their love."[106] Parks did question and criticize the Nation of Islam's beliefs, suggesting that he had no intention of joining: "I sympathize with much of what they say, but I also disagree with much of what they say."[107] "Nevertheless," he added, "to the Muslims I acknowledge that the circumstance of common struggle has willed us brothers."[108]

Of the articles offering alternative representations of the Nation of Islam, perhaps the best known after Parks's feature in *Life* was "Letter from a Region in My Mind" by the black novelist James Baldwin, which appeared in the 17 November 1962 issue of the *New Yorker*. "Whether in private debate or in public," he explained with frustration, "any attempt I made to explain how the Black Muslim movement came about, and how it has achieved such force, was met with a blankness that revealed the little connection that the liberals' attitudes have with their perceptions or their lives, or even their knowledge—revealed, in fact, that they could deal with the Negro as a symbol or a victim but had no sense of him as a man."[109]

"Letter" was Baldwin's response to this "blankness." While not necessarily a sympathizer like Parks, Baldwin certainly empathized with the Nation of Islam. As such, his essay serves as an indirect critique of dominant journalistic representations. Like the ex-convict Clarence Cooper, Baldwin refused to distinguish the Nation of Islam from "true" religions. Nation of Islam theology, he asserted, was no different from any other theology in that "it had been designed for the same purposes; namely the sanctification of power."[110] Indirectly criticizing depictions of the Muslims as dangerous insurrectionists, Baldwin suggested that they only elicited fear because, "the power of the white world is threatened whenever a black man refuses to accept the white world's definitions."[111] In sharp contrast to C. Eric Lincoln's assertion that nonviolence was a preferable form of protest requiring a certain level of sophistication, Baldwin argued that "the real reason non-violence is considered to be a virtue . . . is that white men do not want their lives, their self-image, or their property threatened."[112]

Baldwin argued that the movement's beliefs, as eclectic and racist as they seemed, were based in the everyday experiences of its membership. In one passage, Baldwin recounted a dinner at Elijah Muhammad's house. Baldwin failed to realize that the white man was the devil, Muhammad suggested, because he had been "too long exposed to white teaching and had never received true instruction."[113] Baldwin wrote that he wanted to tell Muhammad of several good white friends whom he trusted deeply and of a few more who were "trying to make the world more human." "But how could I say this?" Baldwin mused, "One cannot argue with anyone's experience or decision or belief. All my evidence would be thrown out as irrelevant to the main body of the case, for I could cite only exceptions."[114]

Baldwin's views, as well as the others noted above, contrasted with those in larger national news and general-interest magazines. Whether in *Time*, *Reader's Digest*, *Esquire*, or any number of other periodicals, journalists' preferred readings made the "Black Muslims" out to be subversive others, a potential or present threat to all that was "American." However, one alternative representation did occasionally appear within this frame as a submotif. Journalists sometimes viewed the Nation of Islam as a social mirror, a group spawned from poverty and racism and thus reflecting and stemming from larger societal problems. Like Lincoln's quote in "Recruits Behind Bars," the social mirror motif challenged the dominant frame of subversion. It offered readers other interpretations.

For example, one article in *Christian Century*, "Despair Serves Purposes of Bizarre Cults," juxtaposed Hofferian fears of mass movements with social criticism. The anonymous author argued that "white and Negro leaders who slough off the black Mohammedan movement in the United States as though it were a mere passing fad popular only among Negroes on the fanatical fringe should pay close attention to what is now happening in the slums of Kingston, Jamaica."[115] The editorial noted that the "gaunt, ragged, sickly people who live in an area of Kingston aptly called 'Back-to-the-Wall'" were "turning increasingly to the leadership of the Rastafarians a wild, violent, cruel band of insurrectionists."[116] "These malcontents," the magazine continued, "are African Nationalists, a sect of lawless, marijuana-smoking Negroes who follow the back-to-Africa movement launched in Jamaica and in the United States by Marcus Aurelius Garvey in 1914."[117] After eliciting reader's fears by detailing Rastafarian growth among Kingston's impoverished, the periodical warned that the Nation of Islam could make similar inroads if inner cities remained neglected. "Meanwhile," the editorial concluded, "our own great cities are spotted with 'Back-to-the-Wall' slums in which desperate people will turn to any leader who offers escape. Continued neglect by society and the church will turn these people into pariahs—lost to society, to the church, and to themselves."[118]

Alex Haley's 1960 article in *Reader's Digest* similarly used the Nation of Islam to critique American social inequality. He concluded that "as long as inequity persists in our democratic system, Elijah Muhammad—or some variation of him—will be able to solicit among the Negro population enough followers to justify the title, 'the most powerful black man in America.' It is important for Christianity and democracy," Haley continued, "to help remove the Negro's honest grievances and thus eliminate the appeal of such a potent racist cult."[119]

Haley, like the writers in *Christian Century*, offered poignant social criticism that countered the preferred reading of the Muslims as subversive others. Simultaneously, however, the social mirror motif legitimized the dominant frame in two ways. First, it denied that Nation of Islam membership could ever be a rational choice by implying that members of the black working class "naturally" gravitated toward the group because of racism and poverty. This indirectly supported the journalistic view of poor blacks as overly emotional and susceptible to the lure of mass movements. Second, this motif tacitly called the Nation's beliefs into question by implying that its theology was wholly a reaction to material circumstances.[120] These motifs combined to confirm journalists' views that the Nation of Islam was a "false" religion, or perhaps not even a religion at all. Most journalists assumed that the Nation of Islam's existence was solely an expression of black existential angst. While this might seem sociologically sound to some readers, it is telling that journalists (and scholars) seldom applied such interpretations to Methodists, Catholics, Episcopalians, or other groups that they considered mainstream.

Just an Overblown Splinter Group: Representational Change and the Cessation of Coverage, 1964–1965

On 21 February 1965 Malcolm X, whom the Nation of Islam considered an apostate, was assassinated. He was shot several times by a Black Muslim, Talmadge Hayer, with the assistance of two other members, as he began a speech at the Audubon ballroom in Harlem. On 8 March 1965 *Newsweek* reported the story, titling it "Death of a Desperado." More striking than any details of the incident is the article's description of the Nation of Islam as "never more than an overblown splinter group."[121] The same magazine that earlier portrayed the Nation as a group of dangerous subversives now viewed it more as an annoyance than a threat. Even more strikingly, by 1966 the movement temporarily disappeared from *Newsweek* and other news and general-interest magazines altogether. From 1959 to 1965 the *Reader's Guide to Periodical Literature* listed thirty-two articles about the movement (excluding several book reviews of Lincoln's *Black Muslims in America* and four articles about Malcolm X). By consulting other bibliographical works and various magazines, I uncovered sixty-five articles on the Nation of Islam for the time period.[122] From 1966 to 1968, however, I found only four articles, and they were all on the boxer Muhammad Ali. Several factors combined to produce this diminished magazine coverage of the Nation of Islam.

First was the expulsion of Malcolm X from the group in 1964 and his assassination in the following year.[123] These events directly correlate with diminished coverage of the Nation of Islam in at least three ways. As noted by several scholars, the news media tend to focus more on personalities than abstract ideas or movements as a whole.[124] This practice creates "news celebrities," and Malcolm X was certainly one. While I have noted that journalistic depictions of the American religious fringe in this period tended to downplay personality and focus on the "mass movement" aspects of certain groups, Malcolm X was an exception. For example, while (as noted above) the *Reader's Guide* lists thirty-two articles from 1959 to 1965 about the Nation of Islam in general, it lists thirty-seven stories specifically on Malcolm X. Twenty-three of these appeared in 1964–65. Simply put, Malcolm's break with the group and later murder left journalists without their favorite source for incendiary quotes about the Nation. Malcolm X's departure similarly left the Nation of Islam without its primary public spokesperson. The group did not temper its racialized theology or fiery rhetoric immediately after Malcolm's expulsion. However, it did become more insular. Without Malcolm X, its members spoke less to the press, and the press paid less attention to them.

Malcolm X's assassination at the hands of his former group correlated with diminished coverage. An article on the murder in *U.S. News* in 1965 was revealingly titled "Now It's Negroes vs. Negroes in America's Racial Violence." The story asserted, "the Nation's racial strife suddenly has taken on a new character."[125] It continued, "the turning point came with the murder—by Negro assassins—of Malcolm X, a Negro leader who preached the use of armed force against whites. It was part of a round of murder, bombing and

For journalists in the 1960s, Malcolm X was a favorite source for incendiary quotes. (Library of Congress)

arson involving Negroes who proclaim hatred for all white men, spurn integration, and want to set up a segregated State of their own.[126]

U.S. News went on to contrast this "new violence" with standard civil rights "clashes between white segregationists and Negroes." It also tempered the position, taken years earlier by the magazine, that the Nation of Islam presented a growing threat. The assassination revealed deep rifts among black separatist groups and no doubt led white journalists to see the Muslims as less of an organized threat to American (read white?) society.

But Malcolm X's departure and murder were not the only incidents that coincided with diminished coverage. Though Malcolm X was certainly a favorite Nation member for TV and newspaper journalists to quote, few news and general-interest magazine articles relied exclusively on Malcolm X for stories about the Nation of Islam. Recall that from 1959 to 1963, the *Reader's Guide to Periodical Literature* contains only four articles that focus on Malcolm X. So while Malcolm X's presence certainly attracted journalistic interest, his absence alone is insufficient to account for the drop in coverage. In fact, several major events in the mid-1960s took potential column-inches away from the Nation of Islam. One of these was the expanding American war in Vietnam. Stories on the Nation began to wane just as coverage of the Vietnam War began to grow. The *Reader's Guide* lists 107 articles on Vietnam between March 1961 and February 1963, then over 350 between March 1963 and February 1965, with additional stories in another twenty related categories.

Perhaps more significant than expanding coverage of Vietnam was the onset of urban rioting. Beginning with the earliest civil rights protests in the 1950s, journalists warned of potential violence in the streets. Perhaps it was therefore to be expected that the Nation of Islam gained initial media attention in the midst of civil rights struggles. Two years before their appearance on *Newsbeat* in 1959, President Dwight Eisenhower called federal troops into Central High School in Little Rock to desegregate it. That same year, 1957, saw the first of several civil rights bills pass. The March on Washington in 1963, featuring Martin Luther King Jr.'s famous "I have a dream" speech, coincided with the height of Nation of Islam coverage. I found, for example, seventeen articles on the Nation in 1963, more than double the number for 1961 and 1965, the years of the second-highest totals. Journalists in the largest news and general-interest magazines mostly wrote favorably of the civil rights movement. Henry Luce's *Time*, showing its support of a moderate civil rights agenda, made Martin Luther King Jr. its "Man of the Year" in 1964.[127] But most journalists viewed the Nation of Islam—with its separatist ideology, apocalyptic eschatology, and anti-passivist rhetoric—as a rabble-rousing group inclined at any moment to transform peaceful protests into violent revolution. In chronicling and monitoring the Nation of Islam, journalists, as well as public officials, revealed their fears of violence and social disorder.

Beginning in 1964, the fears came true. During the summer, rioting erupted in Harlem and seventeen other inner cities. The summer of 1965 proved even worse, with Watts and thirty other urban areas exploding with violence. Despite the fears of journalists and the FBI, the Nation of Islam was not directly involved in any of the riots. Statistically, we now know that those who rioted didn't fit Nation of Islam demographics. The rioters were better educated than nonrioting ghetto dwellers, with 90 percent having some high school education. They were also more likely to be employed than nonrioters.[128] Faced with present disorder, journalists forgot about the potential disorder of the Nation. With the explosion of rioting, the white media's monitoring of disenfranchised blacks moved abruptly from the religious periphery to the city center.

It is notable that the decrease in Nation of Islam coverage coincided with a dramatic change in how journalists represented the group. By 1965 the once-dangerous subversives of unknown strength had become far less sinister. When *Newsweek* called the Nation an "overblown splinter-group," it undermined the alarmist representation that it had helped to create. Two articles in particular, one based on a national poll and another written by an ex-Muslim, help to illustrate how the media image of the Nation began to change from national threat to minor annoyance.

Newsweek *and the "Negro in America" Poll*

On 29 July 1963, the cover of *Newsweek* featured the dimly lit profile of a black male. "The Negro in America: The First Definitive National Survey," the title announced, "Who He Is, What He Wants, What He Fears, What He Hates, How He Lives, How He Votes, Why He Is Fighting . . . and Why Now?"[129] The title's trope of using the pronoun "He" to describe a collective, essentialized "Negro" was not unusual. This style, like the "Negroes vs. Negroes" headline in *U.S. News*, revealed an assumption of a white readership.[130] Interestingly, this implicit assumption guided even left-leaning religious periodicals like *Christianity and Crisis*.[131] "The Negro in America" reported the results of a poll sponsored by the magazine of 1,350 African Americans.[132] Several of the 252 questions were about the Nation of Islam. "What about the much-publicized Black Muslims and their leaders Malcolm X and Elijah Muhammad?" *Newsweek* asked. The unnamed writers replied to their own question, suggesting, "As a matter of fact, 41 percent of rank-and-file Negroes simply don't recognize the Muslims by name, and even many who are familiar with the name are hazy on the Muslim cause. Mrs. Edna Mae Hutchinson of Philadelphia says: "I don't know nothing about them. Some people say they eat fish and grow beards."[133]

Edna Mae Hutchinson's remark served a couple of purposes. First, the authors of the article ostensibly used it to support poll statistics. The quote provided an example of a "rank-and-file Negro" unsure of Nation of Islam teachings. In choosing it, however, the magazine managed to ridicule both the subject—the Nation of Islam—and the respondent. The journalists' patronizingly used Hutchinson in the same way that prewar Hollywood film makers often cast black actors: for comic relief. Hutchinson therefore resembled a female version of what the film scholar Donald Bogle calls the Hollywood "Sambo"—a figure whose humorousness depended entirely on the acceptance of negative racial stereotypes.[134] In addition to supporting statistics, then, journalists tacitly (and perhaps unwittingly) used Hutchinson's quote to legitimize established representations of working-class blacks as ignorant.

Other poll questions revealed negative attitudes toward the

Nation of Islam. Eight of every nine respondents who knew the movement rejected its validity. Twenty-two of every twenty-three disagreed with its separatist beliefs. Only 29 percent of "rank-and-file" blacks and 17 percent of "Negro Leaders" viewed Elijah Muhammad favorably. This made Muhammad fourteenth among the fourteen blacks who were ranked.[135] With numbers showing that "rank-and-file Negroes"—that amorphous mass of potential true believers—knew little about the group, the *Newsweek* poll made the Muslims look more like an object of derision than fear.

After the poll's publication, only twelve articles appeared on the group between 1963 and 1965. Seven of these reported Malcolm X's defection and assassination, while two were about Muhammad Ali. From 1966 to 1968, as noted above, only four appeared—all on Ali. Given these numbers, it is possible, but hardly provable, that the *Newsweek* poll partly contributed to diminishing coverage of the Nation of Islam. But it is an apostate narrative, published in the *Saturday Evening Post* in 1965, that shows the extent to which the one-time looming menace could be rescripted into an insignificant annoyance.

A Nation Apostate Speaks to the Nation

On 27 February 1965, the *Saturday Evening Post* published "The Black Muslims Are a Fraud," by Aubrey Barnette with Edward Linn. Apostate tales—the stories of those who leave a religious group because of grievances—were part and parcel of coverage of the American religious fringe in the mid- to late 1970s. They were extremely rare, however, in the 1950s and 1960s. Malcolm X discussed his defection from the Nation of Islam on both WNTA television and in his autobiography.[136] But Aubrey Barnette's story is one of only two apostate narratives published during the 1960s in news and general-interest magazines. (The other, in *Ebony* in 1965, was by Ruth Boaz, a white ex-member of Father Divine's Peace Mission Movement.)[137] Barnette's "The Black Muslims Are a Fraud" influenced coverage that came after it. Shortly after its publication, for example, *Newsweek* and *Senior Scholastic* used Barnette's tempered estimates of Muslim membership.[138] Perhaps more significant, Barnette's sharply revised picture of the Muslims appeared right before their disappearance from the national media spotlight.

In most apostate narratives, the author's initial strategy is to win the reader's trust. In Barnette's case, not only was he black, but he was also a former member of an anti-white religion. To connect with the mostly white, middle-class readers of the *Saturday Evening Post*, he distanced himself from the traditional depiction of a Nation of Islam member as poor, ignorant, and racist. "My background," Barnette wrote, "made me a most unusual prospect for the Muslims."[139] He noted that he had been a business student at Boston University, was married with three children, and had been employed at a post office when he first came into contact with the group. He wrote, "More than that, I had never known the hardships that drive Negroes to desperation. My father, a post-office worker, was always able to make a better-than-average living. We never lived in ghettos, but in well-integrated areas. One of my brothers not only went to Columbia University on a full scholarship but was elected president of his sophomore class."[140]

Accompanying photographs also depicted Barnette as middle class. One photo showed him in front of the ten-room house he had to sell after joining the group.[141] Barnette told readers that his $5,200 yearly salary as a secretary for the Nation of Islam also forced him to trade in his 1959 Chevrolet for a 1949 model[142] (he stated that he made $7,200 in the year before joining the movement). Another picture placed Barnette in a familiar journalistic image of postwar domesticity. He and his wife were posed sitting on a couch, flanking their five smiling, neatly dressed children. The caption noted that "free of Islam's fierce demands, Barnette and his wife Ruth can spend time with their children."[143]

After situating himself as middle class, Barnette distanced himself from Nation of Islam beliefs. Never once did Barnette suggest that he found the Nation of Islam's racialized theology appealing. Nor did he suggest that his wife's conversion a year before his own influenced him. Instead, he described his membership in terms of opportunities to use his college education to aid other blacks: "I joined for a combination of reasons. Ruth felt that since I had a college degree I should be making some kind of contribution to the Muslims' program for educating Negro children. The opportunity to put my business education to work in the burgeoning black business empire Minister Louis was always telling me about appealed to me. And most important of all, I suppose, I did have my own guilt feelings about remaining on the sidelines at a time when the racial situation was finally coming to a boil."[144]

Barnette listed another reason for joining. The minister of the Boston Temple, Louis X (Louis Farrakhan), told Barnette that he wanted him to do national publicity for Louis's touring musical, *Orgena*. Barnette described the plot, "in which the white man was put on trial for creating the conditions that led to the black man's degradation."[145] Predictably, Barnette never suggested to his readers that he agreed with the play's message, but only that he was interested in doing promotion for it. This section of Barnette's tale was like the rest in that he never discussed Nation of Islam beliefs—let alone note that he held any himself.

A traditional element in many apostate tales—from nativist tomes against antebellum Catholics to stories from "cult" defectors in the 1980s—is the illicit detailing of atrocities. These sometimes included sex, conspiracy, and even murder. As noted in Chapter 1, a number of scholars have recognized that similar horrific stories have been told about a variety of religious groups throughout American history. Over the past three centuries, they argue, Catholics, Jews, Mormons, and members of ISKCON and the Unification Church, among others, have all been the subjects of strikingly similar tales of sex, murder, and conspiracy. Harvey Cox, for example, argues that four historically recurrent themes emerge in narratives told about "marginalized" and feared religious groups. These are the beliefs that the group is politically subversive, that sexual and behavioral deviancy occurs within the group's confines, that the group presents a false façade of benignity, and that the group somehow brainwashes its members and transforms them into zombies.[146] The sociologists David Bromley and Anson Shupe also note similar recurring motifs. "The themes," they write, "that we have found to be common in old and new controversies include (1) deception and coercion used to recruit and hold members, (2) illegitimacy of beliefs, (3) sexual perversion, (4) political subversion, (5) and financial exploitation."[147]

While Barnette certainly denounced his former group, his

charges against the Nation of Islam differed markedly from traditional atrocity tales. It also differed from reporting on the group in the early 1960s. Barnette did focus on financial exploitation, and he briefly questioned the legitimacy of Muslim beliefs by noting they didn't use the Qu'ran much. On the other hand, he played down or even ignored other themes, like political subversion, that journalists in the 1960s often used to represent the group. "The Black Muslims," Barnette asserted, are "just another little money-grabbing scheme feeding on the frustrations and ignorance of American Negroes."[148] In his view, both journalists and scholars—as well as the Muslims themselves—had perpetuated the myth that the group was large, successful, and growing in strength. He asserted that the Nation of Islam's current membership was less than 7,000. Arguing directly against C. Eric Lincoln and Louis Lomax, he suggested that Nation of Islam membership had never exceeded 15,000.[149]

Barnette altogether avoided the familiar journalistic discourse that represented the Muslims as a national threat. "To the white man," he even suggested, "the Black Muslims have been only a minor annoyance." But, he continued, "to the Negro, and this is the final tragedy, they have been another foot on the back, another knock on the door, another ride in the darkness, another beating— yes, another slave master."[150] The "foot in the back," Barnette suggested, was primarily economic. Despite their focus on developing independent black businesses and on general economic uplift, Barnette compared the group to the Ku Klux Klan, saying that both wanted to "keep the Negro in his place." Barnette implied that the Muslims needed ignorant, poor blacks to fill their pews and bank accounts. "It is impossible," he wrote, "to preach total disaffection to anyone who is making his way in the real world."[151]

Barnette asserted that businessmen who joined the Boston Temple soon lost their businesses. "If being a Muslim is the only road to the Hereafter," he commented, "it also seems the quickest road to bankruptcy."[152] He used his own tale of trading down from a ten-room house and a new car as an example. In another section, Barnette criticized Muslim-owned businesses. The problem with them, he implied, was that they were too small to make substantial profits. "My disillusionment," he wrote, "with Islam's business empire came during my first visit to Chicago as a Muslim. I had heard about the modern communal businesses, but all I saw were a small bakery; a small grocery store; a small restaurant; a small cleaning establishment; a small clothing store; a small barbershop, and a small dress factory."[153]

Barnette found other faults with the Nation of Islam. For example, he expressed dismay that the "University of Islam" was only a grade school. Contrary to most other articles on the group—as well as academic studies—he claimed that it was not accredited.

Barnette also began his tale with an accounting of being beaten up by members after he exited the group, though unlike previous journalists he did not focus on the potential violence of the group. He suggested that Muslim leaders were too dictatorial. He also complained that an elaborate complex of offices in Chicago, to be paid for by Muslim tithes, hadn't been built yet. It was completed several years after his story was published.

Barnette's most sustained critique, however, centered on business and economic issues. In Barnette's view, to put it simply, the Nation of Islam consisted of poor capitalists. He did not deny that they had established dozens of black-owned businesses, but he dismissed those stores and shops as too small. Ignoring the economic uplift stories about the majority of members who came from the poorest classes, he focused on the self-employed businessmen whose income dropped after joining the movement. In the early 1960s, the largest news and general-interest magazines had consistently portrayed the Muslims as potential insurrectionists of unknown strength. In 1965 Barnette's narrative in the *Post* rescripted them as "minor annoyances," a "little money-grabbing scheme" out to bilk ignorant African Americans. In an article that corresponded to the virtual end of Nation of Islam coverage, the Muslims had become third-rate capitalists of little significance.

The media scholar Herbert Gans has argued that the news media "supports the social order of public, business and professional, middle-class, middle-aged, and white male sectors of society."[154] Likewise, the religious historian Martin Marty has suggested that after World War II, "magazines like *Life* and *Look*, *Newsweek* and *Time*, *Saturday Evening Post* and *Collier's*, the *Ladies Home Journal* and *McCall's* aspired to speak for and to very wide cultural strands, in semifictional and taken-for-granted 'mainstream America.'"[155] In view of these trends, it is not surprising that journalists in the early 1960s depicted the anti-white, anti-government, and anti-Christian Nation of Islam as the polar opposite of all they considered "American."

Like coverage of the Third Force during the same period, coverage of the Nation of Islam was molded by simultaneous Cold War desires for consensus and worries about lower-class volatility and susceptibility to communistic or otherwise "un-American" mass movements. Stories about the Third Force and California cults revealed journalists' implicit ambivalence and even disdain toward mass movements and lower-class religious enthusiasm. Simultaneously, during the volatile civil rights era, depictions of the Nation of Islam betrayed more explicit fears of black working-class insurrection.

But unlike in other representations of fringe movements in the early 1960s, race was the most important variable in Muslim depictions. At a time when black churches—despite their participation in the civil rights movement—received relatively little attention in national magazine stories about civil rights, the comparatively small Nation of Islam received heightened attention. Tellingly, journalists represented the Muslims quite differently from the newly reestablished Ku Klux Klan. In depicting the Nation of Islam as a societal menace, they frequently quoted the "fanatical" Muslim doctrine that the white man is the devil. However, journalistic representations of the Klan seldom quoted its doctrines, and left out modifiers like "fanatical" in their descriptions. To be sure, reporting on the Klan certainly was not positive. But stories that detailed Klan growth in the American South did not show the movement to be a national threat in the way that they did the Nation of Islam. For example, *Newsweek* assured readers in 1964 that the Klan was small and being held in check by "Dixie's growing acceptance of the inevitability of integration, and stern control measures."[156] In an interesting contrast to the alarmist newsmagazine articles on the Nation of Islam in the early 1960s, *Newsweek* also told readers that "The Klan, indeed, scarcely take a turn without an FBI man hearing about it."[157] Interestingly, articles about the Nation never reported this, thus leaving the potential threat that it posed open for speculation.

In examining the different ways that journalists reported on the KKK and the Nation of Islam, one is reminded of the sociologist Amy Binder's study of print media framing of heavy metal and rap music in the mid-1980s and early 1990s. Binder found that writers in *Time*, *Newsweek*, the *New York Times*, *Reader's Digest*, and *U.S. News* were more likely to view heavy metal as problematic because it could corrupt youth:[158] 65 percent of respondents referred to the corruption of youth or the need to protect youth from corruption.[159] On the other hand, 64 percent of Binder's sample framed rap as problematic because it was a threat to society as a whole, while only 14 percent suggested that rap was a corrupting influence from which youth needed protection.[160] In other words, writers saw heavy metal, which they perceived as "white" youth music, as posing a very different problem from rap, which they perceived as "black" youth music. Similarly, in the Cold War 1960s, it was the black racist subversive more than the white racist subversive who was depicted as a potential threat to the nation as a whole. While the Klan was seen negatively, it was the Nation of Islam that was seen as a potential danger to society.

In the mid-1960s, several factors combined to diminish journalistic monitoring of the Nation of Islam. By 1965 *Newsweek* called the group "overblown" and Aubrey Barnette suggested that its leaders were insignificant money grabbers who only posed a threat to ignorant blacks. Reenvisioned as a small group of third-rate entrepreneurs, the Nation of Islam virtually disappeared from national magazines after 1965. But they reappeared in 1969–70. Curiously, Barnette's poor capitalists had become, in the words of *Time*, "the original black capitalists."[161] "In recent years," the unnamed writers asserted, "the militant Black Muslim movement has been saddled with a falsely fierce image." (They didn't remark that *Time* itself was partly responsible for this image.) Nevertheless, *Time* continued, "the Muslims have always been the bourgeoisie of the black militant movement."[162] Several other magazines concurred. *Trans-Action* referred to the group as "the Black Wasps," while *U.S. News* reported on the Muslims' burgeoning "farm empire."[163] *Fortune* even featured the group in its "Businessmen in the News" section, detailing "Black Capitalism in the Muslim Style."[164] As noted earlier, this representational shift did not coincide with any changes in Nation of Islam theology, rhetoric, or practice. In the wake of the civil rights struggles and black power movement of the 1960s, the Nation of Islam, it appeared, had been representationally reinvented. The former subversives had been domesticated. Once the archetypal "other," the Nation of Islam had become the ultimate Americans: successful entrepreneurial capitalists.

PART II

Reconstructing
an American
Religious Fringe,
1966–1993

chapter three

THE BUDDHA,
THE HOBBIT, AND
THE CHRIST
DEPICTING THE
MIDDLE-CLASS
FRINGE, 1966–1972

On 7 July 1967, *Time* published the cover story "The Hippies: Philosophy of a Movement." The unnamed writers described the movement as "a cult whose mystique derives essentially from the influence of hallucinogenic drugs" and its "professed aim" as "nothing less than the subversion of Western society by 'flower power' and force of example."[1] The article described the movement in detail. The hippies were mostly white, middle-class, educated, and between the ages of seventeen and twenty-five. Their cultural mecca was the Haight-Ashbury district in San Francisco, and LSD was their drug of choice. One page included pictures of Buddha, Christ, Gandhi, and the Hobbit. These, the writers declared, were the movement's heroes.[2]

These figures are emblematic of three movements that garnered substantial attention from the print media in the late 1960s and early 1970s. The Buddha—and even Gandhi—conjured up images of the various guru-based Eastern religions that were becoming visible on the American landscape. The Hobbit, the title character of J. R. R. Tolkien's fantasy novel about the magical elves, dragons, and wizards of Middle-Earth, supposedly evoked the occult groups and practices that received sustained attention in the period. Christ brought to mind the increasingly robust Jesus movement of the early 1970s. Together the gurus, occultists, and Jesus people—often called "Jesus freaks"—made up the bulk of representations of the American religious fringe in the mid- to late 1960s. Depictions of these groups, and thus the fringe itself, changed dramatically between the mid-1960s and late 1970s.

Between 1966 and 1979, as in previous periods, journalists consistently acted as "heresiographers." By identifying inauthentic fringe religion, they set the boundaries of "mainstream" American religion. In this same period, journalistic representations of the periphery darkened. In the mid-1960s, the largest news and general-interest magazines depicted the fringe as exotic and mostly harmless. By 1979, however, the American religious fringe was all but synonymous with the epithet "cult." Several sociologists of new religions have noted this period's increasingly negative coverage of the Unification Church, the International Society of Krishna Consciousness, the Divine Light Mission, and others.[3] The sociologist James Beckford notes that in the 1970s (and 1980s) the media propagated "cult menace" stories in which "allegations of economic exploitation, mental cruelty, the deliberate alienation of recruits from their families, deceptive recruiting practices, harmful diets and lifestyles, sexual abuse and, of course, brainwashing were widespread."[4]

This chapter, covering the period from 1966 to 1972, traces the beginnings of the gradual shift in American religious fringe representations from disdained exotics to dangerous deviants. The historian Tom Schachtman refers to roughly this same period as the "decade of shocks."[5] Political assassinations, the Vietnam war and its atrocities, race riots, the civil rights and countercultural movements, and later the Watergate scandal and an energy crisis, marked the period as one in which the image of a unified American cultural consensus seemed increasingly distant. In addition to covering and commenting on these social upheavals, magazines responded to concern over a growing generation gap, a vocal youth counterculture, and an apparent—though statistically unfounded —"cult explosion" by turning their attention away from working-class and ethnic movements like Pentecostalism and the Nation of Islam. Instead, they increasingly focused on the guru-based Asian religions, Evangelical Jesus movements, and occult practices that were attracting predominantly white, middle- and upper-middle-class youth.[6]

It is now a cliché, but no less true, to say that the 1960s were a time of ferment and change. During this decade, many historians have suggested, the notion that prevailed in the 1950s of an American cultural consensus crumbled amidst turmoil at home and abroad. Magazines sometimes reflected this change, and Henry Luce's *Life* and *Time* provide good examples. As noted in the Introduction, Luce made these publications his mouthpiece from the onset. Among other things, Luce used them to promote American expansionism and support the Vietnam War. Writing about *Life*, the American studies scholar John Gennari notes that the magazine "had arrogated itself to the role of defining an American common project."[7] After Luce's death in 1967, however, Gennari suggests that "with America at war with itself, it became impossible for *Life* any longer to project a clear, unambiguous, and consensual vision of American life."[8] The magazine ceased publication in 1972.

Time, the newsmagazine, also changed after Luce's death. By the end of the 1960s, *Time* had begun, like many periodicals, to question the role of the United States in Vietnam. As the war escalated, documented atrocities committed by American soldiers surfaced. The most infamous and widely reported case was the My Lai massacre in March 1968, in which American troops raped, tortured, and murdered at least 109 Vietnamese villagers, including children and infants. *Life* featured a pictorial on the incident on 5 December 1969. On that same day, its sister periodical, *Time*, ran a cover story titled "My Lai: An American Tragedy." In an editorial accompanying the feature, *Time* put into question American history and destiny in a way foreign to its past coverage. The unnamed writer suggested that there was "a dark underside to American history: the despoliation of the American Indian, the subjection of the black, the unwise and probably immoral insistence on the enemy's unconditional surrender that led to Hiroshima."[9] "My Lai," the sobered writer asserted, "is a warning to America that it, like other nations, is capable of evil acts and that its idealistic goals do not always correspond to its deeds."[10]

The editorial can be viewed as a journalistic example of what the historian Tom Engelhardt has called the "end of victory culture." He suggests that "victory culture," the triumphalist, providence-driven story of inevitable American progress and expansion, ended between 1945 and 1975.[11] He argues that some Americans, especially during the 1960s and early 1970s, grew less comfortable viewing the United States, in Superman style, as the incorruptible good guy fighting evil forces out to destroy truth and justice.[12] Luce's passing certainly helped to change the tone of his magazines. But it was incidents like My Lai—as well as the growing domestic disharmony seen in war protests, various civil rights and liberation movements, and urban rioting—that led not just *Time* and *Life*, but also other magazines, to question or even discard the Cold War notions of a faultless, unified American culture.

Making the Cult Explosion

In addition to social and cultural changes, scholars see the late 1960s as a time of religious ferment. The religious historian William McLoughlin suggested in the 1970s that the period had witnessed the beginning of a "Fourth Great Awakening."[13] Writing in the same period, the sociologist Robert Wuthnow asserted that a "consciousness reformation" characterized the late 1960s.[14] These scholars echoed the era's journalists. In 1970, for example, the increasingly pluralistic *Life* declared that "never before in history has a single society taken up such a wide range of religious and near-religious systems at once."[15] Writing one year later in the Catholic periodical *Commonweal*, the religion scholar Jacob Needleman suggested that "the turning of our young people to mysticism and Eastern religion is a phenomenon so various and pervasive" that it was forming a "new religious mind of young America."[16]

But despite the widely shared perceptions of a spirituality explosion in the late 1960s, several scholars more historically removed from the period suggest that little statistical evidence supports the claim. In terms of new religious movements, for example, the sociologist Rodney Stark and his colleagues assert that the proportion of the population joining new religions—as well as the number of new religions founded—remained relatively stable from the 1920s through the 1980s.[17]

Similarly, the historian Robert Galbreath suggests that perceptions of an "occult revival" in the late 1960s are problematically premised on vague definitions of "occult," a lack of comparison to previous historical periods, and an unexamined model of occult declension.[18] Proposing what he calls a "tentative, rather unwieldy" definition, Galbreath suggests that "modern occultism pertains to matters that are 'hidden' or 'secret' in one or more of the following senses: (1) extraordinary matters that by virtue of their intrusion into the mundane world are thought to possess special significance (e.g. omens, portents, apparitions, prophetic dreams); (2) matters such as the teachings of the so-called mystery schools that are kept hidden from the uninitiated and the unworthy; and (3) matters that are intrinsically hidden from ordinary cognition and understanding but are nonetheless knowable through the awakening of hidden, latent faculties of appropriate sensitivity."[19] Using this broad definition, Galbreath finds no clear evidence that the period's increased media and scholarly attention to the occult corresponded to heightened participation.

Assuming that Galbreath's and Stark's assertions are valid, what accounts for scholars' and journalists' perceptions of religious ferment? I suggest several factors. First, in 1965 the U.S. government lifted the Asian Exclusion Act. Because of this, American religion in the 1960s became more diverse. The anti-immigration law, originally enacted in the isolationist and nativist 1920s, had banned virtually all Asian immigration.[20] After 1965, according to the religious historians Thomas Tweed and Stephen Prothero, nearly 40 percent of all immigrants came from Asia.[21] Among the early immigrants and visitors were an assortment of Asian gurus and spiritual teachers, including C. Bhaktivedanta Swami Prabhupada, founder of the American branch of the Hare Krishnas, and Maharishi Mahesh Yogi, the creator of Transcendental Meditation. So while the proportion of people joining new religions and the number of new religions founded may not have increased dramatically, the visibility of Asian, guru-based groups did.

Second, observers found that the types of Americans who joined Asian, occult, and Evangelical Jesus groups in the late 1960s differed from those who had joined so-called fringe groups in previous decades. Throughout much of the twentieth century, journalists and scholars assumed that the American religious fringe attracted minorities, the poor, the aged, and the dispossessed. In his popular book on sects and cults published in 1961, for example, Richard Mathison asserted that cults "are often refuges for the poor."[22] In the same year, the religion scholar Horton Davies similarly asserted, following H. Richard Niebuhr's *The Social Sources of Denominationalism* (1929), that denominations were middle class while sects were the "churches of the disinherited." Writing as a Christian theologian and sociologist, Niebuhr saw denominationalism as the sacrifice of universal Christian ideals to parochial socioeconomic, political, and ethnic interests. On the other hand, Niebuhr argued that the upstart faiths of the disinherited appeared through divine intervention, asserting that "the rise of new sects to champion the uncompromising ethics of Jesus and to 'preach the gospel to the poor' has again and again been the effective means of recalling Christendom to its mission."[23] While Davies's work partly acknowledged Niebuhr's argument, noting that some sects come into being "to emphasize facets of the Christian faith and life which had been neglected by the Churches," *Challenge of the Sects* departed from Niebuhr's view in that it was primarily an apologetic written to defend "historic Christianity from the attacks of their sectarian critics."[24] Interestingly, writers often held the view that sects and new religions were the refuges of the disinherited even when demographics didn't support them. Davies's *Challenge of the Sects*, for example, included chapters on Christian Scientists and Theosophists, both of whom had mostly middle- and upper-middle-class postwar memberships.[25] Like the hippies, the Americans joining the guru-based Asian movements, occult groups, and Jesus people were overwhelmingly college age, educated, middle class, and white.

These two factors, combined with others detailed in the next chapter, resulted in an altered picture of the fringe. One must wonder if the similar demographics of magazine journalists and those joining new religious movements partly fomented perceptions of the cult explosion. Available numbers show that from 1965 to 1980 journalists at magazines like *Time*, *U.S. News*, and *Newsweek* were 95 percent white, 78 percent middle to upper middle class, 68 percent northeastern, 79 percent male, and overwhelmingly college educated.[26] In the 1950s and early 1960s, when journalists looked at the Third Force and California cults, they saw zealots separated from them by class or region. When they examined the Nation of Islam, they saw an exotic and volatile mass movement of black subversives. But when they reported on the guru-based new religions, occult groups, and Jesus freaks of the late 1960s and early 1970s, they saw their own children—though seldom literally, of course. Journalists' previous story frames of exoticism and otherness— which dehumanized the fringe—would eventually seem inappropriate. But this representational shift was gradual. In many ways, magazine articles of the mid- to late 1960s initially depicted the Asian religions and occult movements of the day as they had the California cults and Third Force earlier—they evoked exoticism and even humor. At the same time, however, articles suggested that these groups were really more banal than exotic.

Gurus, Witches, and Asian Religion: Banal Exoticism and Authentic Religion, 1966–1969

On 5 November 1966, the *Saturday Evening Post* featured John Kobler's essay, "Out for a Night at the Local Caldron." "To her neighbors," Kobler began, "Mrs. Eunice Jenkins (as we will call her, to avoid alarming them) is a plump, cheerful London housewife who exemplifies middle-class, middle-aged British decorum. But at the approach of Halloween, she prepares to perform some of the most bizarre pagan rites to have survived into the 20th century."[27] The article was about British Neopagan Wicca, an eclectic occult religious movement made up of loosely connected groups and individuals who look to nature-oriented, often polytheistic religions and myths for inspiration.[28] Kobler gave a history of the movement and its founder, Gerald Gardner. A retired British civil servant, Gardner is viewed by scholars of new religious movements as one of the "founders" of contemporary Neopaganism.[29] Kobler also interviewed practicing witches like Sybil Leek and Doreen Valiente. Throughout, he depicted the British witches as curiosities who were simultaneously exotic and harmlessly domestic.

Kobler's prose and the accompanying illustrations by the Addams Family creator Charles Addams were lighthearted. The article's subheading announced that "witchcraft in Britain can be fun, one reason there are thousands of real British witches."[30] The first drawing showed dozens of fathers and children standing at the doorways of their homes. They waved to their wives and mothers —who just happened to be wearing pointy black hats and black gowns, and carrying broomsticks. These domestic witches waved back as they walked to their station wagons. The second illustration showed six overweight, middle-aged men and women dancing nude around a caldron. Above them, a younger woman danced in a cage, while a witch in the corner of the castle-like room spun records at a turntable. "Witchcraft a Go Go," the caption read, "more frenzied than most discotheques."[31]

While Kobler noted that exposés on black magic remained "a staple of the British press," he suggested that "Britain's witches are not especially sinister."[32] The characters in Kobler's article appeared humorous, even charming. They were simultaneously exotic and banal: they danced naked around bonfires, but drove to them in station wagons. They cast spells and dabbled in the occult, but they were white, middle aged, middle class, and English. The British witches appeared in the Halloween issue of the *Post* as entertaining holiday curiosities. They were offbeat, but much too familiar to be frightening.

Some Asian religions appearing in the United States received similar journalistic treatment. On 17 January 1969, for example, *Time* published "Sects: The Power of Positive Chanting." The article introduced readers to Nichiren Shoshu Sokkagakkai International of America (NSA), a Japanese Buddhist movement which entered the United States in 1960. *Time* described NSA as "an odd blend of militant Buddhism, the power of positive thinking and showbiz uplift."[33] Unlike other Buddhist groups, NSA focused exclusively on the Lotus Sutra, a Mahayana scripture dating from the first century.[34] Followers chant Lotus Sutra excerpts and practice Daimoku, which consists of repeating the mantra "Nam Myoho Renge Kyo." This roughly translates as "devotion to the Lotus Sutra." Members suggest that chanting this can make one wealthy, cure illnesses, and assure happiness. In addition to these personal benefits, members believe that chanting the Daimoku will also reap global rewards. Participants assert that if a certain portion of

Charles Addams's humorous illustrations for the Saturday Evening Post, *like John Kobler's accompanying text, banalized British witchcraft.* (© 1966 Saturday Evening Post)

the world's population practices chanting, world peace will ensue, called "kosen rufu."

Like Kobler's article in the *Post*, *Time* presented a positive mixture of the exotic and humorous. Evoking the potentially exotic, mysterious "Orient" traditionally associated with Western conceptions of Asia, the article described followers at one meeting in Hollywood sitting "Oriental-style" with Buddhist prayer beads between their fingers.[35] The accompanying photograph showed the group facing a stage, where an Asian priest, dressed in robes, knelt with his back to the audience. The caption read "Soka Gakkai Conversion Ceremony: Doing It with Daimoku." Showing the group in a positive light, *Time* reported that "Negroes who join the movement claim to be impressed by the absence of racial prejudice."[36] "Ultimately, the goal of Soka Gakkai," *Time* noted, "is the establishment of an earthly kingdom come—an era of world peace that will be achieved when at least one-third of mankind adopts the sect's version of true Buddhism."[37]

Though it interpreted NSA as intrinsically oriental, the magazine also represented the movement as familiar. Through vivid description, for example, *Time* humorously recounted that followers enthusiastically sang "Chant Daimoku! Yeah! Yeah! Yeah!" to the tune of the Beatles' "She Loves You." No doubt, relatively few readers in the 1960s would have found Beatle tunes exotic. One article in *Newsweek* directly stated that the movement was "neither exotic nor mysterious."[38] And by reporting on the group's annual convention, *Newsweek* allotted NSA the type of coverage that it usually reserved for established Christian denominations. However, the accompanying photograph—which showed smiling NSA conventioneers performing an elaborate dance in space suits—certainly evoked the offbeat.

Coverage of British witches and Nichiren Shoshu of America in the mid-1960s, like the groups themselves, mixed the exotic and the banal, the domestic and the foreign. In addition, the articles sometimes implicitly distinguished authentic and inauthentic religion, as they did in depicting the Nation of Islam, California cults, and the Third Force. This is most vividly seen in the coverage of Maharishi Mahesh Yogi and his Transcendental Meditation philosophy.

Mahesh Maharishi Yogi first entered the print media spotlight though his interactions with the Beatles, who approached him as a spiritual guide. A university physics student and lifelong spiritual seeker, Mahesh devised a form of meditational practice based broadly on some principles taken from two Indian sacred texts, the Upanishads and the Bhagavad-Gita.[39] He called his system Transcendental Meditation and suggested that by following a few simple techniques, all people could attain "self-realization." This state of enlightenment, in turn, would lead to success in all facets of one's life. The guru became a pop icon when his image appeared with those of other popular culture figures on the cover of the Beatles' famous album *Sgt. Pepper's Lonely Hearts Club Band* (1967). In addition to the Beatles, the Beach Boys, the Rolling Stones, Mia Farrow, and a number of other celebrities consulted Mahesh.

Time, *Newsweek*, and other magazines began reporting on the Beatles' interactions with the guru in 1967. They quickly lost interest, however, and few articles appeared after 1968. During this brief period of attention, articles consistently suggested that the guru's philosophy was too simple. In their initial story on Mahesh in 1967, titled "Mystics: Soothsayer for Everyman," *Time* used humor, sarcasm, and assertions about Hindu orthodoxy to challenge his religious authenticity. In the editorializing style that *Time* made famous, the anonymous writers asserted that Transcendental Meditation's (TM) message "might be summed up as how to succeed spiritually without really trying."[40] They suggested that the guru's message was "a trifle opaque" and reported his claim that meditation need only take a half-hour from the novice's day. Sarcastically noting the Beatles' interest in TM, *Time* suggested that "the Liverpool boys are particularly enthusiastic about the convenience of the Maharishi's method, since they can be regenerated without interrupting their busy schedule."[41] The Maharishi, the magazine continued, "has been sharply criticized by other Indian sages, who complain that his program for spiritual peace without either penance or asceticism contravenes every traditional Hindu belief."[42]

Other stories followed the same general pattern. For example, a story in *Newsweek* in 1967, "The Guru," described Transcendental Meditation as "a vague mixture of self-therapy, Hindu teaching and flower power."[43] Like the article in *Time*, it cited "authentic" Indian holy men to criticize Mahesh. *Newsweek* wrote that "few yogas" had even heard of him until recently. "Further," it continued, "many Indian sages contend that his rather simplified system of meditation is without basis in the Bhagavad-Gita—the epic poem that is Hinduism's most exalted scripture."[44] In 1967 a guest essayist for *Life*, Loudon Wainright, similarly suggested that Mahesh offered an "An Invitation to Instant Bliss" that seemed "astonishingly—perhaps ridiculously—simple in outline and purpose."[45] Not to be left out, *Look* featured a cover article in 1968 on Mahesh's tour of American college campuses, "The Non-Drug Turn-on Hits Campus: Student Meditators Tune In to Maharishi." In it, the magazine's assistant editor William Hedgepeth asserted that "tradition-minded gurus, angrily citing the Bhagavad-Gita, say that self-abnegation and suffering along with rigid concentration are the prescribed pathway to Enlightenment."[46] Hedgepeth noted Mahesh's contrary belief that Enlightenment was compatible with active living and easily available to everyone. "To make this absolutely clear for those who continue to miss the point," Hedgepeth wrote, "his brand-new retranslation and reinterpretation of the exalted Bhagavad-Gita began rolling off the presses in Norway last November."[47]

Journalists' repeated declarations of Transcendental Meditation's religious inauthenticity revealed certain assumptions. First, the coverage mirrored earlier coverage of the Nation of Islam in that writers used appeals to tradition to dismiss Mahesh's philosophy. While stories about "Black Muslims" referred to "True Moslems," those about Mahesh criticized him by citing unnamed Indian holy men, tradition-minded yogis, and sages—"traditional exotics" of the Western imagination. In this manner, the magazines not only questioned the guru's message, but his spiritual credentials and, interestingly, the extent of his exoticism. That TM appealed to modern Westerners, and accommodated Indian meditation practices to them, seemed to banalize it for many journalists. Part of the problem with TM, then, was that it wasn't exotic enough.

Appeals to authentic Hindu tradition revealed assumptions that religion, at least the Indian variety, was inherently static. "Retranslations" and "reinterpretations" of sacred texts and practices, the articles implied, were inevitably false—especially those that make the exotic and mysterious practices of Indian ascetics available to Western pop musicians. Implicitly categorizing Transcendental Meditation as heterodox, the articles referenced an essentialized, orthodox Hinduism. Writers and editors in the largest magazines, by suggesting that TM was too easy to understand and too simple to practice, tacitly suggested that authentic religion must be demanding and difficult. True spiritual enlightenment, for journalists, was a state that only a few could attain. When *Time* called Mahesh the "Soothsayer for Everyman," it was a condemnation, not a compliment.

In faulting Mahesh's Transcendental Meditation for being simple and undemanding, journalists ignored other potential, though less theological, criticisms. For example, writers never discussed the non-egalitarian, even Darwinian aspects of Mahesh's philosophy. In an interview in 1968 in *Ebony* with its editor Era Bell Thompson, the yogi asserted that the poor held full responsibility for their status. "You see," Mahesh told Thompson, "every one is his own responsibility. If I'm poor it is my responsibility. I cannot blame someone if I am poor. If I'm energetic and if I have imagination, and clear thinking, I become wealthy."[48] Later, he suggested that "survival of the fittest is the law."[49] Mahesh also spoke against civil rights demonstrations and intermarriage. He further suggested that "frustrated, tense, and worried" civilians—not the military establishment or politicians—were responsible for the Vietnam War.[50]

Curiously, newsmagazines also chose not to report on the accusations of sexual impropriety against Mahesh that led the Beatles to dissociate themselves from him. In an interview in *Rolling Stone* in 1971, the former Beatle John Lennon recounted that the group left the yogi because they believed the rumors that Mahesh had attempted to rape someone and entice others into having sex with him.[51] Writers never even reported that the group broke with the yogi after only a brief mentorship. Given journalists' historical propensities for following the activities of celebrities and reporting on the possible moral failings of the leaders of fringe groups, these exclusions seem especially curious. Like stories on the Third Force in Christendom, California cults, and the Nation of Islam, those on Transcendental Meditation distinguished authentic and inauthentic religion. Unlike them, however, they ignored the personal activities of the founder and the potentially less palatable aspects of his philosophy—even though writers might have used such things to further their claims of inauthenticity.

Magazine articles mixed exoticism, banality, humor, and sarcasm to depict British witches and the followers of Nichiren Shoshu and Transcendental Meditation. Though writers framed the groups as curiosities, they represented them as harmless—much as they had done with the California cults. That would change. In 1969, for example, *Time* represented the NSA as comical. It even made the movement somewhat familiar to readers by connecting it to "the power of positive thinking," the title of Norman Vincent Peale's bestseller. The writers described the NSA as "militant Buddhism," but not, in contrast to earlier coverage of the Third Force and California cult groups, as zealous and dogmatic. Instead, *Time* asserted that the movement placed few demands on followers. In addition to chanting, the magazine noted, "every member is expected to help expand the roles by the practice of shakubuku—proselytizing—wherever he goes."[52]

When the magazine featured the group again in 1975, however, these earlier assessments had changed. "One of their most debatable practices," *Time* now asserted, "is shakubuku, or forcible persuasion, which some critics charge has often bordered on brainwashing."[53] The low-demand positive thinkers had become manipulative mind benders. What accounted for this representational shift? Not a change in NSA proselytizing. Throughout the 1960s and 1970s, NSA aggressively practiced shakubuku, which translates into English as "break and subdue."[54] Rather, NSA's changing image in *Time* mirrored a larger shift in news and general-interest magazine portrayals. From 1968 to 1972, journalistic coverage of the occult foreshadowed some of the negative fringe representations to come.

Satan Returns: Banal Exotics and Dangerous
Deviants in Occult Coverage, 1968–1972

Robert Galbreath is right to suggest that little evidence exists for an increase in occult participation in the late 1960s. However, using Galbreath's definition of the occult as encompassing secret or hidden matters like omens, apparitions, psychic abilities, secret societies, and mystery schools, there is also no doubt that it received heightened commercial and media attention. Movies like *Rosemary's Baby* and television shows like *Dark Shadows* appeared. A plethora of mass-market books on the occult were also published, ranging from sympathetic popular overviews like John Godwin's *Occult America* to scathing critiques like Owen Rachleff's *The Occult Conceit*.[55] Always on the lookout for heresy, Evangelicals contributed dozens of polemics against the occult, and their most visible periodical, *Christianity Today*, reviewed dozens of texts on it.[56] Children's board games even reflected growing attention to the occult. In 1967, for example, Parker Brothers' Ouija board game moved ahead of Monopoly as the most popular game as measured in yearly sales.[57] Other children's games of the period included "Mystique Astrology" and "Prediction," both purporting to allow the players to foretell future events.[58] The religious historian Robert Ellwood correctly suggests that the occult had become popular culture in the 1960s.[59]

As part of mass culture in the 1960s, the occult received attention from the print media. Like the Third Force and California cults, occultism was a malleable and inclusive rubric that connected a wide range of disparate groups, including Anton LaVey's Church of Satan, a colorful movement in southern California that attracted celebrities like Sammy Davis Jr. and Jayne Mansfield; Puerto Rican Espiritismo, a laity-based Afro-Caribbean faith that used herbs, healing, and spells; and American Neopaganism.[60] Just as the occult could refer to a plethora of groups, journalistic representations contained a variety of framing motifs. Strikingly, occult depictions in the largest news and general-interest magazines simultaneously evoked exotic curiosity and dangerous deviancy.

On 19 June 1972, for example, the cover of *Time* featured an unidentified hooded figure. Two nondescript eyes gazed at the reader from the dark pointed hood, which was decorated with a pentagram and goat. Large white letters announced, "The Occult Revival: Satan Returns." Like the article on British witches in the *Saturday Evening Post* in 1966, the story opened with a scene that mixed the domestic and the exotic. In the first paragraph, the magazine's unnamed writers described neatly dressed people gathered in a "comfortable split-level home" in Louisville, Kentucky.[61] The hosts were a young Army officer and his wife, and their guests included a computer programmer, a dog trainer, and a college student. This seemingly reputable group, *Time* recounted, proceeded solemnly to the vinyl-floored recreation room. But instead of talking over coffee, watching television, or playing cards, the group had another activity planned. It ritually invoked Satan. "This recent scene—and many a similarly bizarre one—," *Time* warned, "is being re-enacted all across the U.S. nowadays."[62]

The article proceeded to discuss crystal balls, Spiritualism, witchcraft, the history of the devil, and prophecies, among other topics. Sixteen accompanying photographs also ran the gamut, showing everything from a nude witchcraft coven to a Protestant youth group called the "Evangelical Teen Challenge Jesus People," pictured exorcising a demon from a young woman. Whether it was paintings of the devil or Satanists in full costume, the photos evoked the exotic. But like Kobler's British witches, *Time* suggested, some occultists were only exotic in appearance. Writing about LaVey's Church of Satan, for example, the magazine asserted that the most striking thing about the members was "that instead of being exotic, they are almost banal in their normality."[63] For *Time*, it seemed, the Church of Satan—like Mahesh Maharishi Yogi—was just not exotic enough.

Time described the Church of Satan as banal and, by implication, harmless. But the magazine also suggested that the occult had a more seamy and dangerous side. "But the darker, more malevolent Satanists," the article claimed, "give only rare and tantalizing hints of their existence."[64] The most famous of these groups, the magazine asserted, was Charles Manson's "family," the group that committed the widely publicized torture and murder of the actress Sharon Tate and three of her friends in 1969. The murder and court case were the subject of a bestseller by Vincent Bugliosi and Curt

Gentry titled *Helter Skelter* (1969).[65] *Time* continued its discussion of underground Satanism by suggesting that "now and again other grisly items in the news reveal the breed."[66] *Time* related that "in New York this spring, police were searching for possible Devil worshipers in a grave robbery incident. In Miami last summer, a 22-year-old woman Satanist killed a 62-year-old friend, stabbing him 46 times. Convicted of manslaughter, she drew a seven-year sentence, thanked Satan for her light penalty, and said that she had 'enjoyed' the killing. In April she escaped from prison, and has not been recaptured."[67]

In 1970, in an article titled "Cult of the Occult," *Newsweek* had evoked similar foreboding. As the writers at *Time* later would, the *Newsweek* reporter Nick Kazan called LaVey's Satanic Church banal, "'a highly stylized, arcane bore.'"[68] But the article warned, "the farthest-out cults that glorify evil are pervaded by an air of secrecy and aberration. Tales of murder and human sacrifice sometimes surround them."[69] In supporting this claim, *Newsweek* included rumors about a police raid in Houston on a "satanic sanctum" that uncovered the bones of sacrificed animals. It also quoted the popular author Arthur Lyons Jr., who suggested that "intense devil dabblers 'are insane—really dangerous.'"[70]

The "breed" of Satanist described by *Time* and the "farthest-out cults" in *Newsweek* closely resembled those later portrayed in the Satanic cult legends of the 1980s. As several scholars have noted, and as I discuss more in Chapter 5, the decade saw a number of rumor panics about underground Satanic cults who robbed graves, abducted children, and practiced human sacrifice.[71] The sociologist Jeffrey Victor has identified sixty-two panic-inducing rumors about devil-worshiping cults in the United States between 1982 and 1992.[72] This figure does not include the hundreds of allegations since the late 1980s by individuals of ritual child abuse at the hands of Satanist parents.[73] The most striking thing about all these rumors and claims was that they lacked confirming evidence. Despite sympathetic police and favorable coverage in local newspapers, as well as a prime-time television special in 1988 in which the host, Geraldo Rivera, affirmed the existence of an immense underground Satanist network, no such groups were ever uncovered.[74]

The evidence hinted at in *Time* and *Newsweek* of "the darker, more malevolent Satanists" followed the legendary, "friend of a friend" (FOAF) tales that fueled many rumors of the 1980s. The magazines failed to name any specifics about the grave robbery in New York or the discovery of animal bones in Houston—or even tell why the police would suspect Satanists. No specific sources were named, making it impossible for readers to investigate the stories further. *Time*, for example, gave no details about the Satanic murderess in Miami. The magazine's closing note that she escaped from prison and had yet to be caught mirrored the portentous endings of many contemporary FOAF legends.

The magazines' assertions that dangerous, even murderous, Satanic groups lurked about the landscape in the late 1960s was based more on rumor and supposition than on material evidence. But inclusion of these phantom-like Satanists in occult stories served to darken depictions of the periphery, adding dangerous deviancy to American religious fringe discourse. For example, while no one would question that the members of the Manson "family" were dangerous deviants, stories about them also proclaimed them to be Satanists, but never explained why. In so doing they connected the Manson family to occult religion—and thus to the religious margins as a whole. Previously, Cold War journalists had depicted the members of the Nation of Islam as potential threats to the American social order. Representations of the group in the largest magazines revealed fears of the black, lower-class other. For some journalists, the Nation of Islam was a visible Cold War enemy that could be distinguished by both race and dress. For most writers, the Muslims were also inherently associated with urban ghettoes. Thus, like the Third Force and California cults, the Nation of Islam was safely contained by being associated with people and places outside an assumed "American mainstream." But dangerous occultists were nameless, faceless, and everywhere. Worse yet, the few occultists identified in articles were often, like the couple in Louisville, middle-class whites wholly indistinguishable from the magazines' writers and readers. Though left unwritten, Satanist rumors in magazines implied that cultic evil now lurked in the shadows of America's tree-lined suburbs.

Social Mirror and Genuine Realm of Magic:
Journalists Interpret the Occult

In *Religion in the Age of Aquarius* (1971), the Christian philosopher John Cooper asserted that by examining the more "alienated and hostile" occultists, "we will be able to see some of the
demonic and destructive forces that are operating in our country because of the failure of organized religion, so far, to meet the
needs of human beings in the age of Aquarius."[75] The failure of
the "Church" to meet the needs of young Americans, Cooper argued, had led to increased occult dabbling, drug abuse, Satanism,
nymphomania, homosexuality, murder, and "the use of aggressively offensive language such as four-letter words."[76] To diminish these things, Cooper asserted, Christianity needed to wake up
and "get with it."[77] It must become, he argued, more experimental
and emotional. "What I am saying," Cooper concluded, "is that the
Church should be the kind of agency that could meet the needs of
the people."[78]

Cooper's book was a jeremiad. This genre, the literary historian
Sacvan Bercovitch argues, has been prevalent in American history
since the 1600s, when the Puritans occasionally used it to structure
sermons.[79] Named after the Hebrew prophet Jeremiah, this literary
form shocks listeners and readers with litanies of social evils and
then reassures them that spiritual remedies exist. Cooper's work,
and its list of occult atrocities, resembled Puritan clerical attacks
on the lay practice of magic in the latter 1600s.[80] But it differed
from them in one significant way: while Puritan clergy warned
members of the laity to change their ways, Cooper, like many of his
religious contemporaries, suggested that Christianity itself needed
to change. Strikingly, Cooper's jeremiad, a religiously based criticism of organized religion, was partially echoed by "secular" journalists, who suggested that interest in the occult reflected an American spiritual crisis. In other words, the occult, like the Nation of
Islam in the early 1960s, was sometimes seen as a social mirror,
stemming from and reflecting the problems of American society.
But while the "Black Muslims" were thought to be born of social
ills, journalists viewed occult interest as symptomatic of spiritual
sickness.

On occasion, magazine interpretations of the occult, like Cooper's book, directly faulted organized religion. In an essay published in 1968 and titled "That New Black Magic," for example, *Time* asserted, "as organized religion loses its appeal through stuffiness or sterility, people seeking faith increasingly turn to mystical religions, such as Zen and Zoroastrianism."[81] Likewise, a cover story in *Time* in 1972 on the occult declared it a "substitute faith" born of "religious impulse."[82] The occult's status as a stand-in implied that it had replaced some former, presumably inadequate religion. *Newsweek*, however, viewed occult practices as social mirrors reflecting larger cultural inadequacies—of which organized religion was only a part. "But both the young and old who have turned seriously to the invisible and supernatural," *Newsweek* concluded in 1970, "seem not so much a group apart from the rest of society as an enlarged picture of its troubles."[83] This sentiment had religious parallels as well. It recalled Herman Hughes, assistant editor of the Jesuit periodical *America*, who in 1968 asserted that "in our modern materialistic, scientific and unspiritual age, witchcraft and demonology have suddenly become intriguing to many."[84]

The jeremiad is a predictable literary form. It begins with a condemning list of problems. It ends with the author offering hope for the fallen society. For Cooper, America's salvation stemmed from a greater openness within organized religion to emotion and experimentation. *Time*, however, suggested that salvation could be found in the harmonious joining of religion and science. In 1972 the magazine wrote, "perhaps, eventually, religion, science, and magic could come mutually to respect and supplement one another. That is a fond vision, and one that is pinned to a fragile and perpetually unprovable faith: that the universe itself is a whole, with purpose and promise beneath the mystery."[85]

Though the article left it up to readers to decide the "purpose and promise" of the universe, the claim that such metaphysical drives existed was itself a theological statement affirming transcendent intentionality. But *Time* went even further. In discussing spiritualism, it asserted that "no skeptic has proven spiritualism to be valid, but there is a residue of the unexplained in these claimed psychic events, some occurrences that seem to defy the laws of chance or mere coincidence."[86] If any readers were uncertain whether *Time* had just asserted the reality of the supernatural, a statement several paragraphs later ended all doubts. "Beyond all the charlatanism," it suggested, "there is a genuine realm of magic, a yet undiscovered territory between man and his universe," one that possibly could "be accepted as a legitimate pursuit of knowledge, no longer hedged in by bell, book, and candle."[87]

In general, interpretations of the occult in these select articles from *Time* and *Newsweek* resembled the period's religious jeremiads on the subject. Both religious writers and newsmagazine journalists presented readers with long lists of occult practices. Both suggested that some esoteric groups—like underground Satanists—were dangerous, and both blamed society and organized religion for the burgeoning interest in the occult. Both even offered hope for the future. Most strikingly, both affirmed the existence of a transcendent world beyond. In its article, *Time* affirmed the existence of the supernatural; it suggested that the universe moved purposefully and held promise. The magazine's interpretation of the occult, and its testimony on the reality of the preternatural, reveals what the religion and media scholar Mark Silk calls "the unsecular media."[88] In this case, journalists in the largest newsmagazines acted not only as heresiographers, but as apologists confirming the reality of the supernatural and transcendent.

The Jesus Movement Is upon Us:
The Generation Gap and Religion, 1971–1972

On 9 February 1971, a headline in *Look* magazine announced that "The Jesus Movement Is upon Us." The pictorial introduced readers to the youthful California-based religious revival that mixed the music, fashions, and communes of the hippie movement with conservative Evangelical Protestant Christianity. The frame was positive. Nine photographs showed young, overwhelmingly white Californians smiling, singing, preaching, and lifting their hands into the air in praise. One caption quoted a minister who described "the greatest awakening in the history of the church."[89] Another caption accompanied a photo of girl standing in the ocean, hands raised, and "Jesus" and a heart drawn on the back of her shirt. It read, "Her costume is informal, but there is nothing off-hand about her faith as she awaits baptism."[90] The two photographers on the assignment, Jack and Betty Cheetham, were so impressed by what they saw that they converted, while the writer, Brian Vachon, said that he had seriously considered doing so.[91] "Look out you other 49 states," Vachon concluded, "Jesus is coming."[92]

Like *Look*, most of the largest news and general-interest magazines portrayed the Jesus movement favorably. In a cover story in June 1971, *Time* concluded that "in a world filled with real and fancied demons for the young, the form their faith takes may be less important than the fact that they have it."[93] *U.S. News and World Report* wrote of a "supercharged evangelism . . . the latest version of an American pietism that has erupted periodically since colonial times," and quoted the evangelist Billy Graham praising the movement.[94] In an article in *Reader's Digest* tellingly titled "We *Need* Their Faith!" Norman Vincent Peale asserted that the Jesus people were full of love and joy, and that "sober, settled Christians have a lot to learn from these incandescent young people."[95] Peale granted that the Jesus people were sometimes "emotional to the point of hysteria, or dogmatic to the point of rudeness," but he suggested that the "established church" could provide the "maturity" and "enlightened leadership" needed to quell these things.[96] "Look beneath some of the exuberance and the long hair and the odd clothing," Peale reassured his readers, "for the true hallmarks of Christianity, the love and joy and fellowship that have astounded observers ever since the first century."[97]

While writers and journalists in these periodicals lauded the Jesus movement, many parents held more negative views—and these also appeared in mass-market magazines. Peale's essay, for example, was a response to letters from parents concerned about their children's new faith commitments. One mother contacted Peale to ask for help because she felt that her eighteen-year-old son had become a "fanatic." She lamented that "he carries a Bible everywhere and quotes from it constantly. He embarrasses his father and me by greeting our friends with religious slogans and questions. We are church-going people ourselves, but we cannot understand the intensity of our son's obsession. Please, please tell us how to handle this thing."[98]

In 1971, Time *proclaimed a "Jesus Revolution" on its June cover.*
(© Time, Inc./Timepix)

The mother's concern reflected some Americans' views that a growing generation gap divided them from their children. While small in numbers, the hippie movement spurred new fashions and styles. Few teens and young adults participated actively in the communalist and political activist parts of the counterculture, but many more partook in the commercial counterculture of clothing and music that merged with them. Some also experimented religiously, reading about Asian religions or, as in the Jesus movement, participating in charismatic, conservative Evangelicalism. While the number of youths actually joining a new religion, an Asian religion, or the Jesus movement was quite small, some parents viewed their children's fleeting interests and fashions portentously—and sometimes accurately—as a rejection of their own faiths and values.

Like Peale, other Protestant writers addressed the issue of a spiritual generation gap. In 1968, for example, a college chaplain, David Edman, published his sermon, "Are You Disturbed by the 'New Religion?'" in *Reader's Digest*. Responding to readers concerned over the incorporation of rock music, coffee houses, and nightclubs into youth ministries, Edman's response sounded like Peale's: keep an open mind and realize that ferment and enthusiasm are a sign of life. "Unquestionably, we live in an age of religious revolution, and people of traditional religious beliefs and practices are in for a good many jolts," Edman warned.[99] On the other hand, he predicted, "the merely fashionable will properly perish, but what is of God will endure."[100]

The spiritual generation gap was a particular concern for Catholic writers and periodicals after the Second Vatican Council, known as Vatican II, a series of meetings from 1962 to 1965 that substantially altered Catholic practice and doctrine. Among other changes, the Mass was now celebrated in the vernacular, there was an increased emphasis on the laity, and it was acknowledged that other religions may also hold truths. While some American Catholics felt betrayed by the "modernization" of the church, others hoped that Vatican II would revitalize it and help keep Catholic youth in the fold. In the summer and fall of 1966, the Jesuit weekly *America* published a series of editorials and letters addressing the generation gap. Reflecting its liberal view and sympathy for

Vatican II, *America* suggested three factors moving youth to leave the faith. First, "it seems clear, however, that since 'religion' fits all too comfortably into that total world of their parents which young people, not without reason, consider phony and a menace to their freedom, this religion cannot survive the demise of the rest of that fading universe."[101] Second, youth were becoming increasingly intellectual and literate: "They are discovering every day that the faith-world of their childhood is regarded by many creators of contemporary life as a mythological relic, irrelevant for the future of mankind."[102] Third, *America* blamed the "failure of organized Christianity to put both its membership and its extensive resources unreservedly behind great humanitarian movements of today."[103]

The editorial in *America* was yet another jeremiad, and it generated a series of letters and additional editorials. These revealed rifts between some parents and youth that seemed as deep as the divide between traditionalists and Vatican II reformers. Edward P. Reid, for example, wrote a letter suggesting that Jesuits, including the staff at *America*, were partially responsible for youths' leaving Catholicism. Reid railed against "mamby-pamby 'accommodations' to the fancied needs of youth," asserting that "we only compound confusion when we advocate guitars and rock-and-roll as a 'special' liturgy for the young."[104] Younger readers responded to opinions like Reid's in kind and in large number. One, Richard R. Russo, proclaimed that "the older generation does not believe in many of the things that it holds true, and that is this hypocrisy which is handed down to the younger generation." Another reader, Patrick Collins, wrote that "by questioning, we will get a fuller and better understanding of what Christianity is than your generation will ever hope to have."[105] *Catholic World*, run by laypeople, published articles on the generation gap that revealed similar sentiments: some adults and youth just didn't understand each other.[106] Some apparently didn't care to.

But this was more than a generational divide. It was also a gap between many journalists—in both religious and nonreligious periodicals—and their readers. While the writers and editors for *Time, Look, U.S. News, Reader's Digest, Catholic World*, and *America* viewed burgeoning religious movements like the Jesus people positively, some readers who had sons and daughters interested or involved in such groups felt differently.[107] These readers' more negative views soon appeared in mass-market magazines, spurred by the emergence of parents who organized to remove their young adult children from certain countercultural religious groups.

Jesus Freaks and Anti-Cultists: Controversy at the Darkening Margins

In the late summer of 1971, William Rambur, a retired navy officer from California, formed the Parent's Committee to Free Our Sons and Daughters from the Children of God after his daughter, a twenty-two-year-old nursing student, joined the group, which was an apocalyptic, Evangelical commune.[108] By the late 1970s, this small parent's group would grow into a loosely organized national coalition of parents, pastors, and psychiatrists who lobbied against "cults." The anti-cult movement, as it was labeled by sociologists, eventually provided a new and dramatic set of idioms for journalists writing about the American religious fringe.[109]

The focus of Rambur's group was the Children of God. Founded by a prophetic leader, David "Moses" Berg, in 1967 as "Teens for Christ," the group was the most countercultural and controversial of those in the Jesus movement.[110] At first, the Children of God was semi-nomadic. Members traveled across the United States and Canada, criticizing institutional Christianity and American capitalist society in theatrical public demonstrations and occasional disruptions of church services. Perhaps most alarming to parents, Berg called on members to sever ties with their biological families in order to better embrace their new, religious one. In the mid-1970s, the group would become even more controversial when Berg introduced free love and "flirty fishing," in which female members witnessed to unconverted males through sex. Some members even engaged in sex with minors in the group.[111] Though these experiments occurred after the founding of Rambur's group, the concerned parents' group cited numerous other complaints against the Children, which they aired in the national print media.

Though the Children of God would later face well-documented

scandal, early magazine depictions of the group only vaguely distinguished it from the larger Jesus movement. In a cover story on the Jesus people in *Time* July 1971, the magazine referred to the Children as "ultra rigid." The writers quickly tempered this assessment in the following sentence, however, asserting that "few are more zealous than Pat Boone," referring to a popular, clean-cut Christian singer who was a staple on television variety shows in the 1960s.[112] *Time* also featured two photos of the group. The first showed several men, gathered in a prayer circle, their hands joined and raised. "Children of God disciples," the caption read, "join hands in celebration of Jesus at Indio, California."[113] The second picture, which future newsmagazine articles would replicate in almost every story about the Children of God, showed men and women wearing sackcloth and holding signs that displayed quotations from the Bible damning the wicked and society. Interestingly, the caption of this more striking image failed to identify the group. Instead it read, "wearing sackcloths, dabbed with ashes, youths conduct a vigil on Los Angeles' Skid Row."[114]

Television news also noticed the group and gave it positive coverage. An edition in January 1971 of "First Tuesday," a one-hour news show on NBC, featured the Children of God. The program's producer, Robert Rogers, said he was so impressed by the communal group that he wouldn't prevent his own daughter from joining. Many younger viewers apparently shared Rogers's assessment. NBC reported that it received responses to the program from youth wanting to contact the group.

On 5 November 1971, the Protestant Evangelical magazine *Christianity Today* published the first report of organized opposition to the Children. "Suspicion, intrigue, charges and countercharges are swirling in a maelstrom of controversy," wrote Edward Plowman, "that involves a growing band of far-out young Christian vagabonds known as the 'Children of God.'"[115] Plowman detailed the history and theology of the Children, as well as the views of the Parents Committee to Free our Sons and Daughters from the Children of God (FREECOG). "Charges against the Children," Plowman noted, "range from hypnotic spellbinding and demon possession to apostasy and hatemongering."[116] In addition to these more religiously based charges, the story in *Christianity Today* detailed accusations against the group that would eventually be picked up by newsmagazines and extended to "cults" in general. These included tight security that allowed members little freedom, the disruption of family ties, censorship of mail, and even the stockpiling of weapons. Among these charges was brainwashing. For example, Plowman reported that one Christian psychiatrist whose daughter had joined asserted that the Children "definitely" used brainwashing.[117] Other parents agreed. Plowman wrote, "parents have complained that their children have been spirited away, held incommunicado for days, and somehow alienated from home ties. Parents of Children at a recent Atlanta meeting said their offspring had undergone dramatic personality changes. Such terms as hypnosis, brainwashing, witchcraft, Satanic influences, and drugs were tossed around freely as possible explanations. Indeed, a number of the children seen in various colonies last month did have glazed eyes and walked about as if in a trance."[118]

While Plowman never directly came out in support of the brainwashing accusation, his suggestion that some Children appeared "as if in a trance" left the question suggestively open. When *Time* reported on the controversy between the Children of God and disgruntled parents on 24 January 1972, the magazine was less ambiguous about brainwashing charges—though its definition of the term may have differed from FREECOG's: "While there seems to be no hard evidence of kidnaping, drugging or genuine hypnotism so far, a broader charge of 'brainwashing' may be closer to the truth, at least in the sense of relentless exposure to the sect's propaganda."[119] With this sentence, *Time* presented its readers with a new idiom for understanding the American religious fringe—one that would eventually dominate representations in the 1970s.

The article in *Time* on the Children of God, unlike that in *Christianity Today*, framed the group positively. Though the magazine referred to the movement as "the storm troopers of the Jesus Revolution . . . its most forceful and criticized zealots," the group was acknowledged to have had more success than many parents in "winning young people from drugs, casual sex and drifting."[120] (The assertion about drifting proves especially interesting, considering the group was semi-nomadic at the time.) *Time* also asserted that the Children had "potent precedents in St. Francis of Assisi and St. Thomas Aquinas, both of whom had to break with their families over their vocations."[121] While *Time* reported FREECOG's charges, it ended its story by citing parents who were happy that their children had joined.[122] An earlier article in *Newsweek* did the same, citing one parent whose two sons had been "cured" of drug addiction by the group.[123] While the larger newsmagazines reported accusations from unhappy parents, they did not necessarily agree with the parents' negative assessments—at least not yet.

If *Time* and *Newsweek* did fault the Children of God in these early articles, it was for the same thing for which they had faulted earlier fringe groups: zealotry and conservative theology. *Time*, for example, not only noted the group's "purer-than-thou attitude" but also questioned its apocalypticism. It asked whether the Children were "prepared to live more fully in the world if doomsday does not come as expected."[124] *Newsweek* also questioned aspects of the Children's fundamentalist theology, particularly their biblical literalism. "The Gospels, of course," *Newsweek* asserted, "are studded with many such stern admonitions which, if followed literally by Christians, would tear conventional society apart."[125] As with the Third Force groups of the 1950s, the Children of God were too zealous and too fundamentalist for some reporters' sensibilities.

However, magazine representations of the American religious fringe from 1966 to 1972 did differ from earlier ones. Writers in the largest news and general-interest magazines depicted the California cults, Nation of Islam, and Third Force as exotic, overly emotional "others" separated by race, region, and class. Depictions of the gurus, occultists, and Jesus people similarly evoked exoticism. But they also suggested its apparent opposite—banality —by asserting that some groups were exotic in appearance but rather ordinary "in reality." This motif partly resulted from the makeup of many of the groups that the journalists were covering, which attracted white, middle-class youth. This population, so close to journalists' own social locations, just didn't seem that exotic. These seekers, after all, were what most journalists thought of when they imagined the "American mainstream." In the early 1970s, when disgruntled parents began accusing various "cults" of moral and physical atrocities, writers and editors in the largest magazines were faced with the task of how to represent the accusations and the conflicts that underlay them. By the mid-1970s, virtually all national periodicals accepted allegations by the anticult movement that various "cults" engaged in brainwashing. They did, perhaps unwittingly, because it allowed them to symbolically and psychologically distance the white, middle-class "mainstream" converts from the exotic fringe groups that they joined. By the late 1970s, brainwashing and the negative "cult" label would become journalistic doxa.

chapter four

MAKING THE

CULT MENACE

BRAINWASHING,

DEPROGRAMMING,

MASS SUICIDE, AND

OTHER HERESIES,

1973–1979

On 10 November 1975, *Time* published a story about parents who were disgruntled about their children's membership in Sun Myung Moon's Unification Church. "Around the country," *Time* wrote, "hundreds of parents have been driven to near hysteria by changes in their convert children's behavior and by reports of brainwashing."[1] Supporting parents' fears, the magazine noted that both ex-members and psychologists confirmed the allegations of brainwashing. *Time* quoted one defector's charges of "psychological abuse" and "subliminal fascism," and reported: "Harvard Psychiatrist John Clark Jr. recently testified in District of Columbia Superior Court that the ex-Moonies he had examined seemed physically and emotionally exhausted; a few were psychotic."[2] The story ended portentously, noting that "Jack Kerry, the Moon watcher in the California attorney general's office, sees the movement as 'extremely dangerous' and adds: 'I think this whole situation is going to explode.'"[3]

The Unification Church, a new religion combining aspects of Christianity with the revelations and biblical interpretations of its founder, the Reverend Sun Myung Moon, was the archetypal cult of the print media in the 1970s. Founded in Korea in 1954, the group, whose full name is the Holy Spirit Association for the Unification of World Christianity, attracted negative attention from some relatives of converts and the mass media in the United States for its aggressive proselytizing, totalistic communal living, and large group weddings. Various stripes of Christians and Jews also attacked Moon's revelatory scripture, *The Divine Principle*, as heretical. The sociologist Anson Shupe suggests that "the Unification Church, among all other new religious movements or 'cults,' has always been the bête noire of the modern anticult movement in America. It offers a veritable archetype of the dimensions that offend, infuriate, and threaten conventional society, thereby calling down accusations of heresy and setting in motion the ritual process of assigning the label 'evil.'"[4] Along with brainwashing motifs, journalists blended tenuous allegations of deviant sex rituals and conspiratorial foreign connections with documented cases of deceptive proselytizing in California and Moon's antagonistic preaching to make captivating—if not alarming—reading. Among other things, journalists repeatedly reported rumors that Moon had engaged in bizarre ritual sex practices while in Korea, had mysterious ties to the Korean intelligence service, and had founded his religion purely for profit.[5] The sociologists Barend van Driel and James Richardson noted that the "Moonies," as journalists called them, received anywhere from two to fifteen times as much press as other new religions like the International Society of Krishna Consciousness (Hare Krishnas), the Children of God, and Scientology, the therapeutic new religion founded by science fiction novelist L. Ron Hubbard in 1954.[6]

But the content of Unification Church coverage was not unique for its time. By the mid-1970s, charges of brainwashing, deception, fraud, and various improprieties appeared in most stories about groups that the journalists labeled cults. During this time, *Reader's Digest* explained to readers "How Cults Bilk All of Us" and detailed a "Rescue from a Fanatic Cult."[7] *Parent's Magazine* asked, "Could Your Child Be Brainwashed?" while *U.S. News and World Report* dared look "Behind the Cult Craze."[8] By the late 1970s the connections between cults, brainwashing, and fraudulence had become naturalized. In other words, these associations became unquestioned truths—not just in magazine articles, but for many Americans. This chapter traces the naturalization of negative cult stereotypes from 1973 to 1979, the period when the American religious fringe became synonymous with what the sociologist James Beckford calls "the Cult Menace."[9]

Explaining the period's negative media coverage of cults, most sociologists focus on the influence of the anti-cult movement (known in the sociology of religion as the ACM), the loosely organized coalition of parents and psychiatrists who lobbied, litigated, and even abducted their sons and daughters to remove them from certain religious groups.[10] The sociologist Andrew Greil credits the anti-cult movement with creating the category "cult" and suggests that "print and broadcast media for the most part uncritically accepted the ACM's analysis" of new religions.[11] While the anti-cult movement certainly played a role in fomenting negative media coverage, journalists were more than uncritical mouthpieces for the movement. Instead, writers and editors in various magazines eventually used the idioms of brainwashing, scandal, and conflict because of a complex variety of factors.

Scholars studying depictions of new religions—mostly sociologists—have focused intensively on the 1970s. At the same time, few have exclusively interpreted coverage in general-interest mass-market magazines, newsmagazines, and special-interest magazines of subjects like deprogramming, cult atrocity stories, and Jonestown. A few scholars have noted that journalists showed contempt for deprogramming. Here I suggest that the reason for this lies in a long-standing journalistic disdain for strongly held views, as seen in stories about Third Force and California cults in the 1950s. And while several scholars have examined cult atrocity tales—those shocking stories of cults' immoral and criminal activities—none have examined the intrinsic connection between their content and placement in special-interest magazines geared toward homemaking and family interests. While this chapter visits familiar subject matter, it considers neglected variables and new interpretations of cult depictions in the 1970s.

Cults, Brainwashing, and the Business of Journalism

Though hard to indisputably prove, one could posit that magazine articles promoted charges of brainwashing leveled by the anti-cult movement partly because of the social locations of their writers and editors. When journalists in the largest magazines reported on what, in Chapter 3, I called the "middle-class fringe," they saw a population of converts demographically resembling their own sons and daughters. Brainwashing motifs allowed journalists, their readers, and distraught parents of new religion members to symbolically separate "mainstream," white, middle-class converts from the cultic "fringe" groups that they joined. The religion theorist Bruce Lincoln argues that "anomalies remain always a potential threat to the taxonomic structures under which they are marginalized, for in the very fact of their existence they reveal the shortcomings, inadequacies, contradictions, and arbitrary nature of such structures."[12] "Mainstream" individuals in "fringe" groups constituted just such a threatening anomaly—and one that brainwashing addressed. If cults coercively brainwashed converts—as the anti-cult movement asserted—then young, white, middle-class adults couldn't possibly be responsible for their own positions on the religious periphery.

On the other hand, most newsmagazine writers and editors seemed inclined to accept brainwashing theories long before they came into contact with anti-cultists. The brainwashing concept emerged during the Korean War. According to the anthropologist Catherine Lutz, the term was coined in 1953 by Edward Hunter, a journalist employed by the CIA.[13] "Ostensibly describing a new Chinese Communist psychological weapon," Lutz notes, "the term appeared in a flood of media pieces to account for P.O.W.'s actions: confessing to war crimes, signing peace petitions, and otherwise collaborating with the enemy."[14] Brainwashing, a Cold War creation, served to account for American soldiers who in some way renounced their American, capitalist allegiances in Chinese and Korean prison camps. In the 1950s and 1960s a number of books appeared on brainwashing, including the journalist Virginia Pasley's *Twenty-One Stayed: The Story of the American GIs Who Chose Communist China—Who They Were and Why They Stayed* (1955), which won a Pulitzer Prize.[15] The "twenty-one" in Pasley's title refers to the number of American POWs who, at the end of the Korean War, had chosen to give up their American citizenship and remain in Korea. Interestingly, Pasley's argument sometimes parallels the discourse of the 1950s on converts to Third Force and California cult groups. Among other things, she argued that the twenty-one all shared characteristics of "broken homes, brutal treatment, serious emotional problems and scanty education." In addition to books, brainwashing also appeared in television and films, especially B-grade science fiction movies.[16] As noted in Chapter 1, the term was so common in the 1950s that some parents and politicians accused Hollywood movies, popular music, and comics of brainwashing teenagers.[17]

In popular culture and entertainment, brainwashing motifs continued through the 1970s. On television, *James at 15* showed a young protagonist brainwashed by a cult and later deprogrammed. The concept was even a familiar trope in children's cartoons. One such example occurred on *Godzilla*, a Saturday morning cartoon of the late 1970s featuring the famous lizard concocted by Toho Studios in Japan. In one episode, an evil underwater dragon uses "eye rays" to temporarily brainwash Godzilla's human friends. The victims appeared zombie-like, talking like robots and moving stiffly. This animated depiction of brainwashing, complete with blank stares and monotone speech patterns, was replicated in several television movies and "cult survivor" autobiographies of the period.

Magazines first picked up brainwashing as a subject in the mid-1950s and published occasional stories through the late 1960s. Some appeared in special-interest periodicals. In 1966, for example, *Esquire* published A. J. Budrys's "Mind Control Is Good/Bad." Budry interviewed behavioral psychologists and concluded that "mind control is a fact."[18] "It is no news," he wrote, "that men can be conditioned in a random way; but now we can be conditioned with a purpose by 'brainwashing,' a more sophisticated manipulation of the brain than most of us would think."[19]

As a Cold War concept associated with communism, one newsmagazine put brainwashing to propagandistic uses. On 14 April 1967, *Time* published "Hanoi's Pavlovians." The article suggested that the signed confessions of several American pilots captured by the North Vietnamese "raised fears that the Communists were once again resorting to the inhuman brainwashing techniques whose widespread use during the Korean War horrified the world."[20] The pilots confessed, *Time* reported, that they had been commanded to bomb civilian targets. "The obvious conclusion," the unnamed authors wrote, "is that the confessions are written by Hanoi's commissars and taped by American-educated announcers."[21] *Time* continued:

> One artful dodger who beat the system was Lieut. Commander Charles Tanner . . . who solemnly declared that two fellows pilots refused to fly their missions, were court-martialed and dishonorably discharged. The officer's names, subsequently trumpeted by Hanoi: Lieut. Commander Ben Casey and Lieut. Clark Kent. . . . However the confessions are concocted, or even extracted, the North Vietnamese clearly have not yet succeeded in washing horse sense or humor from many Americans brains . . . Hanoi's efforts so far only accentuate North Viet Nam's endemic ignorance of Western idiom, intellect and ideology.[22]

Time soon tempered its support of the Vietnam War. But in "Hanoi's Pavlovians," it created a classic Cold War dichotomy of good versus evil. The communists, the article implied, might capture Americans, but they would ultimately fail to break their spirit or use brainwashing to transform them into traitors. The story also assumed that the American war effort was good, ethical, and noble, and therefore any confessions by American soldiers about targeting Vietnamese civilians must have been false. As noted in Chapter 3, however, this attitude would change with the media's discovery of the My Lai massacre in 1969, after which brainwashing accounts disappeared from war reports.[23] Apparently for journalists, the confessions that the North Vietnamese obtained from POWs through alleged brainwashing no longer seemed implausible.

But brainwashing's absence from war coverage didn't mean that journalists had abandoned the concept. It merely reappeared as a domestic problem. On 4 February 1974 Patty Hearst, the millionaire heiress to the expansive Hearst Publishing Corporation, was kidnaped by a leftist terrorist group, the Symbionese Liberation Army (SLA). She reappeared later that spring, when she committed several armed bank robberies as a member of the group. After her arrest, Hearst contended that the group had brainwashed her.

Both *Time* and *Newsweek* picked up the brainwashing angle and produced stories on it. These articles revealed the magazines' firm beliefs in brainwashing. On 6 October 1975, *Time* published "Was She Brainwashed?" The article interviewed several psychologists, asking them whether they believed Hearst had been brainwashed. The Yale psychologist Robert Jay Lifton, "who closely analyzed the mind-bending methods used on American prisoners of war in Korea and by Chinese Communists on their countrymen," stated that the threats, isolation, and chiding dealt by Hearst's captors were "all classic techniques of brainwashing."[24] Another psychologist, Rona Fields, and the psychiatrist Louis J. West agreed, while the political scientist Chalmers Johnson did not. "No one can convince me," *Time* quoted him as saying, "that Cinque [SLA chief Donald Freeze] was bright or skilled enough to brainwash anyone."[25] Apparently for Johnson, as well as for *Time*, the question was not whether brainwashing existed, but whether the SLA subjected Hearst to it.

A related article in *Newsweek* in 1976, "What Is Brainwashing?" initially appeared to take a more skeptical tone. "To both psychiatrists and lawyers," the correspondents wrote, "brainwashing is a loaded word, one that has come to mean almost any way of persuading people to behave in a prescribed way."[26] *Newsweek* even quoted Marvin Ziporyn, a psychiatrist from Chicago, to the effect that "brainwashing is a myth perpetuated on the American public."[27] The newsmagazine's skeptical pretense, however, quickly disappeared. The section immediately after Ziporyn's quote described how "real" brainwashing worked. "Unlike propaganda or advertising," *Newsweek* asserted, "brainwashing relies on mental and physical coercion to force a person into doing what society and his own moral scruples scream out against doing."[28]

In the 1950s and early 1960s, several psychology researchers produced studies of Chinese communist "brainwashing." While some American POWs reported that their captors during the Korean War tortured them to elicit political confessions, the classic brainwashing studies dealt mostly with "ideological reform schools" where civilians and prisoners were forced to participate in communism classes and public self-criticism. These psychological works influenced both journalists and anti-cultists who later charged cults with brainwashing. At the same time, however, the early studies were ambiguous about brainwashing's nature and effectiveness. The most famous of these studies is Robert Jay Lifton's *Thought Reform and the Psychology of Totalism* (1961).[29] The religion scholar Larry Shinn calls Lifton's book "the canonized handbook for anticult activities as they have sought explanations for the conversion of American youth to the cults."[30] Although he would later side with anti-cultists in suggesting that cults did enact some process akin to "brainwashing," Lifton's early study actually criticized the term and argued that forced confession and education were the two basic elements in what he called Chinese "thought reform."[31]

In another well-known study, *Coercive Persuasion: A Socio-Psychological Analysis of the "Brainwashing" of American Civilian Prisoners by the Chinese Communists* (1961), the psychologist Edgar Schein suggested that the "process of coercive persuasion as observed in Chinese Communist prisons has its counterpart in various kinds of total institutions in our own society and elements of it exist in any influence relationship in which there are physical, social, or psychological constraints which tend to force the person to expose himself to the pressures of the influence agent."[32] Issuing a warning against the indiscriminate use of the term "brainwashing," Schein suggested that "there is a world of difference in the content of what is transmitted in religious orders, prisons, educational institutions, mental hospitals, and thought reform centers. But there are striking similarities in the manner in which influence occurs, a fact which should warn us strenuously against letting our moral and political sentiments color our scientific understanding of the Chinese Communist approach to influence."[33]

Today in religious studies, particularly in the sociology of religion, brainwashing is not only an ambiguous but a politically charged concept. At issue among specialists is whether there even is such a thing. Since the late 1970s, many sociologists, psychologists, and religion scholars have produced studies repudiating charges of brainwashing leveled against new religious movements.[34] New religions like the Unification Church, Hare Krishnas, and Children of God, they argue, use the same forms of social and psychological persuasion that established religions and other social movements do. Whether something is considered brainwashing or conversion, they suggest, is often more a matter of personal views about the religious group in question than significant differences in methods of proselytizing. But while a majority of scholars question brainwashing's usefulness in studying religious groups, a small but vocal minority believes that the term does have descriptive value. The sociologist Benjamin Zablocki, for example, argues that brainwashing is a useful concept, but one that has been "blacklisted" as unacceptable among scholars of the sociology of religion.[35] This academic debate became so heated in the 1990s that lawsuits and court battles ensued.[36]

I agree with several researchers who suggest that brainwashing, rather than describing an actual process, is in most cases best viewed as a rhetorical term that marks certain movements negatively. David Bromley, for example, argues that brainwashing and conversion should be viewed as competing political and moral terms that judge the validity of particular groups and activities. Bromley argues that "if there are not single processes or patterns of behavior that correspond to what are termed brainwashing and conversion, then what the terms provide are symbolic umbrellas that positively or negatively sanction diverse phenomena."[37] In other words, brainwashing and conversion are used as antonyms that among other things distinguish authentic from inauthentic religion. Individuals convert to groups that one finds acceptable; individuals are brainwashed into joining groups that one finds unacceptable.

The view of brainwashing as a rhetorical device marking groups that one doesn't like is supported by an experiment conducted in the early 1990s by the social psychologist Jeffrey Pfeiffer. He asked three groups of university undergraduates to read a story. The story related the experiences of Bill, a young college student who left school to join a social movement. Members of the group, the passage suggests, allow Bill little contact with friends and family and make him feel guilty if he questions their actions and beliefs. The narrative was exactly the same for all three groups but for one exception: the name of the movement that Bill joined. When the story suggested that Bill had joined the Unification Church (called the "Moonies" in the experiment), students had a much more negative view of his experiences than when the group named was either the U.S. Marines or a Roman Catholic seminary:[38] 71 percent of the respondents thought that Bill had been brainwashed by the Moonies, while 44 percent used that term to describe his experiences in the Marines and only 29 percent did so to describe his experiences with the Catholic seminary.[39] Taken as a whole, the study shows that brainwashing is a term most often reserved for groups that one already views negatively, whether it be a new religion, an established religion, or a branch of the military.

Though critics of brainwashing like Marvin Ziporyn were vocal in the 1970s, magazine journalists used the concept as if it were an undisputed scientific fact. One article in *Newsweek* in 1976, for example, referred to psychiatrists' "solid evidence" that the Unification Church "systematically programs converts into a state of mental dependency upon Moon."[40] An article in *Time* in 1974 likewise asserted that the Children of God's new openness to free love, polygamy, and sexual proselytization "might be amusing if the Children were not so efficient in their indoctrination of converts, who still go through months of spiritual brainwashing."[41] In 1976 *Seventeen* magazine similarly warned its teen readers that young people "emerge" from cults "with severe mental disorders after they have been programmed to do desperate things."[42] Mark Silk accurately calls brainwashing "the most characteristic feature of the coverage of 'cults'" in the 1970s.[43]

Business and professional obligations, in addition to journalists' propensities to believe in brainwashing, fomented the use of brainwashing in cult menace stories. By the early 1970s, magazine production had become an extremely costly big business. Increased printing costs and competition from television brought about the demise of two photojournalism newsmagazines, *Look* in 1972 and *Life* in 1973. The *Saturday Evening Post* also ceased publication, temporarily, in 1969. For-profit news reporting—largely spurred by increasing media monopolization—led many magazines to search for marketable human interest stories and exposés with high shock value.[44] The journalism historian J. Herbert Altschull suggests that "vast" corporate media "enterprises dedicated to profit and expansion have inevitably concerned themselves less than did editors of the past with 'hard' news and more with marketable commodities: 'soft' features, human interest, gossip about celebrities, and heavily dramatized stories of conflicts and confrontations."[45]

Several studies show that conflict has long been a preferred motif for news about religion, and coverage of cults in the 1970s seemed especially rich in marketable contestation.[46] For example, the sociologists Barend van Driel and James T. Richardson argue that reporting on cults in the 1970s and early 1980s was not uniformly negative, but could "be described as a 'stream of controversies' approach" with "legal conflicts and criminal allegations the most frequent topic."[47] Interestingly, the media scholar Herbert Gans, in his study of *Time, Newsweek*, the CBS *Evening News*, and NBC *Nightly News* from 1967 to 1975, found that investigative reports on crime and scandals dramatically increased while stories on "fads" and "cults" simultaneously decreased.[48] Taken together, these studies help to explain and demonstrate what should not be surprising: most stories about cults in the 1970s included scandals and other controversies. In the mid-1970s, journalists found such controversy in the stories of disgruntled parents who had hired "cult deprogrammers" to abduct their children from new religious movements.

Deprogramming

Deprogramming, the process of forcibly removing individuals from religious groups and confining them until they deconverted, was, like brainwashing, as much a part of popular culture in the 1970s as disco. Television shows like "Cannon" produced episodes about it. Popular nonfiction books such as Ted Patrick's *Let Our Children Go!* dramatically depicted it.[49] One network news show even did a special report on the subject. In August 1973, CBS was allowed to film the abduction, and the subsequent deprogramming over a period of 107 hours, of a nineteen-year-old from the Church of Armageddon commune in Seattle; the result was a twenty-six-minute documentary in three parts broadcast on the CBS *Evening News*, called *The Deprogramming of Kathy Crampton*. All forms of mass media broached the subject of deprogramming, but newsmagazines "discovered" it first.

On 12 March 1973, *Newsweek* published "Defreaking Jesus Freaks." "What's a parent to do," *Newsweek* asked, "when their children leave college, home or job to start a new life in a com-

mune of Jesus Freaks?"[50] Some, the newsmagazine answered, hire
the cult deprogrammer Ted Patrick, who "spirits Jesus Freaks away
from their communes and harangues them into changing their
ways."[51] The article detailed the activities of Patrick, a devout fundamentalist Baptist and former government official under Gover-
nor Ronald Reagan in California, who forcibly removed hundreds
of young converts from new religions—at their parents' request.
An African American, Patrick had attained the nickname "Black
Lightning" for his fast abductions of cult converts. After taking
them, Patrick "deprogrammed" them, which he described as "a
way of showing the kid that what the religious group taught him
just will not stand up to what the Bible really tells us."[52] In deprogramming, the abducted convert was locked into a home or
motel room, and then repeatedly told that he or she held false religious beliefs and had been misled by a corrupt spiritual leader.[53] In
his interview with *Newsweek*, Patrick estimated that "'it takes an
average of two to three days to deprogram a kid, but sometimes I
will keep a person in my house for a month or so."[54] Patrick originally became a deprogrammer in 1971 after his fourteen-year-old
nephew was proselytized by Children of God missionaries. After
investigating the group, he concluded that it was dangerous and, as
Newsweek paraphrased, "sounded suspiciously like the 'witchcraft
and voodoo' he has encountered in black ghettoes."[55]

Newsweek quoted Patrick several times, giving him a voice that
articles seldom allowed to representatives of new religions. At
the same time, however, the overall frame of "Defreaking Jesus
Freaks" was negative. This was apparent in the magazine's commentary on criminal charges filed against Patrick by an unsuc-
cessful "deprogrammee." According to the magazine, Dan Voll, a
twenty-one-year-old Yale student who had "joined a small, quite
respectable sect called the New Testament Missionary Fellowship," claimed that he had been injured when Patrick and his father
violently dragged him into a car for deprogramming.[56] Voll responded to his abduction from the Pentecostal group by filing
criminal charges. *Newsweek* revealed its opinion on the case—and
Patrick's deprogramming in general—by ending the story with a
quote from a civil liberties attorney, John LeMoult: "'What we've

got here is an outfit that does not discriminate between a legitimate church fellowship and the phonies.'"[57] ·

Deeply committed to First Amendment issues like freedom of the press, writers and editors at the largest newsmagazines might have been expected to dislike deprogramming.[58] Despite their apparent acceptance of accusations about cult brainwashing, articles framed deprogramming as a violation of religious freedom. For example, one article in *Time* in 1977 favorably reported a New York State Supreme Court judgment against deprogramming, titling the article "The Freedom to Be Strange."[59] Articles frequently went further to suggest that deprogramming was not only a violation of religious freedom but was also brainwashing. One issue of *Time* in 1973 compared it to "that brain-blowing treatment administered to Alex, the anti-hero in Anthony Burgess's *A Clockwork Orange*."[60] In the subcultural novel of the 1960s and later the movie, the socially deviant Alex is put through a series of violent, Pavlovian treatments to make him less violent and antisocial. "In the process," *Time* commented, "Alex also lost his free will."[61]

Like their secular counterparts—and no doubt partly because of their investment in religious liberty—liberal Protestant, Evangelical Protestant, and Roman Catholic periodicals came out strongly against deprogramming. On 2 May 1973, the *Christian Century* published William Willoughby's "'Deprogramming' Jesus Freaks and Others: Can American Tolerate Private Inquisitions?" Willoughby listed four reasons why deprogramming was wrong. His argument resembled newsmagazine stories in that it appealed to religious liberty and questioned Patrick's ability to distinguish "bad" groups. First, Willoughby argued that even if all the groups from which Patrick abducted people were harmful, it was still not his right to force someone to alter a person's religious views. Representing deprogramming as brainwashing, he suggested that deprogrammees were "prisoners" who were kept sleep-deprived and put through "encounter-group techniques" used to "induce a sense of guilt and to convince the victim that he or she is a phony."[62]

While Willoughby conceded that some religious groups might indeed use "questionable means to recruit members," he asserted that unless the recruit was physically detained or coercively forced to take up beliefs, the issue was strictly a matter of religious liberty.[63] "If this is not so," Willoughby wrote, "every American's religious liberty is in jeopardy."[64] His third reason echoed *Time*: "Patrick's organization is totally incompetent to exercise censorship and decide which group is 'good' and which 'bad.'"[65] The New Testament Missionary Fellowship and the Alamo Foundation—another group from which Patrick had abducted members—were "indistinguishable from accepted fundamentalist churches."[66] "The fact is," Willoughby continued, "one almost gets the impression that Patrick is carrying on a vendetta against any association which does not conform to the standard for church groups."[67] Willoughby ended his essay by arguing that more lawful ways existed for parents to separate their children from religious groups they didn't like. He suggested that parents attempt to sway their offspring by reason. If this didn't work, they should resign themselves to the child's choice. "Anything short of that," he concluded, "is not religious freedom."[68]

The more conservative Evangelical journal *Christianity Today* agreed. In one news brief in 1974 it jeeringly described deprogramming as a "mind-altering treatment" performed to "'liberate' persons from attachment to certain beliefs or persons considered objectionable by one's relatives."[69] Another story—on Ted Patrick's acquittal in the Dan Voll suit—was tellingly titled "Ted Patrick Acquitted: Open Season for Deprogrammers." In it, Edward Plowman echoed Willoughby's critique of Patrick's credentials. Implying that Patrick didn't distinguish between legitimate and illegitimate groups, Plowman noted that the Voll case "involved, of all things, the super straight coat-and-tie New Testament Missionary Fellowship (NTMF), a charismatic community of about forty persons, most of them college students or gainfully employed."[70] While the founding of *Christianity Today* was directly tied to its theological disagreements with *Christian Century*, the stances of the two publications on deprogramming were indistinguishable.

Catholic periodicals mirrored Protestant ones in their condemnation of deprogramming. In an article titled "Kidnapping the Converts," for example, *America* called deprogramming "a process that appears to be a kind of brainwashing designed to counteract the assumed brainwashing of the sect."[71] But unlike *Christian*

Century and *Christianity Today, America* granted that "Mr. Patrick is surely not the only one to whom the enthusiasm of the Children of God or the New Testament Missionary Fellowship seems more like obsessive fanaticism than sound religious faith."[72] On the other hand, the periodical continued, "Religious freedom in our society, however, includes the right to be a fanatic, as long as the rights of others are not violated."[73]

Heresy

Criticism of deprogramming, mainline churches, and secular society certainly did not preclude denunciations of cults as heretical in all three periodicals. While they differed one from the other in their implicit definitions of heresy, they also remained consistent with their own earlier views. For example, the denunciation by *America* of the fanatical "enthusiasm" of the New Testament Missionary Fellowship and the Children of God closely resembled Catholic coverage of the California cults and Third Force sects in the 1950s. As I noted in Chapter 1, Catholic writers in *Commonweal* and *Catholic World* in the 1950s blamed Protestantism's "artistic barrenness" and lack of institutional authority for the proliferation of "enthusiastic sectarians" and California's "strange Oriental seedlings." In its cult and deprogramming articles in the 1970s, however, *America* did not directly fault Protestants. Instead, recalling commentary on the growth of occult spirituality in the 1960s, it blamed secular society and mainstream religions in general. In "Kidnapping the Converts," for example, *America* asserted that "if put in the context of current interests in the occult and various forms of Eastern mysticism, the appeal of these sects may be another reflection of the need to fill the vacuum at the heart of the secularist society."[74] In another article on the Unification Church, it assigned "part of the blame" to "the mainline Christian churches, which seem incapable of stimulating even a fraction of the interest and devotion among idealistic young people that Mr. Moon and similar 'prophets' have called forth."[75]

While *America* merely found "difficulties" in Moon's biblical interpretation, *Christianity Today* explicitly focused on Unification doctrine, calling it "complex, coherent, and heretical."[76] As in its coverage of cults in the 1950s and 1960s, *Christianity Today* ignored the scandalous accusations against the Unification Church recorded by newsmagazines. In "By the Light of a Masterly Moon," for example, the Presbyterian minister Harry Jaeger Jr. rebutted accusations that the Unification Church brainwashed members. The "successful graduate" of the church, he wrote, "has not only an extensive knowledge of the Bible set within a fully charted and diagramed scheme of interpretation but also an equally extensive scheme of history, psychologically sound method of approach to the unconverted, and a sense of destiny for this present hour."[77] For Jaeger and *Christianity Today*, the problem was not that Sun Myung Moon brainwashed and exploited unsuspecting victims, but that he held heretical religious views.

In *Christian Century*, Dean Peerman, the magazine's managing editor, faulted Moon's church on other grounds. Like the criticisms found in *Christianity Today* and *America*, his were consistent with the magazine's earlier coverage of the religious fringe, specifically earlier criticisms of the Third Force by the liberal ecumenist Henry Van Dusen, a regular contributor to *Christian Century*. Van Dusen had alleged that the Third Force was anti-intellectual and faulted its simplistic theology. Peerman contended that the Unification Church's message appealed to "those who hunger" for "clear and simple answers."[78] Van Dusen had suggested that one international Third Force sect, Brazilian Spiritism, was "a strange amalgam that mixes Catholic belief with elements of Voodooism, primitive animism, and extreme emotion."[79] Peerman characterized "Moonism" as "a strange amalgam of Oriental family worship, Eastern religious teachings, spiritism, and dubious interpretations of history and Christianity."[80] Van Dusen had denounced Third Force sectarians for their bigotry, intolerance, and lack of ecumenism. Peerman condemned the Unification Church for its "far-right politics" and argued that its "tactics will bring further disruption and division" to Christianity.[81] Though separated by twenty years and their subjects' marked theological differences, the writers at *Christian Century* described the Third Force and the Unification Church in strikingly similar ways.

Stories about deprogramming in newsmagazines, like those in

religious periodicals, contained implicit conceptions of heresy that mirrored earlier fringe reporting. As with coverage of Third Force groups in the 1950s and the Nation of Islam in the 1960s, the major heresy which journalists found among both cults and deprogrammers was zealotry. Newsmagazine critiques of deprogramming often focused less on religious freedom issues and more on the zealous nature of deprogrammers like Ted Patrick. For example, in a 1973 *Time* article, "Open Season on Sects," the writers called Patrick a "a zealot who despises zealots."[82] Earlier that year, the same periodical had pondered whether Patrick was "obsessed by heresy" and criticized him for lacking the proper psychology credentials to deprogram people.[83] *Newsweek* was even more explicit in its disdain for Patrick and deprogramming. Criticizing deprogramming through the words of unquoted sources, Eileen Keerdoja suggested that "to many civil libertarians, such tactics are as reprehensible as those used by the cults themselves to indoctrinate their members."[84] For Keerdoja's unnamed civil libertarians, deprogramming was reprehensible because it resembled cultic brainwashing.

For writers and editors in the largest newsmagazines, then, cults and deprogrammers were equally guilty of zealotry. For example, while *Newsweek* considered the New Testament Missionary Fellowship respectable, *Time* quoted unnamed critics who found them "insufferably elitist."[85] In an anti-deprogramming article in *Time* in 1977, "Freedom to Be Strange," the writers not only supported the court ruling against deprogramming but concurred with the judge's suggestions that Hare Krishna indoctrination and constant chanting "may create 'an inability to think, to be reasonable or logical.'"[86]

In denouncing the zealotry of both cult members and deprogrammers, journalists yet again acted as heresiographers, demarcating high levels of commitment and conviction as illegitimate. As noted in an earlier chapter, Mark Silk argues that the media tend to "be interested in good order, and therefore are made uneasy by strong beliefs that threaten to disrupt society."[87] The media scholar Herbert Gans similarly argues that much national news focuses on forms of social, moral, technological, or natural disorder and attempts by officials to restore order.[88] In magazine coverage of the 1970s, the social order was equally threatened by the zealotry of cults and that of deprogrammers.

Atrocity Tales: "Moonies," Broken Families,
and Print Media, 1976–1979

Despite their ambivalence and occasional hostility toward new religions, both newsmagazines and religious periodicals denounced deprogramming as a civil rights violation. For both "secular" and religious journalists, neither zealotry nor doctrinal heresy constituted grounds to violate an individual's religious liberty. But some special- and general-interest magazines—particularly family-oriented "homemaker" periodicals like *Good Housekeeping*, *McCall's*, and *Reader's Digest*—took the opposite view. These journals, recounting parents' heroic rescues and deprogrammings of their cult-victimized children, foreshadowed the cult menace frames that all magazine genres would use after the mass suicide at Jonestown in 1978.

The media scholars S. Elizabeth Bird and Robert Dardenne argue that the news always follows certain narrative forms, and "a consideration of the narrative qualities of news enables us to look more critically at whose values are encoded in news—whose stories are being told."[89] Much coverage of deprogramming in special-interest magazines of the mid- to late 1970s encoded the views, values, and concerns of parents and cult defectors through a narrative form that sociologists have called "atrocity tales."[90] These narratives, usually scripted by disgruntled former members of cults or their parents, simultaneously explained the defectors' former cult membership and accused the religious group of various moral atrocities and criminal activities.[91] As a narrative genre, such stories followed certain plot rules and shared recurring motifs. The religion scholar Mary Maaga notes that atrocity tales "share certain particulars that 'explain' the estrangement of former members from their families: food and sleep deprivation; chanting, frequent prayer, unrelenting harangues from the charismatic leader; threats to people's safety if they should leave the group."[92] The parents, ex-members, and sympathetic journalists who published atrocity tales in magazines like *Esquire, McCall's, Reader's Digest*, and *Good Housekeeping* fully accepted charges of brainwashing and considered cult leaders criminal deviants. Because of this, these authors—and by extension the magazines they wrote for—promoted deprogramming as liberating.

Parental anguish was the most common motif in these deprogramming articles. This was perhaps inevitable, since parents wrote several of the articles between 1976 and 1979. In April 1976, for example, the large general-interest magazine *Reader's Digest* published Charles Edwards's "Rescue from a Fanatic Cult." An accompanying illustration dramatically depicts a deprogramming abduction. Edwards and Ted Patrick sit on either side of Edwards's son, Chris. In the background, a dark, snarling cultist paws at the passenger's side door. "Unless it happens to you," Edwards began, "you can't possibly imagine the anguish of losing a son or daughter to one of the extremist religious cults."[93]

Edwards's story recounted his son's conversion to the Unification Church and subsequent alienation from his parents, their fears that he was brainwashed, and his eventual abduction and successful deprogramming by Patrick. A literal and symbolic violation and reconstitution of the domestic family sphere frames Edwards's narration. Edwards and his wife become convinced that their son Chris has been brainwashed when he refuses to come home for Thanksgiving and neglects to attend his great-aunt's funeral. Because of these incidents, the parents perceived Chris as both physically and mentally removed from the family unit. After his abduction and deprogramming, Chris returned home, but Unificationists continued to intrude into their home through constant phone calls. Fearing that "Moonies" would kidnap his son or attack his home, Edwards hired armed bodyguards. In doing so, Edwards physically and symbolically buttressed the domestic sphere, stating, "we've shown the Moonies that we won't give up our son regardless of their intimidations."[94]

The story in *Reader's Digest*, while representative of the period's atrocity tales in its focus on the Unification Church, concern with protecting the family unit, and accusations of brainwashing, was actually less sensationalistic than many. In "Rescuing David from the Moonies" in *Esquire*, for example, the novelist Warren

Adler evoked Cold War fears of foreign influence and infiltration by suggesting that his son's former religion had been part of a conspiracy by the "Korean C.I.A." [95] Implicating the Unification Church as a foreign threat much more explicitly than journalists had done with the Nation of Islam in the early 1960s, Adler wrote that "the Koreans launched a sinister conspiracy, enlisting Moon, among others, to get Congress to keep 42,000 American troops on Korean soil and to continue pouring money into the country." [96] In Adler's narrative, "Moonies" brainwashed unsuspecting young Americans like his son into "becoming unwitting allies of a tyrannical Korean regime." [97] Part of this brainwashing process, according to Adler, involved "sugar buzzing" the victims by giving them copious amounts of Kool-aid. "I've heard," he explained, "that excessive sugar has a numbing effect on the brain." [98]

Adler's story ended like that in *Reader's Digest*, with the successful deprogramming and return home of his son. Adler noted that the family's life had "simmered down" with David back, and added that his son "fully believes he was subjected to sophisticated mind control, cleverly engineered and orchestrated, a mind rape of mammoth proportions." [99] "How could any religion," Adler asked readers, "that as its first consideration tries to break the biological bond between child and parent be good? How can they pose as Christian, when they reject one of the commandments that underpins the Judeo-Christian philosophy: 'honor thy father and thy mother.'" [100]

Published in the revamped *Saturday Evening Post* in 1976, Lottie Robins's tale of her son Arthur's membership in the Unification Church and his eventual abduction and deprogramming closely resembled those of Edwards and Adler. Robins recounted her distress when Arthur renounced his Conservative Judaism background and informed his mother that "Reverend Moon and his wife are now my true heavenly parents." [101] After much heartache and physical illness, Robins persuaded Arthur to leave the "Moonie" commune and return home for an overnight visit. What Arthur did not know was that his parents had hired deprogrammers to detain him upon his arrival. "After twenty hours of discussing, persuading, loving, crying, and comparing Old and New Testaments with the *Divine Principle*, the crisis broke," Robins recalled. "We were able to convince Arthur that our love for him was genuine, while Moon's was materialistic."[102] Robins concluded the article with an anecdote signaling Arthur's successful deprogramming and return to the family fold. Realizing that she had forgotten about Hanukkah during the traumatic period, she apologized to Arthur, as she had neglected to buy him a present. "He put his arms around Jack and me," she recalled, "'no you haven't,' he said. 'I've already got it—my freedom.'"[103]

Not all published atrocity tales were identical. In a 1976 *Seventeen* article titled "Why I Quit the Moon Cult," it wasn't a parent but a daughter who recounted her seventeen months in the Unification Church for *Seventeen*, a magazine with a readership consisting largely of female teens young adults. The narrative does contain some of the classic "cult" motifs seen in the other stories. For example, the unnamed author raised brainwashing charges, saying that the group had programmed her, among other things by allowing her little sleep and "love-bombing" her with praise, hugs, and good treatment.[104] At the same time, her narrative, written by and for young adults, departed in significant ways from the parent-narrated atrocity tales. Most notably, neither parents nor deprogrammers had any agency in getting the girl to leave. In an anomalous twist that contradicts the traditional cult brainwashing motif, it was the director of her Unification Church center, concerned about her increasingly erratic behavior, who arranged to have the girl picked up by telephoning her mother. Despite this glitch in the standard atrocity tale narrative, the author still blamed the "Moonies" for her problems. Noting that doctors had diagnosed her as psychotic, she asserted that "under the emotional stress and physical pressures of the cult, my mind 'just went.'"[105]

During her stay in what she described as a "mental hospital," the author of the article was "deprogrammed from the cult's beliefs."[106] Her post-membership description of Unification beliefs closely resembled those in other atrocity narratives. All the stories, whether narrated by ex-members or their Christian or Jewish parents, stressed that not only was the group dangerous, its theology was also false and "unbiblical." Brainwashing explained how someone could be "duped" into believing such heresy. "Point by point," she recalled, "I was shown how Rev. Moon's doctrines are based on distorted interpretations of the Bible and his own pernicious philosophy."[107] She continued that "therapists explained the techniques that were used to indoctrinate me—sleep deprivation, protein-deficient food, repetitive drilling, isolation, exploitation of fear and guilt. These are the methods that have been employed to brainwash prisoners of war."[108]

The ending of "Why I Quit the Moon Cult," unlike the happy endings in stories narrated by parents, was ambiguous. The author noted that she had been released from the hospital, but that her medical bills exceeded $20,000. She was now a college freshman getting "A's," but she felt "like a plant that's been yanked out of the soil, then put back in, trying to develop roots again."[109] While the parent-narrated atrocity tales suggested a return to a "normal" family life with loving relations, the article in *Seventeen* failed to mention the author's relations with family at all. Nor did the narrative suggest that her life would soon stabilize. "I wonder," the author concluded, "how long it will be before I feel totally 'me' again."[110]

While in the 1950s apostates from Krishna Venta's WKFL accurately charged him with polygamy and in the 1980s opponents of the Children of God pointed to documented cases of child pornography, pedophilia, and holy prostitution, atrocity tales in the mid- to late 1970s largely relied on more ambiguous accusations. Like "sugar buzzing" and "love bombing," some charges appear puzzling or even humorous to contemporary interpreters. In *Good Housekeeping*'s "The Incredible Story of Ann Gordon and Reverend Sun Myung Moon," for example, the journalist Ann Crittenden reported that members of the Unification Church in New York were *starved* on a "diet of gruel and white bread for breakfast, sandwiches of imitation peanut butter for lunch and pasta casseroles for dinner—hardly nutritious food."[111] While one might agree that these food choices are not the best, few today would consider them so bad as to make one susceptible to mind control. Among other things, perhaps, these kinds of accusations tell us more about some Americans' love of meat in their diets in the 1970s than about brainwashing methods.

Indeed, starvation, sleep deprivation, and brainwashing—as Mary Maaga asserts—are "more a question of perspective than

of accuracy."[112] For parents, cult defectors, and sympathetic journalists, however, specific charges against cults like the Unification
Church were probably less important than the perception that
traditional family structures were endangered. These perceptions
seem validated by statistical data. By 1965, 25 to 35 percent of all
marriages in the United States ended in divorce.[113] This number
had been rising steadily since the turn of the century. More strikingly, between 1965 and 1977 the American divorce rate doubled.[114]
As noted in Chapter 3, the late 1960s and early 1970s also witnessed a growing generation gap between parents and their children. These factors, combined with increased mass media coverage of what *Newsweek* in one cover story called "the broken family,"
suggest that these Unification Church narratives reflected and
symbolically resolved particular stresses about the family.[115] I argue that these atrocity tales, detailing the concerns of parents missing their estranged children or their estranged children's explanations for their former religious prodigality, might be viewed as
domestic dramas: soap opera narratives with happy, Hollywood
endings. Criminal cultists spirit the child away. Parents heroically
retrieve the child and have him or her deprogrammed. Doing this,
they manage to restore the child's free will and the family's tranquility, wholeness, and stability.

In these domestic dramas, the specifics of the cult itself held
little significance. The religion's theology, though inevitably
deemed false, was irrelevant. The cult's ultimate significance
rested in its role as a villain. The religious group was the destroyer
of families, the abductor of children. While the Unification Church
played this part in magazines of the mid- to late 1970s, it could just
as easily have been Hare Krishna, the Divine Light Mission, or any
other fringe group that attracted middle-class whites. Articles entitled "How Cults Bilk All of Us" and "Those 'Guru' Cults: Religion
or Exploitation?" show that magazines like *Reader's Digest* already
presumed all cults to be alike.[116] Cults brainwashed innocent victims, exploited people for financial gain, and lied about their true
motives. After the mass suicide in Jonestown in 1978, this view of
cults moved beyond special-interest, homemaker, and domestic
magazines like *Reader's Digest*, *McCall's*, and *Good Housekeeping* to
permeate all mass-market genres.

Alternatives to Atrocity Tales

While special-interest magazines were dominated by "Moonie" atrocity tales containing what we today see as the classic cult motifs of brainwashing and exploitation, alternative depictions of the Unification Church occasionally appeared. These questioned brainwashing claims and offered less alarmist, more nuanced judgments of the group. Here I briefly focus on the three found in my search of the *Reader's Guide to Periodical Literature*. The first, written by Berkeley Rice, a senior editor of *Psychology Today*, appeared in the magazine in January 1976 and was titled "Honor Thy Father Moon."[117] Calling cults "a new opiate for the youth of the '70s" and featuring a cartoon of bell-bottomed silhouettes walking into the mouth of Sun Myung Moon, who was pictured with a wire halo above his head, the article initially appeared similar to the atrocity tales narrated by ex-members and parents. Rice quoted Moon's aggressive rhetoric: "what I wish must be your wish" and "the whole world is in my hand, and I will conquer and subjugate the world."[118] He also visited meetings of the Unification Church, noting that "Moonies rarely have to think for themselves" and that many looked glassy-eyed, presumably, the author wrote, from a lack of sleep.[119]

Unlike writers of traditional atrocity tales, however, Rice did not conclude that members were unwittingly brainwashed, nor did he recommend deprogramming. While Rice suggested that "much of what happens to Moon's converts during the weekend and week-long initiation workshops does follow the classic steps of brainwashing," he noted that "the term brainwashing implies force and captivity, conditions that do not apply to Moon's recruits."[120] "It might be fairer," Rice continued, "to use the term conversion instead of brainwashing. If conversion requires the suspension of critical faculties, at least the Moonies do so willingly."[121] In addition, Rice criticized deprogramming, asserting that it was "hard to condone the desperate attempts to recover the children by kidnaping and deprogramming, a process openly based on the techniques of brainwashing."[122] Though critics called the Unification Church a fraud, Rice concluded that "except for those who drop out, most Moonies seem genuinely happy in their service to Moon and the Church."[123]

Letters to the editor, responding to Rice's article, showed a broad range of views. *Psychology Today* in May 1976 published seventeen letters on Rice's piece.[124] Though some writers withheld their names, six letters identified their authors as disgruntled ex-members or parents. These letters, along with six others, were negative in their appraisal of the Unification Church. One writer suggested that Moonies were too involved in their cult to have free will, that they were "down deep, much deeper than Rice seems to realize."[125] Another letter expressed negativity not just toward the Unification Church but religion in general. The anonymous author compared her Mennonite upbringing and the Jesus Movement with Moon's group, finding them all troubling.[126] The other four letters all defended the Unification Church. Two were from Unification members, another may have been, and a third was from Lynda Wright of Jeffersonville, Indiana, who met a "Moonie" who was selling candy. Wright noted that she was extremely impressed by the member's "endurance and good cheer." "Not only did he dispel my doubts about Moon," she wrote, "but we discussed the Principles and ended our conversation agreeing that there must be effective dialogue and communication between all faiths."[127]

Two other articles appearing in the same year addressed the subject of young adults in cults in ways that avoided the traditional cult motifs found in atrocity tales. An article in *McCall's* in September by Mark Rasmussen, aged twenty-two, promised to explain "How Sun Myung Moon Lures America's Children," but readers did not learn that he brainwashed them. Instead, Rasmussen asserted, the Unification Church tapped into the idealistic passions of its members in a way that other movements did not.[128] While suggesting that Moon's theology seemed to be a "sham," Rasmussen asserted that the "real danger" of the movement was "not that Reverend Moon is about to take over the world or that his followers are brainwashed zombies, but that many of them have lost track of who they are or what they want to do."[129] He asserted that the Unification Church offered members "an opportunity to be absorbed in a strong family unit and the chance to believe unswervingly and unblushingly in God."[130] Turning his article into a jeremiad, the author blamed the lack of these things in contemporary American society for Moon's popularity, suggesting that "the gap between the legitimate needs of the young people who follow Reverend Moon and the fulfillment of those needs tells us a lot about what is lacking in the shape of the lives of the citizens of our society."[131]

The third piece published in 1976, in *Parent's Magazine*, asked, "Could Your Child be Brainwashed?" but it refused to give a simple "yes" answer. While not focused on the Unification Church, it provides for an interesting comparison with the pieces by Rice and Rasmussen. It consisted of two parts, one written by an psychiatrist who specialized in adolescence and another by an academic whose daughter joined a new religion called the Divine Light Mission. The psychiatrist, Everett P. Dulit, informed readers that "brainwashing is hardly ever what happens to young people."[132] The religious groups that youth were joining, he asserted, varied greatly, with some good, some not. To prevent children from becoming interested in extreme movements, Dulit suggested that among other things children be taught to develop self-respect and "an awareness that life is complicated and to be wary of glib and simple answers to their problems, fears, and desires."[133] The second part of the article differed from most parent-narrated atrocity tales. Winfield Best did not assert that his daughter had been brainwashed, nor did he want her abducted from the group and deprogrammed. Instead he related his and his wife's slow acceptance of their daughter's choice and mused over why young adult children might join movements like the Divine Light Mission. Recalling Rasmussen's jeremiad, he suggested that "the non-material advantages we seek to give our children—to help guarantee them their share of the American dream—probably have a greater bearing on the guru phenomenon than anything financial."[134] He also speculated that "compulsive, competitive overparenting" that forces children into art classes, sports teams, and an array of stressful tasks may make children "feel they cannot live up to their parents' expectations, and feeling guilty about that, they become resentful and eager to avoid the 'trials' that lie ahead."[135] "Surely," he posited, "escape from this guilt and pressure (as they see it) is one thing that converts to guru groups are seeking—aside from whatever positive and noble things they may be after."[136]

Articles of this sort, which blamed parents and American society rather than cultic brainwashing for religious conversions, were rare. And like the anti-deprogramming articles found in newsmagazines and religious periodicals, they would soon disappear. After the mass suicide a Jonestown, all magazine genres offered a similar narrative of the American religious fringe. This narrative closely resembled the Unification Church atrocity tales, but was generalized to the American religious fringe as a whole.

Jonestown and the Cult Menace

On 18 November 1978, 913 residents of Jonestown, a farm commune maintained by the Peoples Temple in the jungles of Guyana, committed mass suicide. Jonestown was the "cult story" that seemed to confirm all the parents' and journalists' worst stereotypes. Jim Jones, the founder and head minister of the Peoples Temple, preached what he called "divine socialism" and openly attacked Christianity and American capitalism as racist and classist. He also performed fake miracle healings, slept with several female members, and occasionally had sinful parishioners severely beaten. At Jonestown, dissidents to the cause of divine socialism were confined and drugged.[137] On that night in 1978, most members killed themselves by drinking poisoned Kool-aid, but they killed their children first—injecting cyanide into those too young to drink from a cup.

The sociologist Eileen Barker accurately notes that after Jonestown, journalists more frequently lumped under the cult rubric new religions that they had previously treated individually.[138] The Peoples Temple mass suicide led to what I call a "cult menace hegemony" in all mass-market print genres. From 1976 to 1978 the most vivid cult atrocity tales appeared in special- and general-interest magazines. By 1979 newsmagazines and religious periodicals similarly described cults with motifs of brainwashing, criminality, and violence. Jonestown sharply limited what Bourdieu calls the "universe of discourse" surrounding the American religious fringe.

Bourdieu writes that "The universe of discourse . . . is practically defined in relation to the necessarily unnoticed complementary class that is constituted by the universe of that which is undiscussed, unnamed, admitted without argument or scrutiny." [139] After Jonestown, it was nearly impossible for a journalist to depict the American religious fringe as anything but dangerously volatile.

The history of the Peoples Temple has been well documented in several useful works, and I will only briefly outline it here. [140] The church was founded by James Warren Jones in Indiana in 1956. In 1960 the group formally joined the Disciples of Christ. The early Peoples Temple stressed interracial worship and civil rights. As the head minister, Jones also practiced faith healing. In 1965 Jones moved the church to California, partly because he feared nuclear war and had read that the state's Redlands area was one place that might be spared from nuclear fallout. By the mid-1970s, church membership was at an all-time high of five to seven thousand, with over 60 percent of the congregation African American. In 1975 Jones was lauded by the mayor of San Francisco for his humanitarian work, and in 1977 he received the Martin Luther King Jr. Humanitarian Award. With the exception of a few apostates, few even noticed the Peoples Temple, let alone saw it as a cultic threat.

During the mid-1970s Jones developed the idea of a farming commune in the South American jungles of Guyana. Believing that American society was too racist and classist, Jones sent the first church members to Guyana in 1975 to create Jonestown. Jones moved there in 1977. In 1978, pushed by the concern of church members' relatives, Representative Leo Ryan of California decided to visit the commune. On his way back to the jungle airport, Ryan and some of his entourage were shot to death by Peoples Temple assassins. Convinced that the U.S. military would respond by invading Jonestown, Jones and a small group of his assistants decided that the whole community should commit suicide. The mass suicide was not carried out on the spur of the moment. Jones for years had preached "revolutionary suicide," killing oneself to protest the world's injustice. Starting in September 1978, members regularly conducted mass suicide drills known as "white nights." The difference about the ritual on 18 November 1978 was that it wasn't a drill.

On 4 December 1978, *Time, Newsweek,* and *U.S. News and World Report* published nearly identical stories on the mass suicide. Both *Time* and *Newsweek* titled their covers "Cult of Death" and featured only slightly different photos of Jonestown's dead. All three suggested that Jim Jones used brainwashing to coerce his followers into committing suicide. Though a recent study by the religion scholar Mary Maaga suggests that Jones's female officers had more control over the commune and its demise than Jones had himself, the newsmagazines offered the traditional sociological and anti-cult view that charismatic cult leaders wield mind-numbing control over their passive followers.[141] Though its estimate of the number of dead was low, one sentence in *U.S. News* aptly summed up all three periodicals' conclusions, asserting that, "in the end, only a cult's bizarre regimen of fear, violence, and unthinking devotion could explain the chain reaction that claimed the lives of at least 784 Americans shortly before sunset on November 18."[142]

Coverage of Jonestown in the largest newsweeklies was both monolithic and striking in its indictment of cults. Editors titled a story in *U.S. News* "Behind the Cult Craze." The article featured an illustration of a hooded skeletal figure standing over a box of bodies labeled "Jonestown Guyana." The figure wore a large amulet imprinted with the word "cultism." The caption read "latest offering."[143] *Time* and *Newsweek* relied on cult apostates and anti-cult movement professionals like the former army psychiatrist Margaret Singer to suggest that most cults "share a number of unusual characteristics" and "use the same methods of indoctrinating converts."[144] *Time,* for example, interviewed Singer and others in "Why People Join." The magazine suggested that once recruits start attending cult meetings, "they are frequently subjected to various drills and disciplines that weary them both physically and emotionally, producing a sort of trance."[145] When this occurs, "personalities change from lively and complex patterns of normality to those of an automaton reciting what he has been taught."[146]

A lengthy article in *Newsweek,* "How They Bend Minds," offered similar conclusions. Cults brainwashed people, according to the writers, through a manipulative, charismatic leader, isolation from family, and "various forms of sense deprivation, inculcated through loss of sleep, low-protein diets and exhausting rounds of

The famous cover of Time, *4 December 1978, depicting the mass suicide of the Peoples Temple. The cover of* Newsweek *for the same date was also titled "Cult of Death" and featured a photo of Jonestown's dead. (© Time, Inc./Timepix)*

chanting, praying and indoctrination in the thought of the new father figure."[147] Photographs accompanying the article associated cults with familiar villains. Pictures included Nazi storm troopers, Japanese Kamikaze pilots, and, as the caption read, "Charles Manson and his ghoulish groupies: mesmerized to murder."[148]

Related articles in religious periodicals closely resembled those in the largest newsmagazines. "Four Steps to Cultic Conversion," appearing in *Christianity Today* in June 1979, was almost indistinguishable from *Time* and *Newsweek* in suggesting why people join cults. The author, Richard Stellway, repeated a list of brainwashing techniques that included sleep deprivation, low-protein diets, and familial isolation. Stellway concluded that it was the duty of the "church" to expose all dangerous cults. "Such action," he asserted, "exposes the danger posed by the cults to potential converts and the rest of society, and glorifies Christ by contrasting unethical cultic procedures with Christian values."[149]

Responding to the Jonestown mass suicides in an editorial on 9 December 1978, the Catholic periodical *America* suggested that "the enormity of evil at Jonestown and the profusion of other equally exotic, if less murderous cults throughout the United States does represent, in part, the failure of the churches and the synagogues to pass on the fire of genuine religious faith to others, particularly, and painfully, their own young people."[150] But, the unnamed editor wrote, "surely the answer to that failure is not to be found in the righteous but naive charge that if religious men spoke with the conviction of a Sun Myung Moon or a Jim Jones, the churches and synagogues would be crowded. Religious faith is an act of freedom. The hypnotic control of the messianic leaders around whom such cults center is a denial of freedom, as are the techniques of environmental control and peer pressure that are part of the process of indoctrination."[151]

In suggesting that Jim Jones and Sun Myung Moon used hypnotic control to snare converts, *America* clearly reversed its previous positions of denying the validity of brainwashing theories and primarily faulting mainline churches for cult membership. Finding it hard to believe that over nine hundred people "in their right minds" would ever willingly commit mass suicide, both *America* and *Christianity Today* followed news and general-interest magazines in promoting the brainwashing thesis and generalizing criminality to all cults. In a December 1978 editorial in the *National Review*, "Cult Taxonomy," the conservative publisher William F. Buckley voiced a position held by most news, general-interest, and religious journalists after Jonestown: "If it looks like a cult, walks like cult, and quacks like a cult, then the chances are it's a cult."[152]

In 1978, several months before the suicides at Jonestown, the International Society of Krishna Consciousnness (ISKCON) published "An Appeal to Reason: Please Don't Lump Us In." The movement, popularly known as the Hare Krishnas, sent the small booklet to various newspapers, magazines, and television stations.[153] A Hindu devotional movement with sixteenth-century roots, ISKCON was brought to the United States by A. C. Bhaktivedanta Swami Prabhupada in 1965.[154] By the mid-1970s, local news media and anticult organizations frequently labeled the group a dangerous cult. "An Appeal to Reason" was ISKCON's response to this negative attention.

The pamphlet set forth to "explain and document some of the significant differences between us and the new groups commonly called 'cults.'"[155] For example, the author suggested that ISKCON featured a decentralized, democratic structure. Cults, on the other hand, were led by authoritarian, often immoral, leaders.[156] The author also suggested that Hare Krishna devotees followed strict moral and ethical codes, while cults "permit and even encourage immoral and illegal practices among their members."[157] In addition, while converts made reasoned decisions to join ISKCON, "one of the most common and well-substantiated criticisms of cults is that their recruitment procedures often involve deception and various other forms of psychological coercion."[158] The Hare Krishnas' message was clear: cults truly are bad—and fortunately we're not one.

By the late 1970s, the American religious fringe had become synonymous with the cult menace. The zealous exotics in Cold War mass movements had been transformed into dangerous, brainwashing criminals. The negative associations carried by the term "cult" had become assumed and thus unquestioned, so much so that a group labeled a cult by some outsiders sought to exempt itself from the category but dared not question the category itself. The pamphlet's strategic placement of Hare Krishna outside the cult classification calls to mind the sociologist Paul DiMaggio's description of Bourdieuian agency: "constrained by habitus and objective reality, individuals are consigned to dart in and out between the cracks of social structure, never questioning the rules, seeking only to manipulate them."[159] For the Hare Krishnas, as for the Catholic and Evangelical writers in the 1950s, the problem was not the religious fringe category itself, but more their own position inside it.

chapter five

ESSENTIALIZING
THE MARGINS
THE AMERICAN
RELIGIOUS FRINGE
INTO THE NINETIES

In the wake of Jonestown, journalists and anti-cultists predicted more cult violence. Like *McCall's* and several other magazines, *Seventeen* warned of a "time bomb—like the one that exploded at Jonestown—that may be ticking away in the Unification Church."[1] Ted Patrick, the first "professional" anti-cult deprogrammer, had long referred to Hare Krishna as "another Charles Manson movement—only many of thousands of members strong," and had predicted cultic murder and mayhem.[2] But all news stories run their course and fade away. As the 1980s progressed, there were no other Jonestowns, no new Manson family. Controversial religious groups like the Unification Church and Hare Krishnas lost members, moved away from strictly communal living, and subsequently lost the media's interest.[3] In the 1980s journalists referred to white, middle- to upper-middle-class baby boomers as "yuppies" (short for "young, urban professionals"). In yuppie depictions—which were constructions as much as stories about the religious fringe were—those demographically most likely to look to cult leaders for guidance in the 1970s now consulted self-help literature, the stock market, and a conservative Hollywood actor turned president. Rather than proselytizing Unification doctrine or chanting Hare Krishna, they sang the praises of economic trickle-down theory. Rather than communes, they lived in gated communities. The cult menace, it seemed, was no longer so menacing.

This view can be seen in one article in *U.S. News and World Report* in 1988 titled "On the Trail of High Weirdness." The story, about *High Weirdness by Mail*, a book on religious fringe groups by an author and radio announcer from Dallas, Ivan Stang, used the trope that prevailed in the 1950s and 1960s—of the fringe as consisting of harmless exotics—to suggest that "cults are on the rise, but they're more odd than menacing."[4] According to Stang, the magazine reported, "there's more to ridicule than to fear in the country's assorted fringe groups, crackpot publications, and cult religions."[5] Detailing some of the movements included in Stang's book, *U.S. News* replicated Cold War regionalization of the fringe by noting that a group called the "Breatharians," like the publishers of the *Flat Earth News*, were "also—surprise!—from California."[6] Rather than conjure a looming cult menace, and much like depictions of the fringe during the Cold War, "On the Trail of High Weirdness" suggested that the religious margins were mostly harmless and offbeat. But more menacing depictions of cults and the religious fringe did not vanish from mass-market magazines, nor did persistent journalistic differentiations of mainstream and fringe religion.

Rather than embark on a full examination of print media depictions in the two decades after Jonestown, in this chapter I briefly discuss coverage of four stories from the late 1980s and early 1990s: the accusations of child molestation leveled against Catholic priests in the early 1990s, the PTL Club televangelism scandal of 1987, the Satanic ritual abuse scare of the early 1990s, and the standoff between the Branch Davidians and the Bureau of Alcohol, Tobacco and Firearms (ATF) in 1993. Coverage of these subjects revealed differences and continuities with coverage of the past. In terms of difference, the 1980s and 1990s witnessed what one might call a partial "marginalization" of groups traditionally depicted as mainstream. By the early 1990s writers and editors in the largest newsmagazines regularly reported mainstream religions' involvements in criminal "fringe" activities (as in the stories of child molestation by Catholic priests). Journalists' changing conceptions of the religion beat partly inspired this.

But many continuities with earlier coverage remained. Newsmagazine reports on the televangelist Jim Bakker's sexual tryst with one of his organization's secretaries, and his subsequent payment of hush money to her, closely resembled classist reporting in the 1950s on conservative Third Force Protestants. Similarly, the limited coverage of Satanic ritual abuse and the plethora of reports on the Branch Davidian standoff revealed the continuing "naturalization" of the cult menace. Spurred by the Jonestown tragedy, the term "cult" became dissociated from certain religious groups, like Hare Krishnas and the Unification Church, and linked instead to a broad yet fixed range of negative associations. In other words, cult, and by extension the American religious fringe in general, became tied not to specific groups, but to dangerous, controversial, and criminal activities like brainwashing, child abuse, and murder. Especially in accounts of Satanic ritual abuse and somewhat recalling coverage of the Nation of Islam during the Cold War, writers and editors essentialized the religious periphery as an evil other. Thus when a conflagration in Waco propelled the Branch Davidians into a media spotlight, news and religious magazine journalists used essentialized cult menace motifs to narrate an ongoing story, one based on little undisputed information.

Marginalizing the Mainstream?: Professionalizing the "Religion Beat" and Reporting Clerical Scandals

In the 1950s, magazines like *Time, Life, Look,* and *Newsweek* sometimes served as pulpits for ecumenical church leaders like Henry van Dusen. Religion pages also sometimes resembled "church pages," reporting about mainline denominations' annual meetings and the activities of "celebrity" clergy. In some ways, especially in newspapers, this kind of reporting continued through the 1970s. According to the media scholar Stewart Hoover, journalists' approach "to religion in the period before 1980 was also one that included a good bit of deference to religious leaders and institutions."[7] At the same time, he notes, writers and editors held a "received view" that "religion was not a serious object of press scrutiny; that it deserved limited and compartmentalized treatment; that the journalists who would cover it were less professional because it demanded less professional treatment; that its readers were largely older, less educated, and less important; and that general readership was low."[8] By the 1990s, journalists—especially those working for newsmagazines—approached religion differently.

As noted in Chapter 4, newsmagazines in the 1970s increased their dedication to exposés, shock journalism, and human-interest stories, spurred by corporate conglomeration and for-profit publishing, not to mention the success of investigative reporting in uncovering the Watergate scandal in the Nixon White House. Incidents like Jonestown, the court battles between deprogrammers and new religions, and the political involvement of conservative Christians in the "religious right" in the early 1980s not only took up religion sections but made for cover stories. One result of this —what van Driel and Richardson call the "stream of controversies approach" to reporting—was the less frequent appearance of groups journalists had previously labeled mainstream.[9] After polling a small group of journalists in the 1980s, the media scholar Benjamin Hubbard reported that most agreed with the statement: "mainline Protestant denominations were under reported because their activities lacked pizzazz."[10] Hubbard's sample was small and unscientific, consisting of only eleven religion writers for newspapers and one reporter for NBC. However, looking at the stories they produced, one might guess that the response he received was common among newsmagazine journalists. In search of controversy, revealing exposés, and scandals, reporters turned away from traditional denominational interest stories—a trend that actually began before the 1980s. My examination of the *Reader's Guide to Periodical Literature* reveals that coverage of specific denominations dropped during the 1970s. For example, thirteen stories appeared on Methodists in the 1961 guide, ten in 1970, and just one by 1976. The trend for Catholics, Baptists, and Lutherans and for Judaism follows a similar pattern. Instead, newsmagazine reporters increasingly covered "mainstream" religion only when controversy erupted. By the 1980s and 1990s, periodicals like *Time* and *Newsweek* more often resembled ABC-TV in their religion reporting, described by one scholar as a "'good grief' style that portrayed religion as just an irrational and out-of-control force."[11]

Apart from their changing conceptions of the religion beat, polls show that journalists' own views about religion likely differentiated them from their precursors in the 1950s. In contrast to the Protestant viewpoint of Henry Luce and the obvious faith commitments of the ministers and priests whom newsmagazines used as commentators, latter journalists were less likely to be religious. In a study by Robert Lichter and several colleagues of newsmagazine and television journalists in the 1980s, *The Media Elite*, 50 percent of all journalists stated they had no religion.[12] Interestingly, the religion and media scholar Mark Silk notes that according to several other surveys, smaller periodicals and regional and local newspapers appeared to have more self-professed religious journalists on staff than Lichter's sample from the "media elite."[13] And of course there were notable exceptions even in the largest newsmagazines. Richard Ostling of *Time*, for example, was a believer who had previously written for the evangelical magazine *Christianity Today*, and Kenneth Woodward of *Newsweek* was Roman Catholic. But the multi-author process of news production, coupled with the increasing professionalization of the religion beat, virtually guaranteed that most stories approached religion more suspiciously than before.

What journalists had traditionally viewed as the religious mainstream could no longer avoid the scrutiny of newsmagazines. Consider the (admittedly limited) coverage of American Catholic priests who were charged with, and conceded, having had sexual encounters with teens. A full decade before the explosion in 2002 of media coverage on the growing number of reported priest sex abuse cases, a smaller number of stories broached the same issue.[14] As noted in Chapter 1, the "mainstream" of newsmagazines of the late 1950s and 1960s expanded beyond the so-called Protestant Establishment to eventually include select others. Catholics, then and now the largest single Christian denomination in the United States, were part of this American religious center.[15] But by the early 1990s, that no longer meant that they were immune to investigative reporting.

Mark Silk notes that journalists covered stories of malfeasance by priests judiciously.[16] "Priest abuse was, in short," he writes, "not a simple and satisfying morality tale, but a complex and deeply troubling set of narratives about sex offenders and institutional failure."[17] The cover story in *Newsweek* on 16 August 1993, "Sex and the Church," provides an example of this judicious coverage. Appearing in conjunction with a papal visit to the United States, the story and related articles in the same issue described a widening gap between U.S. Catholics and the Vatican over issues like birth control, women's ordination, and clerical celibacy. One feature dealt specifically with child molestation cases against priests. Titling the piece "Priests and Abuse," *Newsweek* approached the subject carefully. The magazine did criticize the Roman Catholic leadership, arguing that "the church failed its children" by reacting slowly and inadequately in removing known molesters from clerical positions.[18] On the other hand, *Newsweek* tempered its criticism, suggesting that "now the church has begun to respond" and reporting that the National Conference of Bishops had recently issued a "detailed call for action."[19] Given that the scandals that rocked American Catholicism in 2002 stemmed from conduct that had been covered up for many years, it is interesting in retrospect to note how trusting the magazine seemed of the church hierarchy. *Newsweek* also made clear that it did not support the view that celibacy caused child molestation. It noted that members of the mainline Protestant clergy had been involved in similar recent scandals, quoting one Episcopal priest who lamented that "pedophilia is ecumenical."[20] If there was any question about the magazine's stance, a guest editorial by Andrew Greeley, "A View from the Priesthood: It's Bigotry to Blame Celibacy for Church Problems," cleared all doubts.[21]

In many ways, the coverage of the priest molestation scandals in *Newsweek* suggested that little had changed. First, the magazine upheld mainstream and fringe classifications by asserting no inherent connections between child molestation and Catholicism. Conversely, reports in the same year on the Branch Davidian standoff suggested a natural link between religious cults and child abuse. In arguing that Catholic celibacy had nothing to do with child molestation, *Newsweek* implicitly separated one "mainstream" religion from the criminal activities that it had linked to the religious fringe. Second, the priest abuse story even harkened back to coverage of the 1950s with its use of the well-known priest Andrew Greeley as commentator. On the surface, the cover story in *Newsweek* didn't marginalize the mainstream at all. If anything it seemed to further dissociate it from the fringe by giving the American Catholic Church the benefit of the doubt that it would solve what were isolated problems.

But that news and general-interest magazines reported the priest molestation stories at all did signal a change in journalists' attitudes. Philip Jenkins, who studied media coverage of priest malfeasance, argues that from the 1950s through the 1970s, the "mass media had exercised considerable restraint in investigating or reporting news stories involving scandals in the mainstream churches."[22] Jenkins noted that the news media frequently censored themselves, leaving unreported things like the sex scandals of boy scout leaders, clerics, and government officials. In some cases, Jenkins relates, a local Catholic diocese actually requested that the news media not report a priest's malfeasance.[23] The public uncovering of priest scandals, Jenkins argues, came at a time when "media values were in rapid transition," and more organizations were turning to "sensationalist coverage."[24] So while newsmagazine articles on priests' malfeasance were judicious, that they were published at all reflected, in Jenkins's words, "a swift and dramatic reversal of attitude."[25] The Catholic priest molestation cases of the early 1990s brought the nation's largest religious body—one that newsmagazines had considered mainstream since the early 1960s—under the same scrutiny previously reserved for "fringe cults" and sectarian Protestants. While the coverage may not have equated the two, it certainly suggested that "mainstream" groups and figures could be involved in "fringe" activities.

"More K-Mart Than Cartier": "Lowbrow" Religion and the Televangelism Scandal

On 6 April 1987, *Newsweek* titled its cover "Holy Wars: Money, Sex, and Power." The article reported that Jim Bakker, charismatic televangelist and founder of an Evangelical group, the Praise the Lord (PTL) Club, had sexual intercourse with his church secretary, Jessica Hahn, and then had his organization pay her over $250,000 in hush money. Bakker, along with his wife Tammy Faye, had built the PTL Club into a vastly successful institution that included the television show, books, videos, and a theme park outside Charlotte, North Carolina, called Heritage, U.S.A. Reporting on the scandal, *Newsweek* proclaimed that "there was glee among the unbelievers."[26] Examining the magazine's cover stories and book on the scandal, one wonders if the quote was unwittingly self-referential.[27]

Mark Silk argues that the news media gave the televangelism scandal maximum coverage because of its irresistible "topos of religious hypocrisy."[28] Indeed, both *Time* and *Newsweek* published stories that quoted Bible verses to condemn Jim Bakker's sexual tryst and opulent lifestyle. On 6 April 1987, for example, the cover story in *Time*, "TV's Unholy Row: A Sex-and-Money Scandal Tarnishes Electronic Evangelism," began with a verse from Ephesians 4:1–3: "Live a life worthy of the calling to which you have been called, with all the lowliness and meekness, with patience, forbearing one another in love, eager to maintain the unity of the Spirit in the bond of peace."[29]

Perhaps more interesting, *Time* and *Newsweek* went beyond condemning Jim and Tammy Bakker to include the whole of television evangelism. Once again, journalists acted as heresiographers by distinguishing acceptable from unacceptable religious styles, activities, and institutions. On 4 May 1987, for example, *Newsweek* published "What Profits a Preacher? Revealing the Lifestyles of the Rich and Pious." Like *Time*, *Newsweek* began by citing a Bible verse. The passage, from Genesis, described the Tower of Babel, which the newsmagazine likened to televangelism as a whole. "Like the Tower of Babel," Kenneth Woodward and Mark Miller wrote, "the electronic church was erected on the American landscape more than a decade ago through an unholy alliance of religion, television, and mass marketing."[30] The reporters noted the claim by some televangelists that the electronic church in itself was not bad, but Woodward and Miller concluded that "the evidence was not entirely convincing."[31]

In other articles, *Time* and *Newsweek* described televangelism as they might have described cults and their leaders a decade earlier. In one article, for example, *Time* described the Pentecostal evangelist Jimmy Swaggart—an early outspoken critic of the Bakkers who himself later confessed to having sex with prostitutes—as a "Louisiana spellbinder."[32] As noted in Chapter 3, early seventies anti-cultists and journalists alike used terms like "hypnotic spell-binding" to describe how cult leaders mesmerized their hapless victims. *Newsweek* even anticipated news media descriptions of the Branch Davidian communal building when it described Swaggart's million-dollar estate as a "compound."[33]

But journalists' most consistent critique of televangelism concerned money. *Newsweek* suggested that televangelists lavished "wretched excesses" on themselves that made them "by Gospel standards—ungodly comfortable."[34] In addition to using biblical passages to condemn their wealth, articles repeatedly published lists of the televangelists' possessions. Both *Time* and *Newsweek*, written mostly by journalists based in the Northeast, seemed particularly preoccupied with the mostly southern televangelists' use of air conditioning. Both magazines mentioned the Bakkers' air-conditioned dog house more than once, and *Newsweek* also noted that Jimmy Swaggart's grandson played in an air-conditioned tree house.

Focusing on the combination of wealth and religion, journalists questioned televangelism's religious authenticity. Like the Nation of Islam, whose mixture of politics and religion led journalists to question its status as a "true" religion, televangelists appeared to merge material riches and religion, two things that journalists deemed incompatible. Though slightly less explicit, the views of periodical reporters accorded with those of the ABC news commentator George Will, who suggested that televangelists lacked the dignity associated with "true religion."[35] Much as they had done with the Nation of Islam, Transcendental Meditation, and other beliefs, writers and editors, in judging televangelism a "false religion," had implicitly removed "religion" from any material, historical base by positing it as a transcendent, text-based collection of universalized morals.

The *Christian Century*, a liberal Protestant periodical that might be expected to be among the least likely to defend televangelism, responded to negative newsmagazine coverage with an editorial titled "Preacher-Bashing and the Public Life." *Christian Century* agreed with *Time* and *Newsweek* that "certainly there is much to be deplored in the situation: exploitative methods of raising enough money to stay on the air; extravagant lifestyles; the us-against-them mode of proclamation; and what seems to many to be a serious distortion of the Christian message."[36] On the other hand, the *Century* charged, the tone of the news media attack on televangelism "smacks of nothing less than a gleeful attack on 'holy rollers.'"[37] I suggest here that this criticism was correct. In critiquing televangelism, journalists negatively judged certain types of religion. But they did more. In a manner that resembled coverage of the religious fringe in the 1950s, newsmagazines also negatively assessed the people whom they associated with televangelism.

In the postwar era, newsweeklies linked working-class Pentecostals, Fundamentalists, and sectarian groups to "lowbrow" religion and culture. In *Life*, for example, Paul Hutchinson, editor of the *Christian Century*, through the process of articulation, attributed overt emotionalism, snake-handling, country music, and other so-called lowbrow diversions to the Third Force.[38] Over thirty years later, newsmagazine journalists' depictions of televangelists' audience were nearly indistinguishable. *Newsweek*, for example, referred to televangelism viewers as a "species," one that was "rural, relatively low income, often somewhat alienated from mainline America."[39] These demographic assertions are partially supported by a polling study conducted in 1990 by the religion scholar Bobby Alexander. He found that 34 percent of televangelism viewers had incomes below $30,000 and 23 percent more below $16,000. At the time, $13,000 was the government's poverty line for a family of four.[40] The assertion in *Newsweek* about alienation from "mainline society" also has some support. Numerous studies have indicated that Evangelical, Pentecostal, and other conservative Christians—those whom Alexander identifies as televangelism's primary audience—tend to think of themselves as outsiders in what they view as a secular mainstream society. The sociologist Christian Smith, for example, suggests that American Evangelicalism might best be viewed as a self-identified subculture.[41] On the other hand, Smith suggests that polls and studies of Evangelicals have frequently exaggerated their underclass socioeconomic status. He also asserts that studies have too often relied on the biographies of Evangelical leaders to generalize about the whole subculture.[42]

But while there was some demographic and sociological support for the initial assertions in *Newsweek* about televangelism viewers, the magazine's explanations of why some Americans watched televangelists' programs relied more on class stereotypes than statistics. For example, *Newsweek* quoted a newspaper editor who condescendingly suggested that "little people are impressed by wealth."[43] In another article, the periodical repeated this assertion, noting about the Bakkers that "Jim and Tammy live the way most of their followers would like to."[44] But rather than a "respectable" middle- to upper-middle-class show of wealth, *Newsweek* implied that the Bakkers' style was inherently lowbrow, that "despite all the flash and cash, their lifestyle is more K-Mart than Cartier."[45] To support this claim, it offered photographs of a ceramic dog and a Tammy Bakker doll, possibly assuming that readers would find these items tacky and unsophisticated. *Newsweek* explicitly tied the Bakkers' tastes to those of their viewers by suggesting that "outlet stores throughout 'Middle America'" were filled with "the kind of people who belong to Jim and Tammy's flock."[46]

Newsweek also condemned the emotional, enthusiastic style of televangelists. In every article, it correctly noted that most supporters of the Bakkers were "charismatics, emotional Christians who believe in faith healing and speaking in tongues."[47] But the magazine then proceeded to postulate that charismatic religion may have been to blame for Jim Bakker's tryst. "'Pentecostal religions in particular have strong emotional content, and they provide for emotional release,'" the magazine quoted the historian David Harrell, who added "'I don't think evangelists mean to be sex symbols, but they are frequently handsome and highly masculine in behavior.'"[48] *Newsweek* presented Harrell's judgment about the attractiveness of televangelists without comment.

Overall, in its coverage of the PTL Club scandal, *Newsweek* utilized a classificatory strategy that connected class and consumer taste with certain religions. In asserting that the Bakkers—and by association their viewers—were more "K-Mart than Cartier," it implicitly classified televangelism's culture and religion as "white trash," what Gael Sweeney defines as that "denigrated aesthetic of a people marginalized socially, racially, and culturally."[49] This classification, in some ways synonymous with the delineation in the 1950s of high culture and "lowbrow culture," served two purposes. First, it rhetorically separated televangelism's populace from the more "discerning" readership of *Newsweek*. The story frame clearly was about "them," literally a "species" apart from those who read the magazine. Second, dual attention to televangelism's viewer demographics and aesthetics welded together "white trash culture" with "white trash people," with the implication, in Sweeney's words, that "better people have better taste, they are 'naturally' tasteful and discerning, while Trash just as 'naturally' seeks trash."[50] In other words, *Newsweek* implied that rural, working-class people supported televangelists because they were "naturally" predisposed to do so. Criticizing televangelism, the writers and editors at *Newsweek* exercised the media's symbolic power to legitimize cultural, religious, and class differences as natural.

Because televangelists, unlike Catholic priests, inhabited the religious periphery, marginalizing the culture of televangelism didn't entail—at least for newsmagazine journalists—marginalizing the religious mainstream. News and general-interest magazines had labeled Pentecostal and conservative Protestants "fringe" for decades, and televangelism coverage supported a long-standing, class-based differentiation between fringe and mainstream. At the same time, however, the scandal coverage appeared at a time when the numerical minorities and majorities of American religion were shifting dramatically. Statistics reveal that conservative Protestantism, and especially Pentecostalism, grew exponentially from 1965 to 1989. At the same time "mainline" denominations like Lutherans, Methodists, Congregationalists, Episcopalians, and Presbyterians lost between 8 and 32 percent of their membership.[51] By the 1990s, Pentecostals, Southern Baptists, and conservative charismatics combined may have made up approximately 32 percent of the religious population of the United States. Though journalists dismissed them as culturally peripheral, televangelism viewers, Pentecostals, and Evangelical Protestants made up a significant portion of the American population. In the largest news and general-interest magazines, however, numbers seldom determined who was mainstream and who was fringe.

Televangelism features also served to marginalize groups that journalists had traditionally labeled mainstream. The plethora of coverage—part of a larger editorial policy that foregrounded stories of conflict and wrongdoing—pushed stories of the "religious mainstream" out of the periodicals. The result was what the social theorist Anthony Giddens calls an "unintended consequence of action." Giddens writes that people "have reasons for what they do, and what they do has certain specifiable consequences which they do not intend."[52] Journalists' desires to "professionalize" the religion pages by making stories fit the editorial standards of "hard" news resulted in the increasing exclusion of mainline denominations, which writers saw as lacking "pizzazz." More and more, only scandal could guarantee column inches. Religious groups that avoided, or were better at hiding, dramatic conflict and controversy seemed less "newsworthy."

On 6 April 1987 *Newsweek* published an article related to the televangelism scandals titled "It Isn't the First Time." "A steamy brew of religion and sex," it suggested, "is virtually an American tradition."[53] The authors cited the Pentecostal minister Aimee Semple McPherson and the Fundamentalist Billy James Hargis as examples of clergy caught in improper sexual situations. But in addition to these "fringe" representatives, *Newsweek* also recalled figures and events from what many traditional church historians would have considered "mainstream" American religious history. The authors referred to the Second Great Awakening as a period marked by "so-called camp meetings" where "religious fervor would turn into carnal delight."[54] They also noted that one of America's most famous nineteenth-century preachers, the Congregationalist minister Henry Ward Beecher, stood trial for an affair with a married parishioner. Both these assertions had support. Beecher did have an affair, and there apparently were trysts at camp meetings. But the important point is that the manner of reporting had changed since the Cold War decades: historical icons of American religion were no longer immune from scrutiny and criticism.

Essentializing the Fringe: From Cultic Groups to Cultic Activities

At the same time that journalists partially marginalized the mainstream, they fully essentialized the fringe. In the 1980s and early 1990s, many magazine articles dissociated the fringe from groups and instead identified it with activities. Indeed, this focus on actions over specific movements can be seen in religion coverage of the 1950s and 1960s, which implied that overly emotional and dogmatic religion, regardless of the denomination, was part of the fringe. But the point was much more explicit in the latter period. The word "cult," then the most common term for what were labeled fringe groups, was no longer restricted to groups like the Unification Church and Children of God. Instead, it conjured images of brainwashing, financial exploitation, child abuse, and sexual impropriety that might be attributed to any group. In the article "Cultic America: A Tower of Babel" in 1993, the religion correspondent for *Newsweek*, Kenneth Woodward, and other reporters suggested that the "best working definition of a cult distinguishes the destructive from the benign," with cults being those groups inherently destructive and dangerous.[55] Indeed by the early 1990s, American religious fringe discourse in some ways resembled the late-nineteenth-century Orientalist discourse studied by the scholars Edward Said and Timothy Mitchell.[56] Said and Mitchell argue that the European images and conceptions of the Middle East posited an essentialist view of the Orient as the polar opposite of the "West." Mitchell asserts that the Oriental other was depicted as "passive rather than active, static rather than mobile, emotional rather than rational, chaotic rather than ordered."[57] Separated from specific groups and theologies, the American religious fringe, depicted as the cult menace, similarly stood for irrationality and emotionalism. It was also portrayed as a haven for criminality and coercion. At its most extreme, journalists represented the religious fringe as some had portrayed communism in the 1950: as an evil other that stood against everything good, true, and American. Like communism, the cultic fringe broke up families, took away individuality, and, through brainwashing, destroyed free will.

As noted in Chapter 3, during the mid- to late 1980s, small-town newspapers across the United States ran occasional stories about local, underground Satanist groups that reportedly abducted children and practiced human sacrifice. The subject also appeared on television. In 1988, for example, a prime-time special hosted by Geraldo Rivera, "Satan's Underground," attracted 20 million viewers with its warnings about a national network of murderous underground Satanists. Sociologists, folklorists, and criminologists who studied these stories—which in every case turned out to have no supporting evidence—suggested that the rumors amounted to a "Satanism scare" having its roots in socioeconomic stresses afflicting traditional family and community structures.[58] The sociologist Jeffrey Victor, for example, asserts that the rumors about subversive Satanic cults threatening to kidnap and sacrifice children were best thought of as contemporary legends believed and transmitted most widely by rural, economically stressed whites.[59] Rather than stories about actual events, Victor suggests that "threat rumors about satanic cults are . . . metaphors for a dangerous heresy which threatens the legitimate moral order of American society, and which is the destruction of traditional American values."[60] Similarly, in *Raising the Devil*, the folklorist Bill Ellis historically traces the legend and rumor motifs, transmitted in various media, that made up the Satanism scare and suggests that for some people, "satanic cult beliefs may well be cultural language that allows them to express emotions and experiences that they might otherwise not be able to handle."[61]

While television talk shows, radio call-ins, and local newspapers featured rumors of Satanic cults, national news and general-interest magazines generally ignored the Satanism scare, producing only a few articles. One of these, "Nightmares on Main Street" in *Vanity Fair*, is a good example of the genre. In it, Leslie Bennetts related stories of people like Aubrey, who came to believe that her Midwestern farm family was part of a murderous Satanic cult. Bennetts told readers how Aubrey was repeatedly impregnated as a young child in order to produce sacrificial babies—infants that she was later forced to eat as part of cannibalistic rituals.[62] "But Aubrey isn't the only one with such memories," Bennetts suggested. "All over the country, what seems to be an astonishing number of women are coming forward with similar stories of satanic cults and ritual abuse."[63] A therapist herself, Bennetts asserted that claims of Satanic ritual abuse were well founded, that "the sexual abuse of children is now acknowledged to be shockingly widespread at every level of society, and many therapists believe there will be a similar evolution in attitudes toward ritual abuse."[64]

Arguing for the plausibility of ritual abuse, Bennetts used familiar negative tropes of the American religious fringe to remind readers that "the fabric of American society is far darker and more complex than many people would like to admit."[65] She asserted that "Americans have always accepted the existence of bizarre religious sects in their midst, most of them representing some form of Christianity. Many cults are known to have practiced some of the brainwashing techniques and forms of child abuse alleged by satanic-cult survivors. But in general it is only when a self-appointed messiah leads his flock into mass suicide, as Jim Jones did at Jonestown, or mass murder, as Charles Manson did, or armed defiance of law-enforcement authorities, as David Koresh did in Waco, Texas, that social tolerance evaporates."[66]

Another exposé, even more striking in how it connects child abuse and Satanic murder to cults in general, is the 1993 piece by Elizabeth S. Rose published in *Ms.*, titled "Surviving the Unbelievable: A First-Person Account of Cult Ritual Abuse."[67] By the time of the article's publication, numerous academics, psychologists, and law enforcement officials had conducted research that seriously questioned the reliability of stories by purported survivors of Satanic ritual abuse. Studies revealed that most of the accusers only developed their memories after coming into contact with therapists who firmly believed in the existence of underground Satanist groups. While some patients undoubtedly showed signs of mental trauma and child abuse, no evidence ever supported claims that their childhood experiences were tied to participation in murderous Satanist cults.[68] In one case, recounted in Lawrence Wright's *Remembering Satan*, a deputy sheriff in Olympia, Washington, who was accused by his daughters of sexual abuse came to believe, through therapy, that he was part of an extensive Satanic movement in his community.[69] Despite the serious questions about ritual abuse and evidence of "false memory syndrome" available at the time of the article, *Ms.* presented Rose's story as undisputed. Positioned in a self-identified feminist journal, Rose's tale described the misogynistic abuse and murder of women.

Rose alleged that she had been reared and ritually abused in her family's "generational satanic cult," suggesting that her "thought patterns were altered through brainwashing and severe psychological abuse."[70] "Even as an adult," she confided, "I sometimes find myself trapped in the lies and threats the cult used to indoctrinate and control me."[71] Forced into the cult by her mother, Rose recounted horrific stories of rape, murder, and child sacrifice—including the sacrifice of her baby sister. These murderous rituals, Rose noted, were not religious at all, but part of a strategy used by group leaders "expressly for the purpose of control and intimidation of cult followers."[72]

In *Threatened Children*, the sociologist Joel Best notes that concern about victimized children grew dramatically during the 1980s.[73] According to Best, "popular magazines published an average of one story about abused, molested, or missing children each week."[74] Interestingly, though, Best found no evidence that crimes against children had increased from previous decades. Rose's narrative, filled with child torture, murder, and endangerment, fits the "threatened child" genre. Initiated into the macabre group at the age of four, Rose says that she lived in fear of being killed, a worry "typical of children who are exposed to cults."[75] In addition to all these atrocities, Rose added that children in cults are also socially abused. "This is the term," she wrote, "I have coined to describe how a cult takes children out of mainstream society and socializes them in such a way that they cannot return."[76] In Rose's narrative, the children not killed by cults were marginalized by them, made permanent members of a lunatic fringe.

While Elizabeth Rose's narrative in *Ms.* stood out as extreme in relation to most national magazine coverage, it illustrates some trends in evidence in the 1990s. First, like Bennetts's article in *Vanity Fair*, it showed an essentialization of the term "cult." Early in the piece, Rose drops "satanic" and starts commenting on cults in general. One can read "Surviving the Unbelievable" and conclude that cults are groups that brainwash, torture, and murder. What makes this essentialization so complete is that these activities are attributed to a cult that by most evidence doesn't exist.

Second, Rose's representation of cults mirrored that of the anti-cult movement in the late 1980s. The sociologists David Bromley and Anson Shupe have shown that certain anti-cult groups were crucial conduits in transmitting Satanism scare rumors. They note, for example, that the Cult Awareness Network, a clearing-house of anti-cult literature and deprogrammer contacts based in Chicago, sponsored and participated "in workshops and seminars to 'educate' a wide range of professionals about this Satanic cult threat."[77] Indeed, Rose's story was directly influenced by anti-cult literature. She cited *Combating Cult Mind Control*, by the prominent deprogrammer and Unification Church apostate Steven Hassan, as "helpful" and listed the American Family Foundation, a large anti-cult organization, as a group to contact.[78]

One year after the exposé in *Vanity Fair* and one and a half years after Rose's article in *Ms.*, *Redbook* in June 1994 published "Blame It on the Devil."[79] The article, by A. S. Ross, took the information available at the time of the other two articles and came to a different conclusion. "At last the tide may be turning against SRA," Ross wrote, using the acronym for Satanic Ritual Abuse.[80] Ross listed lawsuits against therapists by accused parents, increasingly skeptical law enforcement agents, and the second thoughts of former "SRA" proponents as reasons for its demise. At the same time, however, the readers of this debunking article had recently experienced a media onslaught of cult menace motifs much larger than the few Satanic cult survivor stories that had appeared before. The voluminous media coverage of the Branch Davidian standoff in Waco used the most negative images of the American religious fringe to narrate an ambiguous event. Unlike the debunked Satanic cult rumors, these images would last.

Depicting the Waco Branch Davidians:
Explaining the Ambiguous through Motifs
of the Essentialized Margin

On 19 April 1993, the Branch Davidian commune outside Waco, Texas, burned to the ground with eighty-six people inside. The fiery ending culminated a fifty-one-day standoff between the group and agents from the Bureau of Alcohol, Tobacco and Firearms, which unsuccessfully attempted to raid the commune on 28 February under suspicion that the Davidians were stockpiling illegal guns. From the first day of the standoff, when gunfire was exchanged and casualties suffered on both sides, a large media contingent surrounded the scene. They set up makeshift homes in campers and news vans, becoming citizens of a temporary town that they dubbed "satellite city."

Reporters, federal soldiers, and Branch Davidians were not the only ones present at the standoff. A daily gathering of curiosity seekers, T-shirt peddlers, and concession stand owners created a macabre, voyeuristic carnival. People from all over the United States converged. Most travelers, gawkers, and sales people settled about two miles from the commune at a site known locally as Lamb's Hill, but renamed Holy Hill by journalists struck with the makeup of its new population.

The nickname was fitting, although the journalists who chose it were probably unaware that the Shakers—the celibate nineteenth-century new religion founded by Mother Ann Lee—had used the same name to denote each community's site for special ritualized contacts with angelic entities. A variety of preachers, psychics, and spiritual pilgrims converged at the site. One woman, Altamadad, said that God had told her to come to Waco, plant a wooden cross, and hold prayer vigils until he spoke with her again.[81] Another man, a Seventh-Day Adventist elder from Dallas, handed out religious literature from his car, which had a large cardboard sign taped to it reading "World's Most Dangerous Cult Leader 'The Pope' Revealed."[82] Also present were the Schmaltzes, a family of traveling missionaries who called themselves the "Halalaluyah Gang." They passed out flyers and warned anyone who would listen that the conflict between the ATF and the Branch Davidians signaled the start of a Satanic new world order. Soon, they asserted, an anti-religious global government would begin systematically murdering the world's Christians.[83] For the Schmaltzes and a few others at Holy Hill, Waco was the tip of an apocalyptic iceberg.

Indeed, for many Americans following the events in Texas, the extraordinary situation seemed filled with meaning. But interpretations of what was actually going at the Davidian commune, Mount Carmel, varied. Whereas some, like the Schmaltzes, may have seen apocalyptic portents, others, like the pro-gun lobbyists who demonstrated against the ATF in Dallas, saw the standoff as representing a civil rights issue: it was about the right to bear arms.[84] The very ambiguity of the Branch Davidians and the Waco incident made it a sponge for multiple meanings. Years after the fire, what happened both inside and outside Mount Carmel remains hotly contested. We know that the Branch Davidians were a millennialist group that broke away from the Seventh-Day Adventist Church in 1929.[85] We know that the Davidians possessed a large store of weapons: they funded the commune by selling them at gun shows. We also know that the Davidian leader, David Koresh, was a polygamist who married girls as young as fourteen—legal in Texas with parental consent. Other information is contested. Did child abuse occur within the commune? A visit by the Texas Child Protective Service in 1992 found none, and bugs planted inside the commune by the FBI during the standoff did not reveal any either. Davidian apostates, however, insisted that there was plenty, and Attorney General Janet Reno listed child endangerment as the main impetus to gas the commune on the final day.[86] And did the Davidians start the fire that consumed them in a mass suicide pact reminiscent of Jonestown? The ATF was convinced that they did and initially suggested that two Branch Davidians had admitted as much. The bureau later acknowledged having been mistaken about confessions and all surviving Davidians deny that any suicide pact was made. But despite the paucity of undisputed information about the Davidians and their final days, the largest news, general-interest, and religious magazines all produced articles during the standoff and immediately after the fire filled with details that they would question or retract in follow-up stories months later.

Newsmagazines and religious periodicals first picked up the Waco story in mid-March and followed it regularly through mid-May. Throughout these two months, journalists of all sorts used essentialized cult menace motifs to depict the Branch Davidians and Koresh as crazed child abusers bent on armed conflict and mass suicide. One article in *Newsweek* in May admitted that there were "conflicting explanations" and "evidence" for what happened before and after the fire, yet the magazine and its competition narrated the standoff and its tragic end in unambiguous detail.[87]

News journalists painted a familiar picture of a fringe cult, aided by consultations with prominent anti-cultists and deprogrammers (four of the five largest multi-story newsmagazine features repeatedly used anti-cult deprogrammers, anti-cult psychiatrists, and the Davidian apostate Marc Breault as expert consultants). For example, *Time* suggested that the group's prophet, David Koresh, was a "preacherly hypnotist" who brainwashed his followers.[88] In another article, the magazine described him as "a type well-known to students of cult practices: the charismatic leader with a pathological edge."[89] The liberal Protestant magazine *Christian Century* mirrored *Time*, referring to Koresh as a "charismatic psychopath who was immersed in apocalyptic literature."[90] The cover photo in *Time* after the fire visually represented this notion, juxtaposing the head of a laughing Koresh over a picture of the flaming commune. The magazine titled the cover "Tragedy in Waco" and placed at its bottom a quote from the Book of Revelation, "His Name was Death, and Hell Followed with Him."[91]

Writers and editors used their assertions that Koresh was insane to invalidate Davidian religious belief as a whole. *Newsweek* asserted that Koresh's preaching constituted little more than the "ramblings of a diseased mind," *U.S. News* called it "biblical gibberish," and *Time* condemned the entire Davidian lifestyle as based on Koresh's "mangled theological rationale."[92] *Christian Century* suggested that Koresh feigned a "religious cover" to avoid federal investigation of his activities.[93] Reflecting its liberal Protestant theology, the *Century* condemned Davidian interest in biblical apocalypticism. Its commentator James Wall called the Davidian readings of apocalyptic texts "dangerously narrow" and "irrational."[94] Rejecting fundamentalist readings of the Book of Revelation, and somewhat recalling Cold War assertions that conservative biblical interpretation could be psychologically unhealthy, Wall noted that "the imagery of Revelation, which scholars trace to an imaginative response to the harsh Roman rule of the first century, has a mesmerizing poetic power. When seen as a biblical promise for the New Jerusalem, apocalypticism may be a sustaining scriptural promise for the believer. But the bizarre imagery can also serve as a dangerous instrument of control in the hands of a charismatic leader."[95]

Journalists' convictions that Koresh was a dangerous brainwasher working under a false religious cover complemented their

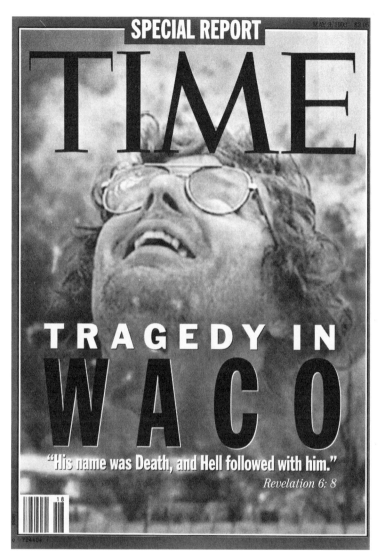

TIME

TRAGEDY IN
WACO

"His name was Death, and Hell followed with him."
Revelation 6: 8

Mixing pictures and a Bible verse, the cover of Time *depicting the "Tragedy in Waco" visually blames the Branch Davidian leader, David Koresh, for the horrific ending to the standoff with the government in 1993. (© Time, Inc./Timepix)* assertions that his followers were a weak-minded, vulnerable lot who committed mass suicide at his command. *Newsweek* suggested that members of all cults were "alienated and vulnerable," while *Christian Century* specifically declared the Branch Davidian rank and file "emotionally wounded."[96] In light of this unanimity, it is unsurprising that *Time, Newsweek, U.S. News, People, Christianity Today*, and *Christian Century* all concluded that the Davidians had burned themselves alive in a mass suicide pact. Four of the six largest multi-story features on the standoff in Waco made some reference to Jonestown. Two months before the fire, *Time* had already titled its story on 15 March 1993, about the initial gun battle between the Davidians and the ATF, "Cult of Death"—the same as its cover story on Jonestown in 1978.[97]

Journalists suggested not only that the Davidians committed mass suicide but that they severely abused their children. According to *People*, for example, Koresh beat children "bruised and bloody."[98] Mirroring reports in *U.S. News* and *Newsweek, Christian Century* suggested that Koresh and the Davidians considered the children within the commune "hostages."[99] *Perspectives*, a publication of the Reformed Church in America, even asserted that millennial beliefs and the victimization of children naturally went together, citing a "dynamic interplay between child abuse and apocalyptic yearning."[100] For all kinds of journalists, cults, mass suicide, and child abuse seemed inseparable.

In fact, journalists relied so heavily on cult menace motifs that articles during and immediately after the standoff made glaring errors later disconfirmed. Seeing Koresh as a manipulative cult leader, for example, *Newsweek* and *Time* both questioned his assertion that he was wounded in the initial gun battle.[101] Yet video recorders sent into the commune by the ATF and brought out before the fire showed that Koresh had two serious bullet wounds that limited his mobility.[102] And despite Koresh's own assertions, virtually all magazines claimed that he believed himself to be Christ. On 15 March 1993, for example, *Newsweek* did note that David Koresh was "growing irritated at reports that he claimed to be Christ . . . Call him a prophet, he said."[103] But on the very next page, *Newsweek* featured a story on Koresh titled "The Messiah of Waco."[104]

One other disconfirmed news items stands out as even more

striking. Without any evidence, *U.S. News and World Report* asserted, apparently influenced by the chronology of Jonestown, that the adult Branch Davidians had shot all their children to death before burning themselves alive.[105] Though no sources confirmed this, it seemed plausible to *U.S. News* because it perceived the Branch Davidians as a cult, and cults—like Elizabeth Rose's satanic family group—naturally abused children. The writers' concluding comments seemed to summarize most magazine journalists' attitudes toward Koresh and the Branch Davidians: "When all the lessons are wrung out of this tragedy, the one that will stand out is that there is no foolproof defense against a fool. There is no leverage to exert on someone willing to expend his life. There is no compromise to strike with someone who sees his own authority menaced by acts of decency. And as awful as it is, the fate of the impressionistic people on whom the fool imprints his will is in his hands."[106]

Branch Davidian Coverage, "True Crime" Narratives, and Cult Menace Motifs

While an extended analysis is beyond the scope of this study, it is useful to briefly compare coverage of Waco in religious periodicals and newsmagazines with some of the "true crime" books produced in the days and weeks after the fire. Just as reports on the Nation of Islam in the early 1960s recalled the image created by the Un-American Activities Committee in Louisiana, depictions of the Branch Davidians in national magazines shared much with the shock tabloid style of true crime works. This type of book, which garners its own section in most chain bookstores, appears soon after major criminal events and claims to use first-hand accounts to construct the "true and inside story" of a tragedy. The genre typically features murderers, especially serial killers, and contains more graphic details than the news media usually include. The four books that I examined were *Massacre at Waco, Texas* by Clifford L. Lindecker, *Fire and Blood: The True Story of David Koresh and the Waco Siege* by David Leppard, *Mad Man in Waco* by Brad Bailey and Bob Darden, and *Preacher of Death* by Martin King and Marc Breault. All the works claim insider information concerning the event but list few or no sources of information. However, one book, *Preacher of Death*, was written by two people who did have contact with the Branch Davidians: Marc Breault was a Davidian apostate and Martin King a journalist who once interviewed members.

The true crime books on Waco were "true" to their genre in that they contained more graphic descriptions than newsmagazine reports did. For example, all four books dwelt at gratuitous length on David Koresh's sexual activities with his many wives. David Leppard described the commune as Koresh's "sexual playground," while Clifford Lindecker added that Koresh kept a "harem" of women in California.[107] All the books suggested that Koresh raped and abused female members and, because of his cruel licentiousness, King and Breault even asserted that the commune suffered an epidemic of sexually transmitted diseases.[108] In addition to detailing Koresh's sexual relations, all four works detailed the weapons that the Davidians may have used in their battle with government agents. Lindecker suggested that the Branch Davidians, in addition to guns, used hand grenades to attack the federal agents, while David Leppard described an assembly line for making machine guns in the "compound."[109]

Some of the details in the true crime book took the form of rumors and legends. For example, Leppard asserted that Koresh abused and even sacrificed commune children in Satanic rituals and that according to two "reliable" ex-members Koresh "advocated ritual child murder." He also reported rumors that Koresh may have "murdered other cult members' babies."[110] King and Breault associated Koresh with Satanism by noting his interest in heavy metal music.[111] The works also reported legend-like rumors of the Branch Davidians' ultimate aims. David Leppard, for example, noted that some believed the communalists were stockpiling weapons for an attack on the city of Waco.[112] Lindecker reported the same, noting that the apocalyptic religious group desired to "massacre the Babylonians, or unbelievers" who lived outside their commune.[113] He added that Koresh had fully intended to kill as many people as possible.[114]

What was striking about these true crime books was not how different they were from the newsmagazines and religious periodicals, but how similar. All three used cult menace motifs in suggesting that the Davidians had been brainwashed by an evil, charismatic leader bent on destruction. All three made conjectures based on little or no evidence. For example, Leppard's suggestion of Satanic ritual abuse was shocking and unconfirmed, but so was the claim by *U.S. News and World Report* that the Davidians killed all their children before burning themselves alive. In narrating the Branch Davidian tragedy, the differences between "tabloid" and "respectable" journalism were narrow indeed, and then more of style than substance.

At the beginning of this chapter, I suggested that all news stories run their course and fade away. By mid-May, the Waco incident had virtually disappeared from national magazines. When it reappeared in two summer articles and several follow-ups in October, the frame had changed: from that of a maniacal leader who led his brainwashed followers to death, to one of the government culpability for the standoff's violent end. In an editorial in *Christian Century* in June, for example, the religion scholar Michael Barkun condemned federal authorities for not taking Davidian apocalyptic belief seriously. The federal authorities, Barkun argued, had let their conviction that they were dealing with a "cult" dictate their actions. "To be called a 'cult,'" Barkun noted, "is to be linked not to religion, but to psychopathology."[115] "The very act of classification itself," he continued, "seems to make further investigation unnecessary."[116] Though he did not mention it, Barkun's condemnation of the federal government's attitude toward the Davidians applied equally to the very magazine in which he wrote.

Another summer article in *Esquire* painted somewhat unflattering pictures of the federal authorities and the media. In "The Last Revelation from Waco," Ivan Solotraff suggested that despite media and government reports to the contrary, the majority of Waco residents who knew David Koresh and the Davidians thought of them as good citizens and neighbors.[117] Solotraff also pointed out the lack of evidence to confirm how the fire started and the falsity of the ATF's assertion that surviving Davidians confessed to starting it.[118] He also described the smug demeanor of journalists living in "Satellite City." Solotraff noted, for example, that after the Branch Davidians hung a banner outside their commune's windows saying "God Help Us We Need the Press," journalists soon appeared with T-shirts reading "God Help Us We Are the Press."[119]

In October, newsmagazines published follow-ups that partially mirrored the pieces published during the summer. In the "Book of Koresh," *Newsweek* used the biblical scholars James Tabor and Philip Arnold to suggest, as Barkun had, that federal authorities had made a grave error in not taking Davidian religion seriously.[120] The follow-up in *U.S. News* somewhat resembled Solotraff's, using statements by the sheriff of Waco to suggest both that the Branch Davidians might have been more even-minded folks than initially thought and that federal authorities had mishandled the situation.[121] Given that journalists have traditionally viewed themselves as government watchdogs, and given that the Waco siege was fraught with apparent government missteps, such coverage seemed belated, but inevitable.

But the magazines' coverage of the incident in the spring had been just as predictable. Faced with an ambiguous situation, journalists relied on cult menace motifs to fill in the blank spaces of a sensationalistic story. Reporters in the largest weeklies consistently consulted professional anti-cultists because, as the media scholar Robert Lichter notes in his study of news journalism, "people gravitate toward sources whose perspectives accord with their own."[122] In doing this, they ignored the opinions of interested Bible scholars and sociologists whom they later quoted favorably.[123] During the standoff, however, reporters disregarded their views because, as David Chidester self-referentially notes, "religion scholars run counter to the dominant discourse of power if they do not accept and reinforce the normative division of the public terrain into the self-evidently 'traditional' and 'nontraditional.'"[124] I have argued throughout this work that journalists in the largest news and general-interest magazines consistently promoted doxic taxonomies of mainstream and fringe that supported such a "dominant discourse of power." Though they may have viewed themselves as disinterested and neutral, journalists covering Waco during the standoff appeared more, in the words of Lichter, "captives of conventional wisdom, carriers of intellectual currents whose validity is taken for granted."[125]

Conclusion

During the standoff at Waco, *Time* published a cover story titled "In the Name of God." The front-page photograph featured elongated head shots of David Koresh and Sheik Abdel-Rahman, a fundamentalist Muslim leader whom federal authorities had implicated in a terrorist bombing of the World Trade Center in New York. The subheading read: "What Happens When Believers Embrace the Dark Side of Faith."[126] "If you scratch any aggressive tribalism or nationalism," the accompanying article asserted, "you usually find beneath its surface a religious core, some older binding energy of belief or superstition, previous to civic consciousness, previous almost to thought."[127] Religious hatreds, *Time* suggested, proved the most "merciless and absolute," and the world's religious zealots "press on, shattering the silence, breaking the foundations."[128]

In *Christian Century*, James Wall took offense. In an article titled "The Media's Dark Side," Wall asserted that David Koresh and the World Trade Center bombing were two "completely unrelated stories of violence" that had nothing to do with "the name of God."[129] He seemed particularly insulted that *Time* had failed to explicitly state that the Branch Davidians were not Christian. Wall wrote that Koresh's group seemed "to owe as much to the National Rifle Association as to any mainstream religious tradition."[130] Koresh, Wall claimed, fit the "classic definition of a 'cult' leader," one whose "aberrant behavior deserves analysis more in psychological than theological terms."[131] Wall continued, "The careless or perhaps intentional manner in which the media connect the psychologically disturbed behavior of Koresh and his use of Christian terminology gives a 'Christian' cast to his cult that is unjustified. Even when the media avoid the adjective 'Christian' in front of 'cult,' the linkage with God (as in 'In the Name of God') coupled with biblical apocalypticism leaves the impression that Koresh is some kind of Christian—which denigrates the faith of millions of believers."[132]

In another critique of the media in *Christian Century*, the American religious historian Martin Marty complained that journalists contacted him and about the Branch Davidians because they viewed them as fundamentalists—and fundamentalism is one of

Marty's subjects. Marty suggested that the Davidians "match none of the scholars' definitions, and we were asked to be experts because we guide studies of other intensely religious people."[133] He concluded that "the study and treatment of religion turns out, like so much else in life, to be a game of inches. These inches can become miles. We try to handle our fundamentalists with care. Some of them say they respect our respect for their differences from one another, which are vast. We do not want to lose that respect by clumping them with the Branch Davidians. No, we are not experts on 'cults.'"[134]

These three articles raise themes visited throughout this work. That in *Time*, for example, pointed to a significant change in journalistic representations since the 1950s. For most of the forty-year period, writers and editors in the largest news and general-interest magazines associated "true" religion with an essentialized, transcendent set of morals and values. In the late 1950s, journalists suggested that the Nation of Islam could not be religious because it was racist and political. In the 1960s, writers questioned Transcendental Meditation's validity because its philosophy was too simple to follow. But "In the Name of God" tied religion in general to violence, suggesting that it had a "dark side." Religion, it seemed, was no longer always a positive thing.

Wall's article in *Christian Century* also demonstrated a recurring theme. Religious writers—as well as some African American journalists in the 1950s and 1960s who wrote about the Nation of Islam —sometimes offered depictions of mainstream and fringe at odds with those of newsmagazine reporters. Strategically interested in placing their own religious faith and values into the American religious center, Catholics and Evangelicals sometimes promoted religious classifications that contradicted those in *Newsweek*, *Life*, and other so-called secular magazines. (Liberal Protestants did so as well, though less often because of their historical influence on the mass media.) Wall's irritation that *Time* connected Christianity to the Branch Davidians and, by association, to violence revealed his desire to keep the boundaries between mainstream and marginality clear. For Wall, nothing truly "Christian" could ever be fringe. At the same time, Wall's article demonstrated that even religious writers—especially after Jonestown, but throughout the forty-year period—worked within the same doxic categories of mainstream and fringe used by journalists at news and general-interest magazines. For Wall, Koresh was a "classic" example of a cult leader and the Branch Davidians a classic example of a cult. There seemed no question that they were part of the fringe, so Wall and *Christian Century* found it doubly important to distance them from their own mainstream faith.

Finally, Martin Marty's article pointed out that recurrent struggles over definitions and classifications occurred, and occur, not just in the print media but in academia. Throughout the period under study, journalists of all stripes, to repeat the words of the social theorist Pierre Bourdieu, "engaged in a specifically symbolic struggle to impose the definition of the world most in conformity with their interests."[135] Marty's earnest desire to protect his academic definition of fundamentalism, while simultaneously not offending his fundamentalist sources, revealed a conscious, articulated engagement with the politics of definition that only appeared unwitting and masked in most journalistic portrayals.

But the article's subject matter also begs the question of how scholars support or contest dominant classification strategies through their scholarship. What exactly do mainstream and fringe labels mean? Those who use such categorizations frequently— though sometimes unwittingly—mark certain groups, beliefs, and practices with more or less social value. Rather than dispassionately organize it, classifications symbolically construct the world as some desire it. The American religious historian William Hutchison suggests that terms like "mainstream," "establishment," and "mainline" could be useful if explicitly used to refer to religious groups wielding dominant, even hegemonic power in society.[136] On the other hand, Hutchison also identified the "persistent lack of clarity" in scholars' use of such terms, noting that they were often used to imply certain normative religious practices, beliefs, and behaviors.[137]

But as Robert Orsi and other scholars of American religion have noted, there simply is no normative American mainstream.[138] To use Orsi's term, religious Americans have always been *improvisatory*, and attempts to designate some beliefs and practices as normal and others as deviant often reveal more about the authors' own views on heresy and orthodoxy than of what some "American mainstream" actually consists.[139] Of course, there are certain beliefs and practices in which only a small minority of Americans ever participated. Polygamy, a nineteenth-century Mormon practice, would be an example. But many other beliefs and rites implicitly relegated to the fringe by scholars have been much more popular than some might expect. For example, Wade Clark Roof's study of the largest single age cluster in the United States, the baby boomers, revealed that as many as 28 percent believed in reincarnation, and between 68 and 84 percent believed in psychic powers.[140] While reincarnation and psychic powers are not official beliefs of most Protestant, Catholic, or Jewish traditions, many adherents in these "mainstream" traditions hold them.[141] Poll results like these, and an increasing number of monographs on the combinative and improvisational religious activities of Americans, suggest that the mainstream, at least as many have traditionally envisioned it, doesn't exist.[142]

The language of encounter and contact can help us re-situate classifications of mainstream and fringe, changing them from tools of scholarship to objects of study. In the last several years, many scholars have argued that to study American religion is to examine multiple groups encountering, contesting, and even borrowing from one another.[143] I agree with some of these writers that we can divide encounters into two separate but interdependent arenas. The first, physical arenas of encounter are those where two or more religious or cultural groups meet face to face. Studying this arena entails examining the history of contacts between various groups, asking what happened when, for example, Native Americans first met Europeans. But, as the historian Joel Martin notes, "contact refers not only to embodied encounters between representatives of different cultures, but also to interpretations of contact manifested on the symbolic level."[144] In other words, those initial contacts between Native Americans and Europeans were conceptual as well. As a result of their physical encounter, each group faced the conceptual task of fitting the "other" into its pre-existing worldview or revising the worldview to incorporate the new contacts. In turn, the images and understandings that the groups produced influenced their relationships and attitudes toward each other. This process was repeated with every new encounter on American soil.

In this work, I examined an aspect of the contemporary period's most important arena of conceptual encounter: the mass media. Focusing on how the American religious fringe was depicted in news, general-interest, and special-interest magazines, I traced how the boundaries of mainstream and fringe changed over time in ways that coincided with larger social, cultural, and magazine industry changes. At the same time, I suggested that large news and general-interest magazines like *Time*, *Newsweek*, *Reader's Digest*, and *Life* consistently labeled religious groups mainstream or fringe in ways that symbolically reproduced and legitimized inequalities of race and class in the postwar United States. While I hope that this work is a good start, I have no illusions that it offers any final statement on its subjects. If it spurs further research and discussion, I'll consider it successful.

Conceptual encounter is a constant theme in American religious history and one that I hope will receive increasing attention. Scholars could focus on how groups perceived each other and constructed classificatory schemes that promoted certain boundaries, identities, and values. To analyze constructions of orthodoxy and heresy, mainstream and margins, authentic and inauthentic, is to study how different groups struggled to create and sustain certain conceptions of the world as preferable, if not natural. Such an approach denaturalizes classificatory schemes and highlights, rather than obscures, issues of power. Studying conceptual encounters in American religion, scholars may find new themes, questions, and narratives.

EPILOGUE

One fall day in 2002 — motivated both by nostalgia and by the need to entertain a very active four-year-old who had worn me out — I watched a television channel that aired retro cartoons. In one episode of *Samson and Goliath* dated 1965, a scheming villager created a robotic "idol" named Ramakish to help enslave "super-stitious" Asiatic mountain people for the evil General Tong, who wore a Chinese communist military uniform. Samson and Goliath, an American boy and his dog who transformed into a muscular giant and lion when trouble arose, saved the villagers from a communist tank invasion and smashed the Ramakish idol. At the end of the fifteen-minute cartoon the grateful villagers responded to their salvation by making a new "idol" depicting Samson and Goliath, much to the heroes' dismay.

Other cartoons from the mid-1960s aired that day mixed exoticism, racism, and action. On *Shazzan*, a fifty-foot-tall Middle Eastern Genie saved his two white American teenage masters by destroying a clay idol to which they were to be sacrificed. On *Johnny Quest*, small, gray, angry creatures identified as "pygmies" practiced ritual sacrifice and tried to kill Anglo scientists, while on *Dino Boy* similarly depicted "pygmies" violently attacked a presumably innocent Native American who rode a pterodactyl. The exotic-looking victim, in consonance with several of the other cartoons, was saved by a young white boy — though this time with the help of his pet dinosaur and caveman friend. Two things struck me as I watched. First, my daughter wouldn't be watching the retro channel much. Second, cartoons like this would not be made today.

When I look back at much coverage of the American religious fringe from the 1950s and 1960s, I come to the same conclusion. The Cold War concern with volatile mass movements of economic, foreign, and racial others led to a style of fringe reporting that in many ways does not fit well with current magazine style, focused as it is on personalizing exposé journalism, promoting diversity, and what Anthony Giddens calls the late modern "project of the self."[1]

At the same time, as I have argued in this work, certain themes and motifs remained. This study examined selected stories and topics from 1955 to 1993. Therefore it would be reasonable to ask what similarities and differences exist in current coverage.

This is an excellent question, but historical training warns me that the here and now can be a hard thing to gauge accurately and thoroughly. The present is an ongoing story in which the end, however predictable at times, is ultimately unknowable. Three current news events, however, recently garnered a wealth of coverage that will eventually provide interesting comparative case studies to the ones offered in this book. First, the terrorist destruction of the World Trade Center Twin Towers on 11 September 2001 has produced a marked increase in coverage of Islam. In the time since the attack, some conservative Christians and politicians have used the media to denounce Islam as a whole, while many American Muslims have appeared in the media to argue that the terrorists could not have been "true" Muslims because of their actions. Still other media presentations have steered clear of both hostile outsider and apologetic insider rhetoric, seeking more nuanced views. One must wonder if there will be a trend in how different kinds of magazines depict Islam, as well as what motifs they will use to discuss its varieties. Will Muslim "fundamentalism," for example, be represented in ways similar to or different from the conservative Protestant groups reported on in this book? Could the dehumanizing Cold War motifs in Eric Hoffer's *The True Believer* be resurrected now that the United States has entered the amorphous "war on terrorism?"

The second news event that will provide for much comparison is the sex abuse scandal embroiling the Catholic Church that exploded into the mass media during the winter and spring of 2002 and garnered front-page coverage. Given the trajectory of coverage in the 1990s, one wonders whether the story will lead to a further "marginalization of the mainstream." One also wonders what kind of coverage and editorializing the recurring topics of sexual abstinence and a male-only priesthood in Roman Catholicism will receive.

The third news event unfolded as I wrote this. In late December 2002 and early January 2003, the Raelians claimed to have successfully cloned and given birth to two human beings. The Raelians, a millennial new religious movement founded in the early 1970s by Claude Vorilhon, believe that space aliens, the Elohim, created humanity by cloning themselves. News reports were quick to suggest that the cloning assertions are suspect, and some suggested that they were a publicity stunt to attract attention to the movement. One wonders whether journalists will use the motif of "exotic curiosity" (1950s and 1960s), the motif of the "cult menace" (1970s through 1990s), some combination of the two, or something altogether new to depict the Raelians. As with the other two stories, time will tell—as will *Newsweek, Christian Century,* and a host of others.

NOTES

Introduction

1 See Christopher Buckley, "This Just In from Our Cult Desk," *New Yorker*, 21 April 1997, 100.

2 One could, of course, argue that the original sociological categories of cult, sect, denomination, and church are problematically based on a hierarchical, evolutionary conception of religious institutions, with "cult" having the weakest organization and the most conflict with the surrounding society, and "church" being the most organized and in harmony with society.

3 For a recent, expansive volume on the historical debates surrounding explanations of religious experience that includes debates on emotional versus rational religion, see Taves, *Fits, Trances, and Visions*.

4 I get the term "heresiographer" from Henderson, *The Construction of Orthodoxy and Heresy*, 175.

5 I address journalist demographics later in this introduction. For an example of the demographics of magazine readership, see *The First Primary and Secondary and Total Audience Report: Demographics 1969*, 36th Annual Media Report of Audiences (Mamaroneck, N.Y.: David Starch and Staff, 1969). The journalism scholar James Baughman notes that magazines like *Life*, the *Saturday Evening Post*, and *Time* had an economically privileged readership. See James L. Baughman, "Who Read *Life*? The Circulation of America's Favorite Magazine," in *Looking at Life Magazine*, ed. Doss, 43–44.

6 See Jacobs, *Race, Media, and the Crisis of Civil Society*, 28.

7 See van Zuilen, *The Life Cycle of Magazines*.

8 I thank Chris Smith for his useful and influential comments about the dissertation version of this work. Also see Smith, *American Evangelicalism*, 91, 92.

9 See Ibid., 105.

10 See Bourdieu, *Outline of a Theory of Practice*, 82–83.

11 Ibid., 82, 72. Bourdieu is a materialist who places prime importance on the economic field, but he rejects essentialist, Marxist definitions of class. David Swartz notes that Bourdieu sees social classes themselves as "contested identities that are constructed through struggle."

See Swartz, *Culture and Power*, 147. "Class, for Bourdieu," Paul DiMaggio writes, "is both a Durkheimian category of groups sharing experiences and collective representations, and a Weberian notion of a set of actors attempting to monopolize markets for different goods and services." DiMaggio describes Bourdieu's classes as "aggregates of optimizers, united by habitus, pursuing parallel strategies toward similar, but not collective, ends." For both DiMaggio quotes, see his "Review Essay," 1470.

12 See Lichter, Rothman, and Lichter, *The Media Elite*, 55. In Bourdieu's social theory, there are not many elite conspiracies to preserve the status quo, nor many subaltern plots to undermine it. The social theorist David Swartz elaborates that "legitimation of social class inequality is not the product of conscious intention but stems from a structural correspondence between different fields.... Actors unwittingly reproduce or change the class distinctions simply by pursuing their own strategies within the sets of constraints and opportunities available to them. When cultural producers pursue their own specific interests in fields, they unwittingly produce homologous effects in the social class structure." See Swartz, *Culture and Power*, 134.

13 See Baughman, *Henry R. Luce and the Rise of the American News Media*, 32, 28.

14 Ibid., 190–91.

15 Ibid., 173.

16 See Lichter, Rothman, and Lichter, *The Media Elite*, 21.

17 See Gans, *Deciding What's News*, 27.

18 The communication scholars Calhoun, Lipoma, and Postone elaborate Bourdieu's position: "Although the economic is crucially determining, it must be symbolically mediated. The undisguised reproduction of economic capital would reveal the arbitrary character of the distribution of power and wealth. Symbolic capital functions to mask the economic domination of the dominant class and socially legitimate hierarchy by essentializing and naturalizing social position. That is, noneconomic fields articulate with, and legitimate class relations through misrecognition." See Calhoun, Lipoma, and Postone, Introduction, in *Bourdieu*, ed. Calhoun, Lipoma, and Postone, 5. For an elaboration of Bourdieu's symbolic capital concept, see Bourdieu, *Outline of a Theory of Practice*, 171–83.

19 Quoted in Swartz, *Culture and Power*, 185.

20 See Bourdieu, "Symbolic Power," 115.

21 See Tweed, Introduction, 1–23; Orsi, "Forum," 1–8.

22 Given this, I agree with David Swartz's assertion that Pierre Bourdieu's social theories can aid scholars in bringing a much-needed "conflict perspective to the study of religion." See Swartz, "Bridging the Study of Culture and Religion," 82.

23 See Silk, *Unsecular Media*, 141.

24 See Susan Mizruchi, Introduction, in *Religion and Cultural Studies*, ed. Mizruchi, xii.

25 In addition to Tweed and Orsi, noted above, see Moore, *Religious Outsiders and the Making of Americans*.

26 See Baird, *Religion in America*. For Sweet's quote, see Moore, *Religious Outsiders and the Making of Americans*, 14. Also see Ahlstrom, *A Religious History of the American People*.

27 See Stuart Hall, Introduction, in *Representation*, ed. Hall, 3.

28 Most of the scholarship comes from the sociology of religion. Even those scholars who have made valuable contributions to the study of new religions have largely failed to define and analyze the media in a systematic way. For two examples, see Shupe and Hadden, "Cops, News, and Public Opinion," 177–202; and Barker, "Will the Real Cult Please Stand Up?" 193–212.

29 See, for example, van Driel and Richardson, "Print Media Coverage of New Religious Movements," 37–61; and van Driel and Richardson, "Research Note," 171–83.

30 For example, van Driel and Richardson choose to leave out coverage of the Peoples Temple in their study spanning 1972–84, yet they include coverage of the Evangelical Youth for Christ and Campus Crusade movements. One wonders how their conclusions might differ had they chosen other criteria for group inclusion. For an example of a study focusing on media coverage of one group, see Shupe, "Constructing Evil as a Social Process," 205–18.

31 See Philip Jenkins, *Mystics and Messiahs*. Although not a study of particular media, Jenkins's expansive work uses print media and paperbacks as sources—some of which I also use—to argue about perceptions of new religions throughout the twentieth century.

32 For a brief history of many of the magazines I use, see Nourie and Nourie, eds., *American Mass-Market Magazines*. They leave African American, sports, and women's magazines out of their encyclopedic work, noting that these were to appear in future volumes. I categorize these periodicals under the heading "special interest."

33 For circulation statistics, see the annual directories published by N. W. Ayer and Sons.

34 See Hartley and Montgomery, "Representations and Power Relations," 236.

35 See Donna Haraway, *Simians, Cyborgs, and Women* (New York: Routledge, 1991), 195, 196. Thanks to Thomas Tweed for initially showing me this source, which he refers to in the introduction to *Retelling U.S. Religious History*, 9.

36 See Tweed, ed., *Retelling U.S. Religious History*, 10.

37 David Bromley, personal correspondence (20 February 1998).

38 See Hudnut-Beumler, *Looking for God in the Suburbs*, 15.

39 See Lichter, Rothman, and Lichter, *The Media Elite*, 8.

40 Ibid., 7.

41 I discovered this by following the circulation statistics of the twenty periodicals I used most in this study. See Ayer's directories, 1955–78.

42 See Lichter, Rothman, and Lichter, *The Media Elite*, 11.

43 See Gans, *Deciding What's News*, xii–xiii. I would differ with Gans when it comes to viewers' reception of these media. Television, incorporating audio and moving pictures, offers a more totalistic experience that must affect reception differently from print media. For a provocative analysis of the differences in print and electronic media reception, see Debray, *Media Manifestos*.

44 Interestingly, newsmagazines like *Time* and *Newsweek* usually used multiple writers and editors to produce a story and left their by-lines blank. By the late seventies the magazines sometimes did list reporters' names, but it was still impossible to tell who wrote and edited specific sections of each story.

45 See Kozol, *Life's America*, 40–41.

46 See Lutz and Collins, *Reading National Geographic*, 12.

47 For examples, see "YMCA for Jews" and "Theology: Good Grief Charles Schulz!" Also see "Anglicans/Baptism: For Babies or Believers?" 36.

48 As would longitudinal studies of a single magazine. For two examples, see Hulsether, *Building a Protestant Left*; and Hart, Turner, and Knupp, "A Rhetorical Profile of Religious News," 58–68.

49 See Kozol, *Life's America*, 15.

50 Ibid., 18. Kozol uses Horace Newcomb's argument on the dialogic aspects of mass communications. Newcomb writes, "None of this should be taken to ignore the attempt on the part of the dominant groups to

consciously or unconsciously impose meaning, to restrict usage and interpretation, to frame the terms of communication process and content, or to manipulate access to interpretive ability . . . but . . . makers and users, writers and readers, senders and receivers can do things with communication that are unintended, unplanned for, indeed, unwished for." See Newcomb, "On the Dialogic Aspects of Mass Communication," 38–39.

51 *Time* suggested that Bach's articles were "too sympathetic" in their portrayals. See "What Price Syncretism?" 88.

52 See "The Judges and the Judged," 551–52.

53 Just how the media influence audiences is the contested subject of a number of reader response studies. McCombs and Shaw, for example, argue that the mass media set the agenda for political campaigns, determining which issues the electorate will deem most important. See McCombs and Shaw, "The Agenda-Setting Function of the Mass Media," 176–87. However, Neuman, Just, and Crigler contest their argument, asserting that audiences bring their own pre-media agendas to political issues. See their *Common Knowledge*.

54 See Stuart Hall, "Culture, the Media, and the 'Ideological Effect,'" 340.

55 See Bourdieu, *On Television*, 21.

56 See Richardson, "Manufacturing Consent about Koresh," 162.

57 See Joel W. Martin, "Forum," 12.

58 See Grossberg, ed., "On Postmodernism and Articulation, 53.

59 See Rodman, *Elvis after Elvis*, 27.

60 See van Driel and Richardson "Print Media Coverage of New Religious Movements," 57.

Chapter One

1 See *Life*, 9 June 1958, 2 (Table of Contents).

2 Ibid., 124.

3 Ibid., 122.

4 Ibid., 124.

5 Ibid.

6 See "The Way of the Cults."

7 Ibid.

8 Ibid.

9 Ibid., 105.

10 See Baughman, *Henry Luce and the Rise of the American News Media*, 45.

11 See, for example, the editorial "To a Greater Christian Church," 24. Al-

though the identity of the writer was not revealed, it was likely the publisher and editor in chief Henry Luce, son of missionary parents.

12 See Stuart Hall, Introduction, in *Representation*, ed. Hall, 6.

13 My use of spatial language like center and periphery, mainstream and fringe, follows R. Laurence Moore's historiographical scholarship, which suggests that American religious historians have always designated "insiders" and "outsiders" in narrating the story of religion in the United States. As I have noted several times, journalists used a variety of taxonomies to designate mainstream and fringe (including musical terminology like "offbeat"), not just spatial language. See Moore's introduction, "Protestant Unity and the American Mission: The Historiography of a Desire," in *Religious Outsiders and the Making of Americans*, 3–21.

14 See Robert Ellwood, *The Fifties Spiritual Marketplace*, 161.

15 I agree with Pierre Bourdieu's assertion that "religion, like all symbolic systems, is predisposed to fulfill a function of association and dissociations or, better, of distinction, a system of practices and beliefs is made to appear as magic and sorcery, an inferior religion, whenever it occupies a dominated position in the structure of relations of symbolic power." See Bourdieu, "The Genesis and Structure of the Religious Field," 12.

16 For a discussion of the distinctions between the mainstream establishment as hegemony on the one hand and as normative on the other, see William R. Hutchinson, Preface, in *Between the Times*, ed. Hutchinson, vii–xv. See Baltzell, *The Protestant Establishment*.

17 See Hudnut-Beumler, *Looking for God in the Suburbs*, 33–38.

18 Quoted in Ibid., 52.

19 See Herberg, *Protestant Catholic Jew*, 39.

20 Hudnut-Beumler describes Herberg's book as a "biblical neo-orthodox jeremiad" against what he perceived as the secularizing religion of "the American way of life." See Hudnut-Beumler, *Looking for God in the Suburbs*, 110–30.

21 See Ellwood, *The Fifties Spiritual Marketplace*, 51–55.

22 See David Morgan, "The Image of Religion in American *Life*, 1936–51," 151.

23 See Hulsether, *Building a Protestant Left*, 61. As the decade progressed, Hulsether suggests, the magazine gradually abandoned this view. See Hulsether, *Building a Protestant Left*, 63.

24 For mention of Peale, see Marty, *Under God, Indivisible, 1941–1960*, 457.

25 See Herberg, *Protestant Catholic Jew*, 84.

26 Mark Silk discusses this article in *Unsecular Media*, 106–7.

27 See the *Look* Magazine Photograph Collection, Look-Job 55–6240, Library of Congress.

28 Silk argues that *Reader's Digest* was especially enthusiastic in its praise of the Mormons. See Silk, *Unsecular Media*, 107. But other magazines represented the movement positively as well. See, for example, "A Church in the News," 90–94.

29 See O'Brien, "Why Do Our Religions Fight Each Other?" 59.

30 Ibid., 64.

31 See Gaustad, *A Documentary History of Religion in America to the Civil War*, 459–62, 442–45.

32 In Chapters 4 and 5 I detail the motifs of these "atrocity tales." For several scholars' delineations of these themes, see David Brion Davis, "Some Themes of Countersubversion," 205–24; Cox, "Deep Structures in the Study of New Religions," 122–30; and Bromley and Shupe, *Strange Gods*, 6–15.

33 See Philip Jenkins, "The Great Anti-Cult Scare, 1935–45," paper presented at the 1999 CESNUR conference at Bryn Athyn, Pa. Quoted by permission. Also see his *Mystics and Messiahs*.

34 Jenkins, "The Great Anti-Cult Scare, 1935–45," 5.

35 See Jenkins, "The Great Anti-Cult Scare, 1935–45," 14. Quoted with permission.

36 See Gilbert, *A Cycle of Outrage*, 11. In newspapers, popular culture critiques could be more ominous. For example, one critic in the *Los Angeles Mirror-News* compared concerts by Elvis Presley to Nazi party rallies. See Doss, *Elvis Culture*, 48.

37 See Robinson, "The Kingdom of King Narcisse," 112.

38 See Brossard, "California's Offbeat Religions," 99–103.

39 Ibid., 102.

40 See Mathison, *Faiths, Cults, and Sects of America*, 216–18.

41 See Brossard, "California's Offbeat Religions," 101.

42 See Carson, "Eccentricity under the Sun," 120.

43 Ibid.

44 Ibid.

45 Ibid.

46 See Foreman, ed., *The Other Fifties*, 2.

47 See *Look*, 29 September 1959, 4 (Table of Contents).

48 See Carson, "Eccentricity under the Sun," 92.

49 Ibid., 112.

50 See "Faith: Healthy v. Neurotic," 78.

51 Ibid.

52 Ibid.

53 Ibid., 80.

54 Ibid.

55 See Englehardt, *The End of Victory Culture*, 91–95.

56 See Elaine Tyler May, *Homeward Bound*, 13–16.

57 See Andrew Ross, *No Respect*, 43, 45–47.

58 Ibid., 47–55. Also see Gilbert, *A Cycle of Outrage*, 109–26. Perhaps the most ardent critic of "mass culture" was Dwight Macdonald. See Hudnut-Beumler, *Looking for God in the Suburbs*, 102–6. Interestingly, Macdonald attacked Luce's publications for cultivating bland "middlebrow" tastes. See Baughman, *Henry R. Luce and the Rise of the American News Media*, 171–72. For the most part, the loudest protests, like Macdonald's, could be found in small literary and political journals like *Diogenes*, *Dissent*, and *Commentary*. Sometimes they appeared in the *New Yorker*, the *Nation*, or the *New Republic*. See Hudnut-Beumler, *Looking for God in the Suburbs*, 102. My analysis suggests that disdain for what was labeled "lowbrow," "popular," and "mass" culture was more latent and ambivalent in large news and general-interest magazines.

59 See Paul Hutchinson, "Have We a 'New' Religion?" 158.

60 Ibid., 138.

61 Ibid.

62 Ibid., 138, 140.

63 See Kammen, *American Culture, American Tastes*, 95. For a full discussion of the essay and an illustration of *Life*'s chart, see 95–100.

64 See Erika Doss, Introduction, in *Looking at Life Magazine*, ed. Doss, 11.

65 See Lawrence W. Levine, *Highbrow/Lowbrow*, 222.

66 See Van Dusen, "Force's Lesson for Others," 122.

67 Ibid.

68 See Van Dusen, "Caribbean Holiday," 948.

69 See "The Healing Ministry," 82.

70 See Richard Carter, "That Old-Time Religion Comes Back," 126.

71 Ibid.

72 Ibid., 127.

73 Ibid.

74 Ibid., 129.

75 Ibid., 130.

76 Ibid., 130.

77 See Fleming, "California Cults and Crackpots," 80.

78 Ibid., 82.

79 Ibid., 80.

80 See Hoffer, *The True Believer*.

81 See James T. Baker, *Eric Hoffer* (Boston: Twayne, 1982), 23, 24–25, 38.

82 See Hoffer, *The True Believer*, 9.

83 Ibid., 81.

84 Ibid.

85 Ibid., 29–56.

86 See Mathison, *Faiths, Cults, and Sects of America*, 33–40. Also see Walter Martin, *Kingdom of the Cults*, 26. The sociologist C. Eric Lincoln also used Hoffer in his study of the Nation of Islam in 1961. See C. Eric Lincoln, *The Black Muslims in America*, 96. I discuss this in more detail in Chapter 2.

87 See Baker, *Eric Hoffer*, 22.

88 See Andrew Ross, *No Respect*, 42.

89 Ibid., 59.

90 See Bach, *Strange Sects and Curious Cults*, 270.

91 See Bach, *They Have Found a Faith*, 300.

92 See Zimmerman, "Where Is the 'Third Force' Going?" 15.

93 Ibid.

94 Ibid.

95 Ibid.

96 Ibid., 18.

97 Ibid.

98 See Walter Martin, *The Rise of the Cults*, 12. Martin's most popular work, selling millions of copies since its initial publication, is *Kingdom of the Cults*.

99 See Spittler, *Cults and Isms*, 12.

100 For an argument for the former, see Hoekema, *The Four Major Cults*, 388–403. For an argument for the latter, see Walter Martin, *The Truth About Seventh-Day Adventism* (Grand Rapids, 1960), 248.

101 See Spittler, *Cults and Isms*, 109–28.

102 Jan Karel Van Baalen asserted that Unitarianism and Modernism were identical. See Van Baalen, *The Chaos of the Cults*, 292–347. Van Baalen never calls ecumenism a cult, but critiques it in his introduction. See 13–14.

103 I say partly because the reversal was not full. Guru-based Asian and

Christian-based sects and new religions remained on the periphery for both evangelicals and news and general-interest magazine journalists.

104 See Lewis, *Confronting the Cults*, 1.

105 Quoted in Lewis, *Confronting the Cults*, 2.

106 See "The Cultic Hordes," 20.

107 Ibid.

108 See Harold Lindsell, "The American Scene: Are Cults Outpacing Our Churches?" 3-4.

109 Ibid., 4-5.

110 Ibid., 5.

111 See "The Challenge of the Cults," 22.

112 See Van Dusen, "Caribbean Holiday," 948.

113 Ibid.

114 See "A New 'Reformation'?" 82.

115 See Letters, *Newsweek*, 12 September 1955, 11.

116 See Cary, "The Land of Itching Ears," 362.

117 Ibid., 360, 362.

118 Ibid., 362.

119 Ibid., 364.

120 Ibid., 362-63.

121 Ibid., 364.

122 Ibid., 365.

123 See Cogley, "The Enthusiasts," 448.

124 Ibid.

125 Ibid.

126 Ibid.

127 See Pierre Bourdieu, "The Genesis and Structure of the Religious Field," 24.

128 Paul DiMaggio, in a synopsis of Pierre Bourdieu's conception of society, explains that "constrained by habitus and objective reality, individuals are consigned to dart in and out between the cracks of social structure, never questioning the rules, seeking only to manipulate them." See DiMaggio, "Review Essay," 1470. This is a theme—and a quote—that I revisit in later chapters.

129 See Jeffrey Sconce, "Brains from Space," 288-89.

130 See Gore Vidal, *Messiah*, 36.

131 See Malcolm X with Alex Haley, *The Autobiography of Malcolm X*, 224.

132 See Walter Martin, *Kingdom of the Cults*, 25.

133 See Gilbert, *A Cycle of Outrage*, 155.

134 See Kozol, *Life's America*, 11.

Chapter Two

1 See "'Black Supremacy' Cult in U.S." 114.

2 Ibid.

3 See Englehardt, *The End of Victory Culture*, 7.

4 Ibid., 99.

5 For the most thorough and acclaimed study of the Nation of Islam, see C. Eric Lincoln, *The Black Muslims in America*. Also see Udom, *Black Nationalism*. Also see the journalist Louis Lomax's *When the Word Is Given*.

6 A search by CBS News through thousands of pages of FBI files on the Nation of Islam, released several years ago through the Freedom of Information Act, produced no evidence of conspiratorial dealings. See the CBS News television documentary "The Real Malcolm X: An Intimate Portrait of the Man" (Fox Video, 1992).

7 See Isaacs, "Integration and the Negro Mood," 490.

8 For a history of Muhammad's early years in the movement, see Clegg, *An Original Man*, 21-27.

9 For a more detailed history of the Nation of Islam and Elijah Muhammad, see Clegg, *An Original Man*. Also see C. Eric Lincoln, *The Black Muslims in America*, 10-17. For a brief list of legend-like rumors about W. D. Fard and his disappearance, see Erdmann Doane Beynon, "The Voodoo Cult among Negro Migrants in Detroit," 896-97.

10 "The Black Man by Nature Is Divine" is a quote from Malcolm X, appearing on WNTA Television's Black Muslim exposé "The Hate That Hate Produced," quoted in C. Eric Lincoln, *The Black Muslims in America*, 71. For an elaboration of the black man as the "Original Man," see Elijah Muhammad's collection of essays taken from his *Muhammad Speaks* columns, *Message to the Blackman in America*, 52-54.

11 For a detailed version of the Nation of Islam's creation story of the Caucasian race, See Muhammad, *Message to the Blackman in America*, 103-22. For a shorter version, see Malcolm X with Haley, *The Autobiography of Malcolm X*, 167-70.

12 See C. Eric Lincoln, *The Black Muslims in America*, 73.

13 See Muhammad quoted in C. Eric Lincoln, *The Black Muslims in America*, 91.

14 See Office Memorandum from Chicago to the FBI Director, 18 September 1953, from Elijah Muhammad FBI files.

15 See Clegg, *An Original Man*, 197–98.

16 See Joint Legislative Committee on un-American Activities, State of Louisiana, *Activities of "The Nation of Islam" or the Muslim Cult of Islam in Louisiana*, 106.

17 Ibid., 108.

18 See Stuart Hall, "Culture, the Media and the 'Ideological Effect,'" 344.

19 See Kozol, *Life's America*, 184.

20 See C. Eric Lincoln, *The Black Muslims in America*, 137.

21 For a narrative on the story's production and the response it received, see Wallace and Gates, *Close Encounters*, 135–38.

22 Ibid., 137.

23 See C. Eric Lincoln, *The Black Muslims in America*, 103.

24 See Oliver, "The Black Muslims," 34.

25 Ibid.

26 Ibid.

27 Ibid.

28 Ibid.

29 Ibid., 35.

30 See "'Black Supremacy' Cult in U.S.," 112.

31 Ibid.

32 Ibid., 113.

33 See C. Eric Lincoln, *The Black Muslims in America*, 224–27.

34 See C. Eric Lincoln, *The Black Muslims in America*, 227.

35 See LaFarge, "The Black Muslims in America," 91.

36 See Balk and Haley, "The Black Merchants of Hate," 68.

37 Ibid., 73.

38 Ibid., 68.

39 See Andrew Ross, *No Respect*, 42.

40 See LaFarge, "The Black Muslims in America," 91.

41 See "The Black Supremacists," 25.

42 See "The Muslim Message," 30.

43 See Krosney, "America's Black Supremacists," 392.

44 See Beynon, "The Voodoo Cult among Negro Migrants in Detroit," 903.

45 See C. Eric Lincoln, *The Black Muslims in America*, 204–6.

46 See Worthy, "The Angriest Negroes," 103.

47 See Thulani Davis, *Malcolm X*, 79. Also see the 1994 "American Experi-

ence" documentary, "Malcolm X: Make It Plain," directed by Orlando Bagwell.

48 See C. Eric Lincoln, *The Black Muslims in America*, 22–25.

49 See Hoffer, *The True Believer*, 31–49, 52.

50 Ibid., 55–56.

51 See "Recruits behind Bars," 14.

52 Ibid.

53 Ibid.

54 Ibid.

55 Ibid.

56 Ibid.

57 See Worthy, "The Angriest Negroes," 103.

58 Ibid.

59 See Joint Legislative Committee on un-American Activities, State of Louisiana, *Activities of "The Nation of Islam" or the Muslim Cult of Islam in Louisiana*, 13.

60 For a useful overview on representational links between cities and ex- oticism, danger, and otherness, see Orsi, "Introduction: Crossing the City Line," 1–40.

61 For examples see "'Black Supremacy' Cult in U.S.," 113–14; "The Black Supremacists," 25; and "The Muslim Message," 30.

62 See Haley, "Mr. Muhammad Speaks," 103.

63 See C. Eric Lincoln, "The Meaning of Malcolm X," 432.

64 See Worthy, "The Angriest Negroes," 102.

65 See C. Eric Lincoln, *The Black Muslims in America*, 211.

66 See Joint Legislative Committee on un-American Activities, State of Louisiana, *Activities of "The Nation of Islam" or the Muslim Cult of Islam in Louisiana*, 106.

67 See "'Go Ahead, Apostle,'" 58.

68 Ibid.

69 See Worthy, "The Angriest Negroes," 102; "The Black Supremacists," 25; C. Eric Lincoln, *The Black Muslims in America*, 166–69. On the other hand, See Lincoln, *The Black Muslims in America*, 220–27.

70 See Hentoff, "Elijah in the Wilderness," 37.

71 See "Enter Muhammad?" 520.

72 See Massaquoi, "The Mystery of Malcolm X," 44.

73 While the term "new religious movement" is now used by a large num- ber of scholars, it is still contested and hazily defined in various ways.

For some works that deal with issues of definition, see Ellwood and
Partin, *Religious and Spiritual Groups in Modern America*, 1–29; Timothy
Miller, ed., *America's Alternative Religions*, 1–9; and Saliba, *Understanding
New Religious Movements*, 107–9.

74 See Bruce Lincoln, *Discourse and the Construction of Society*, 165.

75 See Asad, *Genealogies of Religion*, 28. I agree with Asad's assertion that
   "there cannot be a universal definition of religion, not only because
   its constituent elements and relationships are historically specific, but
   because that definition is itself the historical product of discursive processes" (29).

76 See Silk, *Unsecular Media*, 57.

77 Ibid., 63.

78 See "The Muslim Message," 26.

79 See Southwick, "Malcolm X," 741.

80 See Jonathan Z. Smith, "Religion, Religions, Religious," 276.

81 See "'Go Ahead, Apostle,'" 58.

82 See Hartley and Montgomery, "Representations and Relations," 233.

83 See Stuart Hall, "The Spectacle of the 'Other,'" in *Representation*, ed.
   Hall, 245.

84 In regard to "symbolic power," Bourdieu argues, "Different classes and
   class fractions are engaged in a specifically symbolic struggle to impose the definition of the social world most in conformity with their
   interests." See Bourdieu, "Symbolic Power," 115.

85 See Stuart Hall, "The Spectacle of the 'Other,'" 259.

86 See C. Eric Lincoln, *The Black Muslims in America*, 128.

87 These quotes are taken from "Muhammad Speaks," an editorial on the
   newspaper by James O'Gara in *Commonweal*, 130.

88 See Marcus, *Lipstick Traces*, 168. For the two "manifestoes" of the Situationist movement, see Debord, *Society of the Spectacle*; and Vaneigem,
   The Revolution of Everyday Life.

89 See Marcus, *Lipstick Traces*, 179.

90 Ibid., 170.

91 Malcolm X asserted this frequently in interviews and public speeches.
   For one example, see Hentoff, "Elijah in the Wilderness," 39.

92 See Malcolm X with Haley, *The Autobiography of Malcolm X*, 224, 186,
   192.

93 See Jerry Mahrer, Letter to the Editor, *Nation*, 20 April 1963.

94 See Clarence Cooper Jr., "Aftermath," 165.

95 Ibid., 166.

96 See Crawford, "The Truth about the Black Muslims," 20.

97 See "The Black Supremacists," 25.

98 See Crawford, "The Truth about the Black Muslims," 21–22.

99 Ibid., 20.

100 Ibid., 21.

101 Ibid., 23.

102 Ibid., 22.

103 See Isaacs, "Integration and the Negro Mood," 490.

104 Ibid., 488.

105 See "'The White Devil's Day Is Almost Over,'" 25, 28.

106 See Gordon Parks, "'What Their Cry Means to Me,'" 81.

107 Ibid.

108 Ibid.

109 Baldwin's essay was reprinted in the two-essay collection *The Fire Next Time*, which has since gone through many editions and reprints. See Baldwin, *The Fire Next Time*, 72.

110 See Ibid., 64.

111 Ibid., 83.

112 Ibid., 73.

113 Ibid., 80.

114 Ibid., 86.

115 See "Despair Serves Purposes of Bizarre Cults," 917.

116 Ibid.

117 Ibid.

118 Ibid.

119 See Haley, "Mr. Muhammad Speaks," 104.

120 Because of this representational strategy, the Nation of Islam's image suffered the same fate that William Anselm and Kosta Gouliamos have suggested for ethnic literature. "In the same way, vital ethnic expressions are reappropriated by the hegemonic discourse . . . consider the polarization that occurs between national literature(s) and ethnic writing, in which the ethnic element is considered as a means of existential expression rather than having socio-cultural value." See Anselm and Gouliamos, "Exclusionary Representation: A Hegemonic Mediation," in *Mediating Culture*, ed. Anselm and Gouliamos, 122.

121 See "Death of a Desperado," 25.

122 For some of these additional articles not listed in the *Reader's Guide*, see Mildred Lusk, *Cults in the United States: Selected Bibliography of Sources in the Texas Tech Library* (Lubbock: Texas Tech University Library, 1982).

123 Malcolm X's departure (or expulsion) from the Nation of Islam is detailed in his autobiography.

124 For example, see Lichter, Rothman, and Lichter, *The Media Elite*, 296-97.

125 See "Now It's Negroes vs. Negroes in America's Racial Strife," 6.

126 Ibid.

127 See the "Man of the Year" cover story in *Time* on Martin Luther King Jr., 3 January 1964. For an example from a religious periodical, see "Civil Rights Now!" *Christian Century*, 20 November 1963, 1391.

128 These statistics come from Steigerwald, *The Sixties and the End of Modern America*, 210-11.

129 See "The Negro in America," *Newsweek*, 29 July 1963, cover.

130 See, for another example, "I Like the Word Black," 27-28.

131 See Hulsether, *Building a Protestant Left*, 48.

132 See "The Negro in America," 17.

133 Ibid., 30.

134 See Bogle, *Toms, Coons, Mulattoes, Mammies, and Bucks*, 7-8.

135 See "The Negro in America," 30-31.

136 Malcolm X went back on "Newsbeat" to suggest that Elijah Muhammad had fathered several illegitimate children with his secretaries. See "The Real Malcolm X."

137 See Ruth Boaz, "My Thirty Years with Father Divine," *Ebony*, May 1965, 88-98.

138 See "Death of a Desperado," 25; and "Malcolm X Slain," 21.

139 See Barnette with Linn, "The Black Muslims Are a Fraud," 24.

140 Ibid.

141 Ibid., 27.

142 Ibid., 25.

143 Ibid.

144 Ibid., 24.

145 Ibid., 24. According to C. Eric Lincoln, this is actually the plot of a second Louis X play, titled "The Trial." Lincoln writes that the musical "Orgena" and the play "The Trial" usually appeared together on a double bill. See Lincoln, *The Black Muslims in America*, 1-2.

146 See Cox, "Deep Structures in the Study of New Religions," 122-30.

147 See Bromley and Shupe, *Strange Gods*, 12.

148 See Barnette with Linn, 29.

149 Ibid., 26.

150 Ibid., 29.

151 Ibid., 25.

152 Ibid., 27.

153 Ibid.

154 See Gans, *Deciding What's News*, 61.

155 See Marty, *Under God, Indivisible, 1941-1960*, 7.

156 See "Ku Klux Klan's White Knights," 23. Also see "Next Step: Button-Down Robes," 23; and "The Ku Klux Klan on the Way Back," 51.

157 See "Ku Klux Klan's White Knights," 24.

158 See Binder, "Constructing Racial Rhetoric," 753-67. I found this article through a discussion of it by Michael Emerson and Christian Smith in *Divided by Faith*, 15-16.

159 See Binder, "Constructing Racial Rhetoric," 761.

160 Ibid.

161 See "The Original Black Capitalists," 21.

162 Ibid.

163 See "The Black Wasps," 8-9; and "Whatever Happened to the Black Muslims . . . Negroes Building Farm Empire." *U.S. News and World Report*, 21 September 1970, 83-84.

164 See "Black Capitalism in the Muslim Style," 44.

Chapter Three

1 See "Youth: The Hippies," 18.

2 Ibid., 21. The Hobbit is J. R. R. Tolkien's protagonist in his fantasy book of the same name. The religious historian Robert Ellwood reports that in 1966 *The Hobbit* led the "mass-paperback market with 700,000 copies in print." See Ellwood, *The Sixties Spiritual Awakening*, 134.

3 See, for example, Bromley and Shupe, *Strange Gods*. Bromley and Shupe also give brief overviews of each of these movements. For studies on media coverage of one group, see Shupe, "Constructing Evil as a Social Process," 205-16; and Shinn, *The Dark Lord*.

4 See Beckford, "The Mass Media and New Religious Movements," 104. Beckford's phrase "cult menace"—a term I borrow—appears on page 108.

5 Schachtman writes specifically of 1963-74. See Schachtman, *Decade of Shocks*.

6 The scholar and theologian Harvey Cox accurately noted that many Asian-based new religions like Hare Krishna drew little attention until they started attracting white, middle-class youth. See Cox, "Deep Structures in the Study of New Religions," 124-25.

7 See Gennari, "Bridging the Two Americas," 276.

8 Ibid.

9 See "On Evil: The Inescapable Fact," *Time*, 5 December 1969, 27.

10 Ibid.

11 See Engelhardt, *The End of Victory Culture*.

12 "In 1965," Engelhardt writes, "the time had already passed by when the enemy could prove themselves monstrous to Americans." See Engelhardt, *The End of Victory Culture*, 12.

13 See William G. McLoughlin, *Revivals, Awakenings, and Reform*.

14 See Wuthnow, *The Consciousness Reformation*. For a brief overview and critique of Wuthnow's thesis, see Robbins, *Cults, Converts, and Charisma*, 38.

15 See "The Search for Faith," *Life*, 9 January 1970, 17.

16 See Needleman, "Winds from the East," 188.

17 For Stark's assertion about the stability of numbers between the twenties and seventies, see Stark and Bainbridge, *The Future of Religion*, 234-62. For a similar argument that examines the fifties through the eighties, see Finke and Stark, *The Churching of America, 1776-1990*, 240-44.

18 See Galbreath, "Explaining Modern Occultism," 20-23.

19 See ibid., 18-19.

20 The exceptions were the Philippines and—to a lesser extent—Japan. For a brief description of the Immigration Act of 1924 and an excerpt from it, see Tweed and Prothero, eds., *Asian Religions in America*, 163-64.

21 Ibid., 224.

22 See Mathison, *Faiths, Cults, and Sects of America*, 34.

23 See Davies, *The Challenge of the Sects*, 20-21. Also see Niebuhr, *The Social Sources of Denominationalism*, 21.

24 See Davies, *The Challenge of the Sects*, 9, 7.

25 For a brief discussion of Christian Science's middle-class membership, see Gottschalk, *The Emergence of Christian Science in American Religious Life*, 256-59. For an even briefer mention of Theosophy's mostly middle-class membership, see Ellwood and Partin, *Religious and Spiritual Groups in Modern America*, 81. Stephen Prothero suggests that from its inception the Theosophy society attracted mostly educated professionals. See Prothero, *The White Buddhist*, 48-49.

26 See Lichter, Rothman, and Lichter, *The Media Elite*, 21.

27 See Kobler, "Out for a Night at the Local Caldron," 76.

28 In the United States, Neopaganism, and its largest branch Wicca, is one of the fastest-growing new religions of the early twenty-first century. For three of several book-length studies of the movement, see Pike, *Earthly Bodies, Magical Selves*; Margot Adler, *Drawing Down the Moon*; and Helen A. Berger, *A Community of Witches*.

29 See Aidan Kelly, "An Update on Neopagan Witchcraft in America," in *Perspectives on the New Age*, ed. James Lewis and J. Gordon Melton (Albany: SUNY Press, 1992), 136–51; and Carol Matthews, "Neopaganism and Witchcraft," in *America's Alternative Religions*, ed. Timothy Miller (Albany: SUNY Press, 1995), 339–45.

30 See Kobler, "Out for a Night at the Local Caldron," 76.

31 Ibid., 77.

32 Ibid.

33 See "The Power of Positive Chanting," 51.

34 For more on NSA, see Hurst, "Buddhism in America," 165–67; and Snow, "Organization, Ideology, and Mobilization," 153–72. Also see Hammond and MacHacek, *Soka Gakkai in America*. Nichiren Shoshu and Soka Gakkai International split in 1991. According to Tom Tweed and Stephen Prothero, NSA has 6 temples in the United States with 5,000 active members, while Soka Gakkai International USA has over 60 centers and about 50,000 members. See Tweed and Prothero, eds., *Asian Religions in America*, 281–82.

35 For a definition of Orientalism, see Said, *Orientalism*.

36 See "The Power of Positive Chanting," 51.

37 Ibid.

38 See "Happy Talk," 68.

39 Maharishi is an honorific title. For a brief background on Mahesh and a short history of the Transcendental Meditation movement, see Thursby, "Hindu Movements since Mid-Century," 193–95. For a longer overview of Mahesh and TM, see Mikael Rothstein, *Belief Transformations*, 25–33.

40 See "Soothsayer for Everyman," *Time*, 20 October 1967, 86.

41 Ibid.

42 Ibid.

43 See "The Guru," 67.

44 Ibid.

45 Wainwright, "Invitation to Instant Bliss."

46 See William Hedgepeth, "The Non-Drug Turn-On Hits Campus," 75.

47 Ibid.

48 See Era Bell Thompson, "Meditation Can Solve Race Problem, Says Maharishi Mahesh Yogi," *Ebony*, May 1968, 84.

49 Ibid., 88.

50 Ibid., 84.

51 Lennon later wrote the song "Sexy Sadie" about Mahesh. It contains the line, "What have you done, you made a fool of everyone." See Herbst, ed., *The Rolling Stone Interviews*, 136.

52 Ibid.

53 See "The Super Missionary," 26.

54 See Hurst, "Buddhism in America," 165–66.

55 See Godwin, *Occult America*; and Rachleff, *The Occult Conceit*.

56 See, for example, Melton, "The Other Spiritual Revival," 19–22; and Chandler, "The Occult Tumult," 43–45.

57 See Godwin, *Occult America*, 271–73.

58 See Godwin, *Occult America*, figures 43 and 44 (after p. 242).

59 See Ellwood, *The Sixties Spiritual Awakening*, 202.

60 For an article connecting LaVey's group, Espiritismo, and witchcraft, see "The Cult of the Occult," 96–97. For a book that includes ISKCON and other Eastern new religions under the occult tent, see Godwin's *Occult America*, 204–28.

61 See "The Occult," 62.

62 Ibid.

63 Ibid., 66.

64 Ibid.

65 See Vincent Bugliosi and Curt Gentry, *Helter Skelter: The True Story of the Manson Murders* (New York: W. W. Norton, 1969).

66 See "The Occult," 66.

67 Ibid.

68 See "The Cult of the Occult," 96.

69 Ibid.

70 Ibid.

71 For a broad overview and sociological interpretation of the Satanic cult legends of the eighties, see Victor, *Satanic Panic*. Also see Hicks, *In Pursuit of Satan*; and Richardson, Best, and Bromley, eds., *The Satanism Scare*.

72 For a list, see Victor, *Satanic Panic*, 330–54.

73 For an overview of "ritual abuse" and "cult survivor" narratives, see

Debbie Nathan, "Satanism and Child Molestation: Constructing the Ritual Abuse Scare," in Richardson, Best, and Bromley, eds., *The Satanism Scare*, 75–94; and Philip Jenkins and Daniel Maier-Katkin, "Occult Survivors: The Making of a Myth," in Richardson, Best, and Bromley, eds., *The Satanism Scare*, 127–44.

74 Interestingly, some local newspapers in the early seventies also proved sympathetic to Satanic cult rumors. Curtis MacDougall, for example, noted that on 13 June 1972 the *News-Sun* of Waukegan, Illinois, hinted at devil-worship in the area based on sales of occult books. See MacDougall, *Superstition and the Press*, 399.

75 See John Charles Cooper, *Religion in the Age of Aquarius*, 19.

76 Ibid., 117.

77 Ibid., 139.

78 Ibid., 163.

79 See Bercovitch, *The American Jeremiad*.

80 Cotton Mather's *Wonders of the Invisible World*, a collection of sermons published in 1693, provides a good example of such anti-occult jeremiads. For a secondary source that examines this literature, see Godbeer, *The Devil's Dominion*, esp. 55–84.

81 See "That New Black Magic," 42.

82 See "The Occult," 65.

83 See "The Cult of the Occult," 97.

84 See Herman S. Hughes, "All of Them Witches," 488.

85 See "The Occult," 68.

86 Ibid.

87 Ibid.

88 See Silk, *Unsecular Media*.

89 See Vachon, "The Jesus Movement Is upon Us," 21.

90 Ibid., 17.

91 Though this was not mentioned in *Look*, Edward E. Plowman noted it in the 29 January 1971 issue of *Christianity Today*, page 35.

92 See Vachon, "The Jesus Movement Is upon Us," 20.

93 See "The New Rebel Cry," 63.

94 See "The 'Jesus Movement,'" 60, 59.

95 See Peale, "We *Need* Their Faith!" 139.

96 Ibid., 140.

97 Ibid.

98 See ibid., 139.

99 See Edman, "Are You Disturbed by the 'New Religion?'" 198.

100 Ibid.

101 See "The Faith of the Young," 54.

102 Ibid.

103 Ibid.

104 See "Letters," *America*, 3 September 1966, 215.

105 See "The Answers," *America*, 26 November 1966, 687, 685.

106 See "The Gap between the Generations," 134–38.

107 For the positive view of the Jesus Movement taken by the *Catholic World*, see Jorstad, "The Greening of Revival," 265–68.

108 Rambur's story was briefly recounted in "Generation Gap," 90.

109 For historical and sociological studies of the Anti-Cult Movement, see Shupe and Bromley, "The Modern North American Anti-Cult Movement, 1971–91," 3–31; and Melton, "Anti-Cultists in the United States," 213–33. For an earlier fieldwork study of the movement, see Bromley and Shupe, *The New Vigilantes*.

110 For a brief history of the group, see David E. Van Zandt, "The Children of God," in Timothy Miller, ed., *America's Alternative Religions*, 127–32.

111 See Van Zandt, "The Children of God," 128. Berg's explicit promotion of free love, which he called sexual sharing, also suggested that sex between minors was appropriate. Some members interpreted this to condone sex between adults and children. After some accusations of public pedophilia and incest emerged, Berg—according to the Children of God—officially banned child sex and incest in 1987. See Van Zandt, "The Children of God," 129. For a work that candidly details the history of the group through members' own words, see Chancellor, *Life in the Family*.

112 See "The New Rebel Cry," 61.

113 Ibid., n.p., between pp. 56 and 59.

114 Ibid.

115 See Edward Plowman, "Where Have All the Children Gone?" 38.

116 Ibid.

117 Ibid., 39.

118 Ibid.

119 See "Whose Children?" 51.

120 Ibid.

121 Ibid.

122 Ibid., 53.

123 See "Generation Gap," 90.

124 See "Whose Children?" 53.

125 See "Generation Gap," 89–90.

Chapter Four

1 See "Mad about Moon," 44.

2 Ibid.

3 Ibid.

4 See Shupe, "Constructing Evil as a Social Process," 207. For a general introduction, see Barker, "The Unification Church," 223–29.

5 For a primary source that combines these allegations, see "The Darker Side of Sun Moon," 48–50. For a review of charges against the Unification Church, and suggestions that one of its centers in California did engage in deceptive proselytization, see Bromley and Shupe, *Strange Gods*, 92–127.

6 See van Driel and Richardson, "Print Media Coverage of New Religious Movements," 42–43. Using a selection of four prominent national newspapers and three news magazines, van Driel and Richardson counted a total of 781 pieces on the Unification Church between May 1972 and April 1984. The next-closest group was Scientology with 313. My research in mass market magazines found fewer than a dozen articles on Scientology for the entire period of study, leading me to believe that papers like the *New York Times*, the *Los Angeles Times*, the *Washington Post*, and the *San Francisco Chronicle* covered the group much more extensively.

7 See Carson Williams, "How Cults Bilk All of Us," 237–44; and Edwards, "Rescue from a Fanatic Cult," 129–33.

8 See Dulit and Best, "Could Your Child Be 'Brainwashed'?" 92; and "Behind the Cult Craze," 23–29.

9 See Beckford, "The Mass Media and New Religious Movements," 108.

10 See note 109 to chapter 2, above.

11 See Arthur Greil, "Sacred Claims: The 'Cult Controversy' as a Struggle over the Right to the Religious Label," in *Religion and the Social Order: The Issue of Authenticity in the Study of Religions*, ed. David G. Bromley and Lewis F. Carter (Greenwich, Conn.: JAI, 1996), 56–57.

12 See Bruce Lincoln, *Discourse and the Construction of Society*, 166.

13 See Catherine Lutz, "The Epistemology of the Bunker," 255. See also Edward Hunter, *Brain-Washing in Red China*. The Korean term, according to the psychiatrist Robert Jay Lifton, is "hsi nao," meaning "wash brain." See Lifton, *Thought Reform and the Psychology of Totalism*, 3.

14 See Lutz, "The Epistemology of the Bunker," 255.

15 See Pasley, *21 Stayed*, 227.

16 For examples of brainwashing in popular film, see Sconce, "Brains from Space," 277–302.

17 See Gilbert, *A Cycle of Outrage*, 155.

18 See Budrys, "Mind Control is Good/Bad," 106.

19 Ibid.

20 See "Hanoi's Pavlovians," 33.

21 Ibid., 34.

22 Ibid.

23 For a brief overview of the My-Lai massacre, see Engelhardt, *The End of Victory Culture*, 215–27.

24 See "Was She Brainwashed?" 33.

25 Ibid.

26 See "What Is Brainwashing?" 31.

27 Ibid.

28 Ibid.

29 See Lifton, *Thought Reform and the Psychology of Totalism*.

30 See Shinn, *The Dark Lord*, 127.

31 See Lifton, *Thought Reform and the Psychology of Totalism*, 4–5.

32 See Schein, Schneier, and Barker, *Coercive Persuasion*, 285.

33 Ibid.

34 See, for example, Bromley and Richardson, eds., *The Brainwashing/Deprogramming Controversy*.

35 See Zablocki, "The Blacklisting of a Concept," 97–122.

36 See Allen, "Brainwashed!" 26–36.

37 See David G. Bromley, "A Tale of Two Theories: Brainwashing and Conversion as Competing Political Narratives" (unpublished paper), 16.

38 See Pfeifer, "The Psychological Framing of Cults," 531–44.

39 Ibid., 536–37.

40 See Kenneth Woodward, "Life with Father Moon," 60.

41 See "Children of Doom," 90.

42 The quotes comes from an information box within a larger story on cults. See "Coping with Cults," *Seventeen*, July 1976, 107.

43 See Silk, *Unsecular Media*, 95. Though I argue that his dating is slightly early, I certainly agree about the importance of brainwashing in cult stories.

44 The monopolization of mass media in the last thirty years is well-documented. See Bagdikian, *The Media Monopoly*. Also see Ben Bag-

dikian, "The 26 Corporations That Own the Media," *EXTRA!* June 1987, cited in Schiller, *Culture Inc.*, 35, 177.

45 See Altschull, *From Milton to McLuhan*, 338.

46 For example, a study by Hart, Turner, and Knupp study of the religion page in *Time* from 1947 to 1976 found that 80 percent of all stories involved conflict. See Hart, Turner, and Knupp, "A Rhetorical Profile of Religious News," 61.

47 See van Driel and Richardson, "Print Media Coverage of New Religious Movements," 37, 46.

48 See Gans, *Deciding What's News*, 16, 14.

49 See Patrick with Dulack, *Let Our Children Go!*

50 See "Defreaking Jesus Freaks," 44.

51 Ibid.

52 Ibid.

53 Tom Dulack describes one deprogramming at length in *Let Our Children Go!* See Patrick with Dulack, 11–36.

54 See "Defreaking Jesus Freaks," 44.

55 Ibid.

56 Ibid.

57 Ibid.

58 Van Driel and Richardson also note journalists' negativity toward deprogramming in their study of selected newspapers and magazines. See Van Driel and Richardson, "Print Media Coverage of New Religious Movements," 58.

59 See "The Freedom to Be Strange," 81.

60 See "Kidnaping for Christ," 84.

61 Ibid.

62 See Willoughby, "'Deprogramming' Jesus Freaks and Others," 511.

63 Ibid.

64 Ibid.

65 Ibid.

66 Ibid.

67 Ibid.

68 Ibid.

69 See "Patrick: Deplugged," 38.

70 See Plowman, "Ted Patrick Acquitted," 40.

71 See "Kidnapping the Converts," 456.

72 Ibid.

73 Ibid.

74 Ibid.

75 See "Mr. Moon Waxes and Wanes," 162.

76 See ibid. See also Jaeger, "By the Light of the Masterly Moon," 305.

77 See Jaeger, "By the Light of the Masterly Moon," 308.

78 See Peerman, "Korean Moonshine," 1139.

79 See Van Dusen, "Force's Lessons for Others," 122.

80 See Peerman, "Korean Moonshine," 1139.

81 Ibid., 1141.

82 See "Open Season on Sects," 83.

83 See "Kidnapping for Christ," 83, 84.

84 See Eileen Keerdoja, "Rescuing Cultists," *Newsweek*, 12 February 1979, 17A.

85 See "Open Season on Sects," 83.

86 See "Freedom to Be Strange," 81.

87 See Silk, *Unsecular Media*, 142.

88 In answering the question of whose order is considered the norm, Gans asserts, "with some oversimplification, it would be fair to say that the news supports the social order of public, business and professional, upper-middle-class, middle-aged, and white male sectors of society." See Gans, *Deciding What's News*, 61.

89 See Bird and Dardenne, "Myth, Chronicle, and Story," 79.

90 The earliest sociological studies of cult "atrocity stories" examined newspaper articles on the Unification Church. See Bromley, Shupe, and Ventimiglia, "The Role of Anecdotal Atrocities in the Social Construction of Evil," 139–60. The authors argued that six categories of atrocities were regularly cited, including the physical, psychological, and economic. But they noted that the "core dimension underlying all the atrocities: loss of individual freedom." See p. 143.

91 Barend van Driel and James Richardson define an atrocity tale as "a description of an event or a series of events that has severe negative consequences for individuals, groups or society and that is perceived as being brought about by a new religious movement." See van Driel and Richardson, "Print Media Coverage of New Religious Movements," 52. David Bromley and his colleagues define an atrocity as "an event which is viewed as a flagrant violation of a fundamental cultural value. Accordingly, an atrocity tale is a presentation of that event (real or imaginary) in such a way as to (1) evoke moral outrage by specifying and detailing the value violations, (2) authorize, implicitly or explicitly, punitive sanctions, and (3) mobilize control efforts against the al-

leged perpetrators." See Bromley, Shupe, and Ventimiglia, "The Role of Anecdotal Atrocities in the Social Construction of Evil," 140.

92 See Maaga, *Hearing the Voices of Jonestown*, 25.

93 See Edwards, "Rescue from a Fanatic Cult," 129.

94 Ibid., 133.

95 See Warren Adler, "Rescuing David from the Moonies," 30.

96 Ibid.

97 Ibid., 28.

98 Ibid., 27.

99 Ibid., 30.

100 Ibid., 28.

101 See Robins, "Our Son's New 'Heavenly Father,'" 37.

102 Ibid., 80.

103 Ibid., 117.

104 "Why I Quit the Moon Cult," 117.

105 Ibid., 127.

106 Ibid.

107 Ibid.

108 Ibid.

109 Ibid.

110 Ibid.

111 See Crittenden, "The Incredible Story of Ann Gordon and Reverend Sun Myung Moon," 98.

112 See Maaga, *Hearing the Voices of Jonestown*, 26.

113 See Steigerwald, *The Sixties and the End of Modern America*, 255.

114 See Donald Miller and Arpi Misha Miller, "Understanding Generation X," 4.

115 See the cover of *Newsweek* for 12 March 1973, "The Broken Family."

116 See Carson Williams, "How Cults Bilk All of Us," 237–44; and Cornwell, "Those 'Guru' Cults," 96–100. Cornwell's article is especially interesting because of his position as religion editor for the Associated Press—a huge news bureau supplying national, international, and regional news stories to newspapers nationwide.

117 See Rice, "Honor Thy Father Moon," 36–37.

118 Ibid., 39.

119 Ibid., 41.

120 Ibid., 47.

121 Ibid.

122 Ibid.

123 Ibid.

124 See Letters, *Psychology Today*, May 1976, 8, 11.

125 Ibid., 11.

126 Ibid., 8,11.

127 Ibid., 11.

128 See Rasmussen, "How Sun Myung Moon Lures America's Children," 104.

129 Ibid., 175.

130 Ibid.

131 Ibid.

132 See Dulit and Best, "Could Your Child Be 'Brainwashed?'" 104.

133 Ibid., 126.

134 See Dulit and Best, "Could Your Child Be Brainwashed?" 104.

135 Ibid.

136 Ibid.

137 See Catherine Wessinger, Foreword, in Maaga, *Hearing the Voices of Jonestown*, xii.

138 See Barker, "Religious Movements," 329–46.

139 See Bourdieu, *Outline of a Theory of Practice*, 170.

140 Several useful works exist on the Peoples Temple and the Jonestown incident. See Chidester, *Salvation and Suicide*; John R. Hall, *Gone from the Promised Land*; and Maaga, *Hearing the Voices of Jonestown*.

141 Maaga argues that several of Jones's high-ranking officers, made up almost exclusively of educated, white, middle-class women, controlled the day-to-day activities at Jonestown and were likely responsible for having Jones call upon members to commit suicide. See Maaga, *Hearing the Voices of Jonestown*.

142 See "The Bizarre Tragedy in Guyana," 25.

143 See "Behind the Cult Craze," 23.

144 For the first quote, see "Why People Join," 27. For the second, see "How They Bend Minds," 72. Six journalists wrote the article in *Newsweek*, including Kenneth Woodward.

145 See "Why People Join," 27.

146 Ibid.

147 Ibid., 73.

148 Ibid.

149 See Stellway, "The Four Steps to Cultic Conversion," 26.

150 See "The Dark Night of Jonestown," 420.

151 Ibid., 420–21.

152 See "Cult Taxonomy," 1578.

153 See International Society of Krishna Consciousness, "An Appeal to Reason: Please Don't Lump Us In." The sociologist Eileen Barker gives the pamphlet an alternative name, "Please Don't Lump Us In: A Request to the Media," and identifies an author (Subhananda-das), date (1978), and place of publication (Los Angeles). See Eileen Barker, "Religious Movements," 329–46. I believe that the difference between my copy and Barker's is that mine is geared toward the Australian media.

154 For a general introduction to the movement, see Rochford, *Hare Krishna in America*.

155 See "An Appeal to Reason," 1.

156 Ibid., 13, 5.

157 Ibid., 14.

158 Ibid., 17.

159 See Paul DiMaggio, "Review Essay," 1470.

Chapter Five

1 See Friedman, "Cults," 202. Also see Harrison, "The Struggle for Wendy Helander," 88.

2 See Patrick with Dulack, *Let Our Children Go!* 118.

3 By 1992, for example, two-thirds of ISKCON's members lived outside of communes. See Rochford, "Hare Krishna in America," 219. Beginning in the late seventies, the Unification Church likewise allowed members to live noncommunally. See Barker, "The Unification Church," 228.

4 See "On the Trail of High Weirdness," *U.S. News and World Report*, 14 November 1988, 67.

5 Ibid.

6 Ibid.

7 See Hoover, *Religion in the News*, 23.

8 Ibid., 4.

9 See van Driel and Richardson, "Print Media Coverage of New Religious Movements," 57.

10 See Benjamin J. Hubbard, "The Importance of the Religion Angle in Reporting Current Events," in *Reporting Religion: Facts and Faith*, ed. Benjamin J. Hubbard (Sonoma, Calif.: Polebridge, 1990), 13.

11 See Judith Buddenbaum, "Religion News Coverage in Commercial Network Newscasts," in *Religious Television: Controversies and Conclusions*, ed. Robert Abelman and Stewart Hoover (Norwood, N.J.: Ablex, 1990),

251. Buddenbaum's quote was actually a summarization of another study. See Nimmo and Combs, *Nightly Horrors*.

12 See Lichter, Rothman, and Lichter, *The Media Elite*, 22.

13 See Silk, *Unsecular Media*, 39–42.

14 See, for example, the cover feature in *Newsweek* for 6 May 2002, "Sex and the Church."

15 For 1990 estimates of the American religious population, see Barry A. Kosmin and Seymour P. Lachman, *One Nation under God*, 3.

16 See Silk, *Unsecular Media*, 88.

17 Ibid.

18 See "Priests and Abuse," 42.

19 Ibid., 44.

20 Ibid.

21 See Greeley, "A View from the Priesthood," 45.

22 See Philip Jenkins, *Pedophiles and Priests*, 60.

23 Ibid., 61.

24 Ibid., 63.

25 Ibid., 15.

26 See "God and Money," *Newsweek*, 6 April 1987, 16.

27 For the *Newsweek* book, see Martz with Carroll, *Ministry of Greed*. See also Lichter, Rothman, and Lichter, *The Media Elite*, 22.

28 See Silk, *Unsecular Media*, 87.

29 See "TV's Unholy Row," 60.

30 See Kenneth L. Woodward and Mark Miller, "What Profits a Preacher? Revealing the Lifestyles of the Rich and Pious," *Newsweek*, 4 May 1987, 68.

31 Ibid.

32 See "God and Money," *Time*, 3 August 1987, 50.

33 See Woodward and Miller, "What Profits a Preacher?"

34 See "Heaven Can Wait," 59–60; and Woodward and Miller, "What Profits a Preacher?"

35 *Christian Century* paraphrased George Will's comment in an editorial criticizing media coverage of the PTL scandal. See "Preacher-Bashing and the Public Life," 347.

36 Ibid.

37 Ibid.

38 See Paul Hutchinson, "Have We a 'New' Religion?" 138.

39 For the "species" quote, see "Heaven Can Wait," 65. For the description of the "species," see "God and Money," *Newsweek*, 6 April 1987, 20.

40 See Bobby C. Alexander, *Televangelism Reconsidered*, 182.

41 See Christian Smith, *American Evangelicalism*.

42 See Christian Smith, *Christian America?* Smith provides several examples of recent journalistic and academic representations of Evangelicals. See, for example, 4–9, 92–93.

43 See "God and Money," *Newsweek*, 6 April 1987, 21.

44 See "Heaven Can Wait," 62.

45 Ibid.

46 Ibid., 61, 65.

47 Ibid.

48 See George Hackett with Deborah Witherspoon, "It Isn't the First Time: Scandal Has Rocked the Pulpit Long before Bakker's Fall," *Newsweek*, 6 April 1987, 23.

49 See Gael Sweeney, "The King of White Trash Culture," 249.

50 Ibid., 260.

51 See Richard Ostling, "The Church Search," *Time*, 5 April 1993, 44–49. Also see Wade Clark Roof and William McKinney, *American Mainline Religion* (New Brunswick: Rutgers University Press, 1987).

52 See Giddens, *The Constitution of Society*, 294.

53 See Hackett with Witherspoon, "It Isn't the First Time," 23.

54 Ibid.

55 See "Cultic America," 60.

56 See Said, *Orientalism*; and Mitchell, "Orientalism and the Exhibitionary Order," 289–317.

57 See Mitchell, "Orientalism and the Exhibitionary Order," 289.

58 See Richardson, Best, and Bromley, eds., *The Satanism Scare*; Hicks, *In Pursuit of Satan*; and Victor, *Satanic Panic*.

59 See Victor, *Satanic Panic*. For a definition of legend, see Fine, *Manufacturing Tales*, 1–44. One reservation I have about this definition is Fine's exclusion of memorates (personal experience stories). I agree with the folklorist Linda Dégh that a legend "often assumes the style of experience story, autobiography, rumor, and anecdote, and stresses personal involvement." Also, with Dégh, I suggest that contemporary legends can appear in any oral, literary, or visual media conduits. See Dégh, *American Folklore and Mass Media*, 28–29.

60 Ibid., 54.

61 See Ellis, *Raising the Devil*, 280.

62 See Bennetts, "Nightmares on Main Street," 42.

63 Ibid., 45.

64 Ibid., 48.

65 Ibid.

66 Ibid., 48–49.

67 See Elizabeth S. Rose, "Surviving the Unbelievable: A First-Person Account of Ritual Abuse," *Ms.*, January–February 1993, 40–45.

68 For some of the literature on false memory syndrome and satanic cult survivor stories, see Sherrill Mulhern, "Satanism and Psychotherapy: A Rumor in Search of an Inquisition," in Richardson, Best, and Bromley, eds., *The Satanism Scare*, 145–72. Also see Victor, *Satanic Panic*, 79–101.

69 See Lawrence Wright, *Remembering Satan*.

70 See Rose, "Surviving the Unbelievable," 40–41.

71 Ibid., 41.

72 Ibid., 44.

73 See Best, *Threatened Children*, 1–21.

74 Ibid., 2.

75 See Rose, "Surviving the Unbelievable," 43.

76 Ibid., 45.

77 See Shupe and Bromley, "The Modern North American Anti-Cult Movement, 1971–91," 19–20. For a comparison of Satanist and cult narratives, see David G. Bromley, "The Social Construction of Subversion: A Comparison of Anti-Religious and Anti-Satanic Cult Narratives," in *Anti-Cult Movements in Cross-Cultural Perspective*, ed. Anson Shupe and David G. Bromley (New York: Garland, 1994), 49–75.

78 See Rose, "Surviving the Unbelievable," 44.

79 See A. S. Ross, "Blame It on the Devil," 86.

80 Ibid., 116.

81 See Bailey and Darden, *Mad Man in Waco*, 193–96. This is just one of nearly a dozen "true crime" books to be published in the weeks and months after the fire.

82 See yet another true crime book, Lindecker, *Massacre at Waco, Texas*, photos pp. 120–21.

83 See Bailey and Darden, *Mad Man in Waco*, 185–86.

84 See Lindecker, *Massacre at Waco, Texas*, 184–86.

85 For a history of the Branch Davidians, see William Pitt Jr., "Davidians and Branch Davidians, 1929–1987," in *Armageddon in Waco*, ed. Stuart Wright, 20–42.

86 See Ellison and Bartowski, " 'Babies Were Being Beaten,' " 111–49.

87 See "The Questions Live On," 28–29.

88 See Morrow, "In the Name of God," 34.

89 See Lacayo, "In the Grip of a Psychopath," 34.

90 See Wall, "Eager for the End," 475.

91 See the cover of *Time*, 3 May 1993.

92 See "Day of Judgment," 23; "The Final Days of David Koresh," 28; and Lacayo, "In the Grip of a Psychopath," 34.

93 See Wall, "Eager for the End," 476.

94 Ibid., 475.

95 Ibid.

96 See Gelman, "From Prophets to Losses," 62; Wall, "Eager for the End," 475.

97 See Lacayo, "Cult of Death," 36.

98 See "Zealot of God," 38.

99 See Wall, "Eager for the End," 476. For another example, see "The Final Days of David Koresh," 28.

100 See DeVries, "David Koresh and the Apocalyptic Imagination," 3.

101 See "Thy Kingdom Come," 54; Lacayo, "Cult of Death," 36.

102 Portions of the video recordings can be seen in two documentaries, the PBS Frontline production *Waco: The Inside Story* and the Academy Award nominee *Waco: The Rules of Engagement* (Fifth Estate Productions, 1996).

103 See "Thy Kingdom Come," 55.

104 See "The Messiah of Waco," 56.

105 "The Final Days of David Koresh," 26.

106 Ibid., 34.

107 See David Leppard, *Fire and Blood: The True Story of David Koresh and the Waco Siege* (London: Fourth Estate, 1993), 22; Lindecker, *Massacre at Waco, Texas*, 145.

108 See Martin King and Marc Breault, *Preacher of Death* (New York and Victoria: Signet/Penguin, 1993), 86.

109 See Lindecker, *Massacre at Waco, Texas*, 28; and Leppard, *Fire and Blood*, 5.

110 See Leppard, *Fire and Blood*, 87.

111 See King and Breault, *Preacher of Death*, 44, 62.

112 See Leppard, *Fire and Blood*, 16.

113 See Lindecker, *Massacre at Waco, Texas*, 182.

114 Ibid., 247.

115 See Barkun, "Reflections after Waco," 597.

116 Ibid.

117 See Ivan Solotraff, "The Last Revelation from Waco," *Esquire*, July 1993, 55.

118 Ibid., 54, 118.

119 Ibid., 116.

120 See "The Book of Koresh," 27.

121 See "The Woe Outsiders Brought to Waco," 73.

122 See Lichter, Rothman, and Lichter, *The Media Elite*, 62.

123 A number of scholars contacted both press and government to give assistance—including Tabor and Arnold. See the numerous mentions of this throughout Stuart Wright's *Armageddon in Waco*.

124 See David Chidester, "Forum," 23.

125 See Lichter, Rothman, and Lichter, *The Media Elite*, 297.

126 See the cover of *Time*, 15 March 1993.

127 See Morrow, "In the Name of God," 34.

128 Ibid., 34–35.

129 See James M. Wall, "The Media's Dark Side," *Christian Century*, 24–31 March 1993, 307.

130 Ibid.

131 Ibid., 308.

132 Ibid.

133 See Martin E. Marty, "A Game of Inches," *Christian Century*, 12 May 1993, 535.

134 Ibid.

135 See Bourdieu, *Outline of a Theory of Practice*, 115.

136 See Hutchison, Preface, in *Between the Times*, ed. Hutchison, vii–xv.

137 Ibid., xi.

138 See Orsi, "Forum," 1–8; Orsi, "Beyond the Mainstream in the Study of American Religious History," 287–92.

139 See Orsi, "Forum."

140 See Roof, *A Generation of Seekers*, 71, 85.

141 Reincarnation is of course a widely shared belief in two fast-growing religions in the U.S.: Buddhism and Hinduism.

142 For an essay arguing that combination is a primary theme of American religion, see Albanese, "Exchanging Selves, Exchanging Souls," 200–226. For some examples of monographs that show such religious bricolage, see Braude, *Radical Spirits*; Davie, *Women in the Presence*; David D. Hall, *Worlds of Wonder, Days of Judgment*; and *The Occult in America*, ed. Kerr and Crow.

143 See, for example, Tweed, Introduction, 1–23; Jonathan Sarna, "Introduction: The Interplay of Minority and Majority in American Religion," in *Minority Faiths and the American Protestant Mainstream*, ed. Sarna, 1–11; and Orsi, "Forum," 1–8.

144 See Joel W. Martin, "Indians, Contact, and Colonialism in the Deep South," 159–60.

Epilogue

1 See Giddens, *Modernity and Self-Identity*.

BIBLIOGRAPHY

Abelman, Robert, and Stewart Hoover. *Religious Television: Controversies and Conclusions*. Norwood, N.J.: Ablex, 1990.

"Achievements of Elijah Muhammad, The." *Christian Century*, 26 March 1975, 301.

Adler, Margot. *Drawing Down the Moon: Witches, Druids, Goddess Worshippers, and Other Paganism America Today*. Rev. and expanded ed. New York: Penguin, 1986.

Adler, Warren. "Rescuing David from the Moonies." *Esquire*, 6 June 1978, 23–30.

"After the Raid." *Christianity Today*, 17 May 1993, 84–85.

Ahlstrom, Sydney E. *A Religious History of the American People*. New Haven: Yale University Press, 1972.

Albanese, Catherine L. "Exchanging Selves, Exchanging Souls: Contact, Combination, and American Religious History." In *Retelling U.S. Religious History*, ed. Thomas A. Tweed, 200–226. Berkeley: University of California Press, 1997.

Alexander, Bobby C. *Televangelism Reconsidered: Ritual in Search for Human Community*. Atlanta: Scholar's Press, 1994.

Alexander, Shana. "A Lust for Leadership." *Newsweek*, 7 January 1974, 29.

———. "The Ping Is the Thing." *Life*, 17 February 1967, 31.

Allen, Charlotte. "Brainwashed! Scholars Accuse Each Other of Bad Faith." *Lingua Franca*, December–January 1999, 26–36.

Altschull, J. Herbert. *From Milton to McLuhan: The Ideas behind American Journalism*. New York: Longman, 1990.

"Anglicans/Baptism: For Babies or Believers?" *Time*, 8 January 1965, 36.

"Anguishing Letters to Dad." *Time*, 11 December 1978, 30.

Anselm, William, and Kosta Gouliamos, eds. *Mediating Culture: The Politics of Representation*. Toronto: Guernica, 1994.

"Answers, The." *America*, 26 November 1966, 685–87.

Asad, Talal. *Genealogies of Religion: Discipline and Reasons of Power in Christianity and Islam*. Baltimore: Johns Hopkins University Press, 1993.

Bach, Marcus. "In the Church's Back Yard." *Christian Century*, 8 January 1958, 45–46.

————. *Strangers at the Door*. Nashville: Abingdon, 1971.

————. *Strange Sects and Curious Cults*. New York: Dodd, Mead, 1961.

————. *They Have Found a Faith*. Indianapolis: Bobbs-Merrill, 1946.

Bagdikian, Ben. *The Media Monopoly*. Boston: Beacon, 1983.

Bailey, Brad, and Bob Darden. *Mad Man in Waco*. Waco: WRS, 1993.

Baird, Robert. *Religion in America*. New York, 1844.

"Baiting the Hook." *Christianity Today*, 30 December 1977, 40–41.

Baldwin, James. *The Fire Next Time*. New York: Dial, 1963.

Balk, Alfred, and Alex Haley. "The Black Merchants of Hate." *Saturday Evening Post*, 26 January 1963, 68–75.

Baltzell, E. Digby. *The Protestant Establishment: Aristocracy and Caste*. New York: Random House, 1964.

"Baptism of the 'Jesus People.'" *U.S. News and World Report*, 20 March 1972, 62–63.

Barker, Eileen. "Religious Movements: Cult and Anti-Cult since Jonestown." *Annual Review of Sociology* (1986), 329–46.

————. "The Unification Church." In *America's Alternative Religions*, ed. Timothy Miller, 223–29. Albany: SUNY Press, 1995.

————. "Will the Real Cult Please Stand Up? A Comparative Analysis of Social Constructions of New Religious Movements." In *Religion and the Social Order: The Handbook of Cults and Sects in America*, vol. II, ed. David G. Bromley and Jeffrey K. Hadden, 193–212. Greenwich, Conn.: JAI, 1993.

Barkun, Michael. "Reflections after Waco." *Christian Century*, 2–9 June 1993, 596–600.

Barnette, Aubrey, with Edward Linn. "The Black Muslims Are a Fraud." *Saturday Evening Post*, 27 February 1965, 23–29.

Baughman, James L. *Henry R. Luce and the Rise of the American News Media*. Boston: Twayne, 1987.

Beckford, James A. "The Mass Media and New Religious Movements." In *New Religious Movements: Challenge and Response*, ed. Bryan Wilson and Jamie Cresswell, 103–19. New York: Routledge, 1999.

"Behind the Cult Craze." *U.S. News and World Report*, 4 December 1978, 23–24.

Bell, L. Nelson. "On 'Separation.'" *Christianity Today*, 8 October 1971, 26–27.

Bennetts, Leslie. "Nightmares on Main Street." *Vanity Fair*, June 1993.

————. "Unholy Alliances." *Vanity Fair*, December 1991.

Bercovitch, Sacvan. *The American Jeremiad*. Madison: University of Wisconsin Press, 1978.

Berger, Helen A. *A Community of Witches: Contemporary Neopaganism and Witchcraft in America Today*. Columbia: University of South Carolina Press, 1999.

Berger, Monroe. "The Black Muslims." *Horizon*, Winter 1964, 48–65.

Berry, John. "The Last Revelation from Waco." *Esquire*, July 1993.

Bess, Donovan. "A Rage for Awareness." *Nation*, 20 February 1967.

Best, Joel. *Threatened Children: Rhetoric and Concern about Child Victims*. Chicago: University of Chicago Press, 1990.

Beynon, Erdmann Doane. "The Voodoo Cult among Negro Migrants in Detroit." *American Journal of Sociology* 43 (July 1937–May 1938): 894–907.

Binder, Amy. "Constructing Racial Rhetoric: Media Depictions of Harm in Heavy Metal and Rap Music." *American Sociological Review*, December 1993, 753–67.

Bird, Elizabeth S., and Robert W. Dardenne. "Myth, Chronicle, and Story: Exploring the Narrative Qualities of News." In *Media, Myths, and Narratives: Television and the Press*, ed. James W. Carey, 67–86. London: Sage, 1988.

"Bizarre Tragedy in Guyana, The." *U.S. News and World Report*, 4 December 1978, 25–28.

Bjornstad, James. "America's Spiritual, Sometimes Satanic, Smorgasbord." *Christianity Today*, 23 October 1981, 28–29.

"Black Capitalism in the Muslim Style." *Fortune*, January 1970, 44.

"Black Muslim Hope, The." *Sports Illustrated*, 16 March 1964, 8.

"Black Muslims." *Nation*, 20 April 1963.

"Black Muslims on the Rampage." *U.S. News and World Report*, 13 August 1962, 6.

"Black Supremacists, The." *Time*, 10 August 1959, 24–25.

"'Black Supremacy' Cult in U.S.: How Much of a Threat?" *U.S. News and World Report*, 9 November 1959, 112–14.

"Black Wasps, The." *Trans-Action*, May 1969, 8–9.

Boaz, Ruth. "My Thirty Years with Father Divine," *Ebony*, May 1965, 88–98.

Bogle, Donald. *Toms, Coons, Mulattoes, Mammies, and Bucks: An Interpretive History of Blacks in American Films*. New York: Viking, 1973.

Bonnell, John Sutherland. "The Resurgence of Spiritism." *Christianity Today*, 1 March 1968, 7–10.

"Book of Koresh, The." *Newsweek*, 11 October 1993.

"Bo-Peep's Flock." *Newsweek*, 20 October, 1975.

Bourdieu, Pierre. "Cultural Reproduction and Social Reproduction." In *Knowledge, Education, and Cultural Change*, ed. Richard Brown, 71–112. London: Tavistock, 1973.

———. *Distinction: A Social Critique of the Judgment of Taste*. Trans. Richard Nice. Cambridge: Harvard University Press, 1984.

———. "The Genesis and Structure of the Religious Field." In *Comparative Social Research. A Research Annual. Religious Institutions*, vol. 13, ed. Craig Calhoun, 1–44. Greenwich, Conn.: JAI, 1991.

———. *On Television*. Trans. Priscilla Parkhurst Ferguson. New York: Free Press, 1998.

———. *Outline of a Theory of Practice*. Trans. Richard Nice. New York: Cambridge University Press, 1977.

———. "The School as a Conservative Force: Scholastic and Cultural Inequalities." In *Contemporary Research in the Sociology of Education*, ed. John Eggleston, 32–46. London: Methuen, 1974.

———. "Symbolic Power." In *Identity and Structure: Issues in the Sociology of Education*, ed. Dennis Gleason, 112–19. Dimiffield, England: Nefferton, 1977.

"Boy Guru." *Newsweek*, 2 August 1971, 72.

"Boy Tells of Chaining by Cultists." *Esquire*, March 1970, 114.

Braude, Ann. *Radical Spirits: Spiritualism and Women's Rights in Nineteenth-Century America*. Boston: Beacon, 1989.

"Bringing in the Ancestors." *Time*, 22 August 1969, 52.

"Brisker Status Quo, A." *Time*, 23 October 1972, 87–88.

Bromley, David G., and James T. Richardson. *The Brainwashing/Deprogramming Controversy: Sociological, Psychological, and Historical Perspectives*. New York: Edwin Mellen, 1983.

Bromley, David G., and Larry D. Shinn, eds. *Krishna Consciousness in the West*. Lewisburg: Bucknell University Press, 1989.

Bromley, David G., and Anson Shupe Jr. *The New Vigilantes: Anti-Cultists, Deprogrammers, and the New Religions*. Beverly Hills: Sage, 1980.

———. *Strange Gods: The Great American Cult Scare*. Boston: Beacon, 1981.

Bromley, David G., Anson Shupe Jr., and J. C. Ventimiglia. "The Role of Anecdotal Atrocities in the Social Construction of Evil." In *The Brainwashing/Deprogramming Controversy*, ed. David G. Bromley and James T. Richardson, 139–60. New York: Edwin Mellen, 1983.

Brossard, Chandler. "California's Offbeat Religions: 'We Love You.'" *Look*, 29 September 1959, 99–102.

Buddenbaum, Judith. "Religion News Coverage in Commercial Network Newscasts," in *Religious Television: Controversies and Conclusions*, ed. Robert Abelman and Stewart Hoover (Norwood, N.J.: Ablex, 1990), 251.

Budrys, A. J. "Mind Control Is Good/Bad." *Esquire*, May 1966, 106–9.

Burke, Tom. "Princess Leda's Castle in the Air." *Esquire*, March 1970.

". . . but the Klan." *America*, 9 May 1964, 619–20.

Calhoun, Craig, Edward Lipoma, and Moishe Postone, eds. *Bourdieu: Critical Perspectives*. Chicago: University of Chicago Press, 1993.

Carson, Robert. "Eccentricity under the Sun." *Holiday*, October 1965.

Carter, Lewis F. *The Issue of Authenticity in the Study of Religions*. Greenwich, Conn.: JAI, 1996.

Carter, Richard. "That Old-Time Religion Comes Back." *Coronet*, February 1958, 125–30.

Cary, Diana Serra. "The Land of Itching Ears." *Catholic World*, August 1955, 360–65.

"Challenge of Soka Gakkai, The." *Christianity Today*, 1 March 1968, 29.

"Challenge of the Cults, The." *Christianity Today*, 19 December 1960, 20–22.

Chancellor, James D. *Life in the Family: An Oral History of the Children of God*. Syracuse: Syracuse University Press, 2000.

Chandler, E. Russell. "The Occult Tumult." *Christianity Today*, 15 March 1974, 43–45.

Chidester, David. "Forum: Interpreting Waco." *Religion and American Culture*, Winter 1998, 17–25.

———. *Patterns of Power: Religion and Politics in American Culture*. Englewood Cliffs, N.J.: Prentice Hall, 1988.

———. *Salvation and Suicide: An Interpretation of Jim Jones, the Peoples Temple, and Jonestown*. Bloomington: Indiana University Press, 1988.

"Children of Doom." *Time*, 18 February 1974, 90.

"Children of God: New Revelations." *Christianity Today*, 24 February 1978, 44.

"Children of Moses." *Newsweek*, 28 October 1974, 70.

"Children of the Apocalypse." *Newsweek*, 3 May 1993, 30.

"Christian Science at 100." *Newsweek*, 20 June 1966, 74.

"Church in the News, A: Story of Mormon Success." *U.S. News and World Report*, 26 September 1966.

Clegg, Claude Andrew, III. *An Original Man: The Life and Times of Elijah Muhammad*. New York: St. Martin's, 1998.

"Clergy/Pastor Niemoller's Torpedoes." *Time*, 15 January 1965, 55.

Cogley, John. "The Enthusiasts." *Commonweal*, 2 August 1957, 448.

Cohen, Daniel. *The New Believers: Young Religion in America*. New York: M. Evans, 1975.

Colt, George Howe. "Last Trip to Waco." *Life*, October 1993.

"Comeback for Religious Cults, A?" *U.S. News and World Report*, 24 November 1980, 73–74.

Condit, Celeste Michelle. *Decoding Abortion Rhetoric: Communicating Social Change*. Urbana: University of Illinois Press, 1990.

Cook, Bruce. "Without Broomsticks." *Catholic World*, November 1966.

Cooper, Clarence, Jr. "Aftermath: The Angriest Negroes Revisited." *Esquire*, June 1961, 164–66.

Cooper, John Charles. *Religion in the Age of Aquarius*. Philadelphia: Westminster, 1971.

Cornell, George W. "Those 'Guru' Cults: Religion or Exploitation?" *Reader's Digest*, February 1976, 96–100.

Cowley, Susan Cheever. "Moon Rising." *Newsweek*, 26 May 1975, 63.

Cox, Harvey. "Deep Structures in the Study of New Religions." In *Understanding the New Religions*, ed. Jacob Needleman and George Baker, 122–30. New York: Seabury, 1978.

Crawford, Marc. "The Ominous Malcolm X Exits from the Muslims." *Life*, 20 March 1964, 40–40A.

——— . "The Truth about the Black Muslims." *Jet*, 3 September 1959, 18–23.

Cripps, Edward J. "Listening to Those Who Search." *America*, 18 September 1976, 147–48.

Crittenden, Ann. "The Incredible Story of Ann Gordon and Reverend Sun Myung Moon." *Good Housekeeping*, October 1976.

"Cultic America: A Tower of Babel." *Newsweek*, 15 March 1993, 60–61.

"Cultic Hordes, The." *Christianity Today*, 11 September 1961, 20.

"Cult of the Occult, The." *Newsweek*, 13 April 1970, 96–97.

"Cults: Meddling with Minds?" *Time*, 23 August 1968, 40–41.

"Cult Taxonomy." *National Review*, 22 December 1978, 1578.

Daniel, Walter C. *Black Journals of the United States*. Westport, Conn.: Greenwood, 1982.

"Darker Side of Sun Moon, The." *Time*, 14 June 1976, 48–50.

"Dark Night of Jonestown, The." *America*, 9 December 1978, 420–21.

Dart, John. "Covering Conventional and Unconventional Religion: A Reporter's View." *Review of Religious Research*, December 1997, 144–52.

Davie, Jody Shapiro. *Women in the Presence: Constructing Community and Seeking Spirituality in Mainline Protestantism*. Philadelphia: University of Pennsylvania Press, 1995.

Davies, Horton. *The Challenge of the Sects*. Philadelphia: Westminster, 1961.

Davis, David Brion. "Some Themes of Countersubversion: An Analysis of Anti-Masonic, Anti-Catholic, and Anti-Mormon Literature." *Mississippi Valley Historical Review*, September 1960, 205–24.

Davis, Thulani. *Malcolm X: The Great Photographs*. New York: Stewart Tabori and Chang, 1993.

Dawson, Christopher. "Civilization in Crisis." *Catholic World*, January 1956, 246–52.

"Day in the Life of the 'Children of God,' A" *U.S. News and World Report*, 20 March 1972, 65.

"Day of Judgment." *Newsweek*, 3 May 1993, 22–27.

"Death of a Desperado." *Newsweek*, 8 March 1965, 24–25.

Debord, Guy. *The Society of the Spectacle*. Detroit: Black and Red, 1983.

Debray, Regis. *Media Manifestos*. Trans. Eric Rauth. London: Verso, 1996.

"Defreaking Jesus Freaks." *Newsweek*, 12 March 1973, 44.

Dégh, Linda. *American Folklore and Mass Media*. Bloomington: Indiana University Press, 1994.

"Deprogrammer Patrick: Pressing His Case." *Christianity Today*, 11 October 1974, 50–51.

"Despair Serves Purposes of Bizarre Cults." *Christian Century*, 10 August 1960, 917.

"Devil and Mr. Patrick, The." *Senior Scholastic*, 10 January 1974, 14–17.

DeVries, Mark E. "David Koresh and the Apocalyptic Imagination." *Perspectives*, June 1993, 3–4.

DiMaggio, Paul. "Review Essay: On Pierre Bourdieu." *American Journal of Sociology* (1979), 1460–74.

"Dimensions of the Cult Conspiracy: An Interview with Ronald Enroth." *Christianity Today*, 23 October 1981, 26–27.

Doss, Erika, ed. *Elvis Culture: Fans, Faith, and Image*. Lawrence: University Press of Kansas, 1999.

————. *Looking at Life Magazine*. Washington: Smithsonian Press, 2001.

"Dug In for 'Doomsday.'" *Newsweek*, 18 July 1960, 59.

Dulit, Everett P., and Winfield Best, "Could Your Child Be 'Brainwashed?'"
Parents Magazine, November 1976.

"Echoes of Jonestown." *Newsweek*, 12 March 1979, 14–17.

"Ecumenicism: Chats under a Hot Tin Roof." *Time*, 2 August 1963, 40.

Edman, David A. "Are You Disturbed by the 'New Religion?'" *Reader's Digest*, February 1968.

Edwards, Charles H. "Rescue from a Fanatic Cult." *Reader's Digest*, April 1977, 129–33.

Ellis, Bill. *Raising the Devil: Satanism, New Religions, and the Media.* Lexington: University Press of Kentucky, 2000.

Ellison, Christopher G., and John P. Bartowski. "'Babies Were Being Beaten': Exploring Child Abuse Allegations at Ranch Apocalypse." In *Armageddon in Waco: Critical Perspectives on the Branch Davidian Conflict,* ed. Stuart A. Wright, 111–49. Chicago: University of Chicago Press, 1995.

Ellwood, Robert. *The Fifties Spiritual Marketplace: American Religion in a Decade of Conflict.* New Brunswick, N.J.: Rutgers University Press, 1997.

———. *The Sixties Spiritual Awakening: American Religion Moving from Modern to Postmodern.* New Brunswick, N.J.: Rutgers University Press, 1994.

Ellwood, Robert S., and Harry B. Partin. *Religious and Spiritual Groups in Modern America.* 2d ed. Englewood Cliffs, N.J.: Prentice-Hall, 1988.

Emerson, Michael, and Christian Smith. *Divided by Faith: Evangelical Religion and the Problem of Race in America.* Chicago: University of Chicago Press, 2000.

Englehardt, Thomas. *The End of Victory Culture: Cold War America and the Disillusioning of a Generation.* Amherst: University of Massachusetts Press, 1995.

"Enter Muhammad?" *National Review*, 2 July 1963, 519–21.

"Enterprising Evangelism." *Time*, 3 August 1987, 50–53.

Epstein, Richard. "Teaching Thought Control to Secondary Students." *Education Digest*, October 1975, 57–59.

Ettema, James S., and Theodore L. Glasser. "Narrative Form and Moral Force: The Realization of Innocence and Guilt through Investigative Journalism." *Journal of Communication*, Summer 1988, 8–26.

"Evangelism/God and Man on 800 Campuses." *Time*, 15 January 1965, 55.

"Face of Satan Photographed over Waco Fire!" *Weekly World News*, 18 May 1993, 42–43.

Fackler, P. Mark, and Charles H. Lippy, eds. *Popular Religious Magazines of the United States*. Westport, Conn.: Greenwood, 1995.

"Faith: Healthy v. Neurotic." *Time*, 2 April 1965.

"Faith of the Young, The: An Emerging Problem." *America*, 16 July 1966, 54–55.

"False Prophecy?" *Christianity Today*, 15 February 1974, 49.

"Fastest Growing Church in the Hemisphere." *Time*, 2 November 1962, 56.

"Fatal Prophecy Is Fulfilled, A." *Newsweek*, 10 March 1980, 46.

"Fellow Traveling with Jesus." *Time*, 6 September 1971, 54–55.

"Final Analysis." *Intercom: Published for the Employees of the Dallas Morning News*, June 1993, 2–6.

"Final Days of David Koresh, The." *U.S. News and World Report*, 3 May 1993.

Fine, Gary Alan. *Manufacturing Tales: Sex and Money in Contemporary Legends*. Knoxville: University of Tennessee Press, 1992.

Finke, Roger, and Rodney Stark. *The Churching of America, 1776-1990: Winners and Losers in Our Religious Economy*. New Brunswick, N.J.: Rutgers University Press, 1992.

Fleming, Eugene D. "California Cults and Crackpots." *Cosmopolitan*, May 1959, 80–84.

"Following the Leader." *Time*, 11 December 1978.

Foreman, Joel, ed. *The Other Fifties: Interrogating Midcentury Icons*. Urbana: University of Illinois Press, 1997.

Foster, Lawrence. "Cults in Conflict: New Religious Movements and the Mainstream Religious Tradition in America." In *Uncivil Religion: Interreligious Hostility in America*, ed. Robert Bellah and Frederick Greenspahn, 185–204. New York: Crossroad, 1987.

"Freedom to Be Strange, The." *Time*, 28 March 1977, 81.

Friedman, Robert. "Cults: Are Teens Being Brainwashed?" *Seventeen*, May 1979.

Fry, C. George. "Christianity's Greatest Challenge." *Christianity Today*, 7 November 1969, 9–12.

Fuller, Robert C. *Naming the Antichrist: The History of an American Obsession*. New York: Oxford University Press, 1995.

Fuller, W. Harold. "By the Light of the 'Saviourly' Moon." *Christianity Today*, 1 March 1974, 101–2.

Galbreath, Robert. "Explaining Modern Occultism." In *The Occult in*

America: New Historical Perspectives, ed. Howard Kerr and Charles L. Crow, 11-37. Urbana: University of Illinois Press, 1983.

Gamson, William A., and Andre Modigiliani. "Media Discourse and Public Opinion on Nuclear Power: A Constructionist Approach." *American Journal of Sociology*, July 1989, 1-37.

Gans, Herbert. *Deciding What's News: A Study of CBS Evening News, NBC Nightly News, Newsweek, and Time*. New York: Vintage, 1980.

"Gap between the Generations, The: An Open-Ended Reply." *Catholic World*, June 1967, 134-38.

Gaustad, Edwin, ed. *A Documentary History of Religion in America to the Civil War*. 2d ed. Grand Rapids: Eerdmans, 1993.

Gelman, David. "From Prophets to Losses." *Newsweek*, 15 March 1993, 62.

"General Reno Captures the Capital." *Newsweek*, 3 May 1993, 27.

"Generation Gap." *Newsweek*, 22 November 1971, 89-90.

Gennari, John. "Bridging the Two Americas: Life Looks at the 1960s." In *Looking at Life Magazine*, ed. Erika Doss, 261-77. Washington: Smithsonian Press, 2001.

Giddens, Anthony. *The Constitution of Society: A Theory of Structuration*. Berkeley: University of California Press, 1984.

————. *Modernity and Self-Identity: Self and Society in the Late Modern Age*. Stanford: Stanford University Press, 1991.

Gilbert, James. *A Cycle of Outrage: America's Reaction to the Juvenile Delinquent in the 1950s*. New York: Oxford University Press, 1986.

Gitlin, Todd. *The Whole World Is Watching: Mass Media in the Making and Unmaking of the New Left*. Berkeley: University of California Press, 1980.

Givens, Terryl L. *The Viper on the Hearth: Mormons, Myths, and the Construction of Heresy*. New York: Oxford University Press, 1997.

"'Go Ahead, Apostle.'" *Newsweek*, 13 March 1961, 58-59.

"God and Money." *Newsweek*, 6 April 1987, 16-22.

"God and Money." *Time*, 3 August 1987, 48-49.

Godbeer, Richard. *The Devil's Dominion: Magic and Religion in Early New England*. Cambridge: Harvard University Press, 1992.

Godwin, John. *Occult America*. Garden City, N.Y.: Doubleday, 1972.

Gottschalk, Stephen. *The Emergence of Christian Science in American Religious Life*. Berkeley: University of California Press, 1973.

Gray, Francine Du Plessix. "Exorcising Ourselves." *Vogue*, May 1974, 148-49.

Greeley, Andrew. "A View from the Priesthood." *Newsweek*, 16 August 1993, 45.

Griffith, R. Marie. *God's Daughters: Evangelical Women and the Power of Submission*. Berkeley: University of California Press, 1997.

Grossberg, Lawrence, ed. "On Postmodernism and Articulation: An Interview with Stuart Hall." *Journal of Communication Inquiry*, 1986, 45–60.

"Guru, The." *Newsweek*, 18 December 1967, 67.

Hafez, Kai, ed. *Islam and the West in Mass Media: Fragmented Images in a Globalizing World*. Cresskill, N.J.: Hampton, 2000.

Haley, Alex. "Mr. Muhammad Speaks." *Reader's Digest*, March 1960, 100–104.

Hall, David D. *Worlds of Wonder, Days of Judgment: Popular Religious Belief in Early New England*. Cambridge: Harvard University Press, 1990.

Hall, John R. *Gone from the Promised Land: Jonestown in American Cultural History*. New Brunswick, N.J.: Transaction, 1987.

———, ed. *Reworking Class*. Ithaca: Cornell University Press, 1997.

Hall, Stuart. "Culture, the Media, and the 'Ideological Effect.'" In *Mass Communication and Society*, ed. James Curran, Michael Gurevitch, and Janet Woolacott, 315–48. Beverly Hills: Sage, 1979.

———, ed. *Representation: Cultural Representations and Signifying Practices*. London: Sage, 1997.

Hammond, Phillip E., and David W. MacHacek. *Soka Gakkai in America: Accommodation and Conversion*. New York: Oxford University Press, 1999.

"Hanoi's Pavlovians." *Time*, 14 April 1967, 33.

"Happy Talk." *Newsweek*, 5 June 1972, 68.

Harding, Susan. "Representing Fundamentalism: The Problem of the Repugnant Cultural Other." *Social Research*, Summer 1991, 373–93.

"Hard Lessons from the Ashes." *Newsweek*, 3 May 1993, 31.

Harraway, Donna. *Simians, Cyborgs, and Women*. New York: Routledge, 1991.

Harrison, Barbara Grizzuti. "The Struggle for Wendy Hellander." *McCalls*, October 1979, 87–94.

Hart, Roderick, Kathleen Turner, and Ralph Knupp. "A Rhetorical Profile of Religious News: *Time*, 1947–76." *Journal of Communication*, Summer 1981, 58–68.

Hartley, John, and William Montgomery. "Representations and Power Relations: Ideology and Power in Press and TV News." In *Discourse and Communication,* ed. Teun A. van Dijk, 233–69. New York: Walter De Gruyter, 1985.

"Healing Ministry, The." *Time,* 16 June 1958, 82.

"Heaven Can Wait." *Newsweek,* 8 June 1987, 58–65.

Hedgepeth, William. "The Non-Drug Turn-On Hits Campus: Student Meditators Tune in to Maharishi." *Look,* 6 February 1968.

Henderson, John B. *The Construction of Orthodoxy and Heresy: Neo-Confucian, Islamic, Jewish, and Early Christian Patterns.* Albany: SUNY Press, 1998.

Henrikson, Margot A. *Dr. Strangelove's America: Society and Culture in the Atomic Age.* Berkeley: University of California Press, 1997.

Henry, Carl F. H. "Confronting Other Religions." *Christianity Today,* 1 August 1969, 31.

Hentoff, Nat. "Elijah in the Wilderness." *Reporter,* 4 August 1960, 37–40.

Herberg, Will. *Protestant Catholic Jew.* 2d ed. Garden City, N.Y.: Anchor, 1960.

Herbst, Peter, ed. *The Rolling Stone Interviews: Talking with the Legends of Rock and Roll, 1967-1980.* New York: St. Martin's, 1981.

Hexham, Irving, and Karla Poewe. *New Religions as Global Cultures: Making the Human Sacred.* Boulder: Westview, 1997.

Hicks, Robert. *In Pursuit of Satan: The Police and the Occult.* Buffalo: Prometheus, 1991.

Higginbotham, Evelyn Brooks. *Righteous Discontent: The Women's Movement in the Black Baptist Church, 1880-1920.* Cambridge: Harvard University Press, 1993.

"Hippies, The." *Time,* 7 July 1967, 18–22.

Hoekema, Anthony. *The Four Major Cults: Christian Science, Jehovah's Witnesses, Mormons, and Seventh-Day Adventists.* Grand Rapids: Eerdmans, 1963.

Hoffer, Eric. *The True Believer.* New York: Harper and Row, 1966.

Holifield, E. Brooks. *A History of Pastoral Care in America: From Salvation to Self-Realization.* Nashville: Abingdon, 1983.

Holley, Joe. "The Waco Watch." *Columbia Journalism Review,* May–June 1993, 50–53.

"Home for Christmas?" *Christianity Today,* 17 December 1971, 35.

Hoover, Stewart M. *Religion in the News: Faith and Journalism in American Public Discourse.* Thousand Oaks, Calif.: Sage, 1998.

Hoover, Stewart, and Knut Lundby, eds. *Rethinking Media, Religion, and Culture.* Thousand Oaks, Calif.: Sage, 1997.

Hopkins, Joseph M. "The Children of God: Disciples of Deception."
Christianity Today, 18 February 1977, 18–23.

"Horror Lives On, The." *Time*, 11 December 1978, 28.

Howard, John Robert. "Becoming a Black Muslim: A Study of
Commitment Processes in a Deviant Political Organization." Diss.,
Stanford University, 1965.

"How They Bend Minds." *Newsweek*, 4 December 1978.

"How Vatican II Turned the Church toward the World." *Time*,
17 December 1965, 24–25.

Hoyt, William R. "Zen Buddhism and the Alienation from Nature."
Christian Century, 7 October 1970, 1194–96.

Hubbard, Benjamin J. *Reporting Religion: Facts and Faith*. Sonoma, Calif.:
Polebridge, 1990.

Hudnut-Beumler, James. *Looking for God in the Suburbs: The Religion of the
American Dream and Its Critics, 1945–65*. New Brunswick, N.J.: Rutgers
University Press, 1994.

Hughes, Emmet John. "A Revolution for Christmas." *Newsweek*,
27 December 1965, 11.

Hughes, Herman S. "All of Them Witches." *America*, 16 November 1968,
488–89.

Hulsether, Mark. *Building a Protestant Left: Christianity and Crisis Magazine,
1941–93*. Knoxville: University of Tennessee Press, 1999.

Hunter, Edward. *Brain-Washing in Red China: The Calculated Destruction of
Men's Minds*. New York: H. Wolff, 1953.

Hunter, James Davison. *Culture Wars: The Struggle to Define America*. New
York: Basic Books, 1991.

Hurlup, Elisabeth, ed. *The Lost Decade: America in the Seventies*. Oakville,
Calif.: Aarhus University Press, 1996.

Hurst, Jane. "Buddhism in America: The Dharma in the Land of the Red
Man." In *America's Alternative Religions*, ed. Timothy Miller, 161–72.
Albany: SUNY Press, 1995.

Hutchinson, Paul. "Have We a 'New' Religion?" *Life*, 11 April 1955.

Hutchinson, William, ed. *Between the Times: The Travail of the Protestant
Establishment in America, 1900–1960*. New York: Cambridge University
Press, 1989.

"'I Like the Word Black.'" *Newsweek*, 6 May 1963, 27–28.

"Inside the Mosques." *Newsweek*, 4 November 1963.

International Society of Krishna Consciousness. "An Appeal to Reason:
Please Don't Lump Us In." n.p., n.d.

Isaacs, Harold R. "Integration and the Negro Mood." *Commentary*, December 1962, 487–97.

"It Isn't the First Time." *Newsweek*, 6 April 1987, 23.

Jacobs, Ronald N. *Race, Media, and the Crisis of Civil Society: From Watts to Rodney King*. New York: Cambridge University Press, 2000.

Jacobsen, Douglas, and William Vance Trollinger, Jr. *Re-Forming the Center: American Protestantism, 1900 to the Present*. Grand Rapids: Eerdmans, 1998.

Jaeger, Harry J., Jr. "By the Light of the Masterly Moon." *Christianity Today*, 19 December 1975, 13–16.

Jenkins, Philip. *Mystics and Messiahs: Cults and New Religions in American History*. New York: Oxford University Press, 2000.

———. *Pedophiles and Priests: Anatomy of a Contemporary Crisis*. New York: Oxford University Press, 1996.

Jenkins, Richard. *Pierre Bourdieu*. London: Routledge, 1992.

Jensen, Ros. "Watergate's Elmer Gantry." *Progressive*, April 1974, 6–7.

"'Jesus Movement,' The: Impact on Youth, Church." *U.S. News and World Report*, 20 March 1972, 59–64.

"Jesus People, The." *Newsweek*, 22 March 1971, 97.

"'Jesus Revolution,' The." *Reader's Digest*, December 1971, 135–38.

Johnson, Robert L. "Protestant Hangups with the Counter-Culture." *Christian Century*, 4 November 1970, 1318–20.

Joint Legislative Committee on Un-American Activities, State of Louisiana. *Activities of "The Nation of Islam" or the Muslim Cult of Islam in Louisiana*, Report no. 3, Baton Rouge, 9 January 1963.

"Jonestown Unleashes a Shower of Fallout." *Christianity Today*, 5 January 1979.

Jorstad, Erling. "The Greening of Revival: The Jesus Revolution and Other Signs." *Catholic World*, September 1971, 265–68.

"Judges and the Judged, The." *Christian Century*, 1 May 1957, 51.

"Judgment." *Christian Century*, 7 September 1955, 1027.

Kammen, Michael. *American Culture, American Tastes: Social Change and the 20th Century*. New York: Basic Books, 1999.

Kaplan, Jeffrey. "The Anti-Cult Movement in America: An History of Culture Perspective." *Syzygy*, 1993, 267–96.

Karpel, Craig. "California Evil." *Esquire*, March 1970.

Kerr, Howard, and Charles L. Crow. *The Occult in America: New Historical Perspectives*. Urbana: University of Illinois Press, 1983.

"Kidnaping for Christ." *Time*, 12 March 1973, 83–84.

"Kidnapping the Converts." *America*, 19 May 1973, 456.

Kloman, William. "Banality of the New Evil." *Esquire*, March 1970.

Kobler, John. "Out for a Night at the Local Caldron." *Saturday Evening Post*, 5 November 1966, 76–78.

Kosmin, Barry A., and Seymour P. Lachman. *One Nation under God: Religion in Contemporary American Society*. New York: Crown, 1993.

Kozol, Wendy. *Life's America: Family and Nation in Postwar Journalism*. Philadelphia: Temple University Press, 1994.

Krosney, Herbert. "America's Black Supremacists." *Nation*, 6 May 1961, 390–92.

"Ku Klux Klan on the Way Back, The." *U.S. News and World Report*, 19 October 1964, 51–52.

"Ku Klux Klan's White Knights." *Newsweek*, 21 December 1964, 22–24.

Lacayo, Richard. "Cult of Death." *Time*, 15 March 1993, 36–39.

————. "In the Grip of a Psychopath." *Time*, 3 May 1993, 34–35.

LaFarge, John. "The Black Muslims in America." *America*, 8 April 1961.

Lamont, Michelle, and Marcel Fourier, eds. *Cultivating Differences: Symbolic Boundaries and the Making of Inequality*. Chicago: University of Chicago Press, 1992.

Lang, Frances. "The Mormon Empire." *Ramparts*, September 1971, 37–43.

"Law and Ted Patrick, The." *Christianity Today*, 8 August 1975, 35–36.

"Legal Kidnaping." *Newsweek*, 20 August 1973, 52.

"Lesson of Malcolm X, The." *Saturday Evening Post*, 12 September 1964, 84.

"Letters: Problems and Hopes." *America*, 3 September 1966, 215.

Levine, Faye. "Where Marriages Are Arranged." *Harpers*, May 1974, 9.

Levine, Lawrence W. *Highbrow/Lowbrow: The Emergence of Cultural Hierarchy in America*. Cambridge: Harvard University Press, 1988.

Lewis, Gordon R. *Confronting the Cults*. Grand Rapids: Baker Book House, 1966.

Lichter, S. Robert, Stanley Rothman, and Linda S. Lichter. *The Media Elite*. Bethesda, Md.: Adler and Adler, 1986.

"Life with Father Moon." *Newsweek*, 14 June 1976, 60–66.

Lifton, Robert Jay. *Thought Reform and the Psychology of Totalism: A Study of "Brainwashing" in China*. New York: W. W. Norton, 1961.

Lincoln, Bruce. *Discourse and the Construction of Society*. New York: Oxford University Press, 1989.

Lincoln, C. Eric. "The Black Muslims." *Progressive*, December 1962, 43–47.

———. *The Black Muslims in America*. 3d ed. Grand Rapids: Eerdmans, 1994.

———. "The Meaning of Malcolm X." *Christian Century*, 7 April 1965, 431–33.

Lindecker, Clifford. *Massacre at Waco, Texas: The Shocking True Story of Cult Leader David Koresh and the Branch Davidians*. New York: St. Martin's, 1993.

Lindsell, Harold. "The American Scene: Are Cults Outpacing Our Churches?" *Christianity Today*, 19 December 1960, 3–5.

Lippy, Charles H., ed. *Religious Periodicals of the United States*. New York: Greenwood, 1986.

Logan, Daniel. *America Bewitched: The Rise of Black Magic and Spiritism*. New York: William Morrow, 1974.

Lomax, Louis. *When the Word Is Given*. Westport, Conn.: Greenwood, 1979.

"Lord Krishna's Children." *Newsweek*, 8 July 1974, 50.

"Lotus Power." *Newsweek*, 19 January 1970, 46.

"Lower Religions, The." *National Review*, 6 December 1974, 1394–95.

Lutz, Catherine. "The Epistemology of the Bunker: The Brainwashed and Other New Subjects of Permanent War." In *Inventing the Psychological: Toward a Cultural History of Emotional Life in America*, ed. Joel Pfister and Nancy Schnog, 245–67. New Haven: Yale University Press, 1997.

Lutz, Catherine A., and Jane L. Collins. *Reading National Geographic*. Chicago: University of Chicago Press, 1993.

Maaga, Mary McCormick. *Hearing the Voices of Jonestown: Putting a Human Face on an American Tragedy*. Syracuse: Syracuse University Press, 1998.

Maas, Peter. "What Might Have Been." *Parade*, 27 February 1994, 4–6.

"Mad about Moon." *Time*, 10 November 1975, 44.

"Magic Mountain, The." *Newsweek*, 30 July 1973, 40.

Malcolm X, with Alex Haley. *The Autobiography of Malcolm X*. New York: Ballantine, 1965.

"Malcolm X Slain: Vendetta by Rivals Feared." *Senior Scholastic*, 11 March 1965, 21.

Marcus, Greil. *Lipstick Traces: A Secret History of the Twentieth Century*. Cambridge: Harvard University Press, 1989.

Martin, Joel W. "Forum: Interpreting Waco." *Religion and American Culture*, Winter 1998, 8–17.

———. "Indians, Contact, and Colonialism in the Deep South: Themes for a Postcolonial History of American Religion." In *Retelling U.S. Religious History*, ed. Thomas A. Tweed, 149–80. Berkeley: University of California Press, 1997.

Martin, Walter. *Kingdom of the Cults*. Grand Rapids: Zondervan, 1965.

———. *The Rise of the Cults*. Grand Rapids: Zondervan, 1955.

———. *The Truth about Seventh-Day Adventism*. Grand Rapids, 1960.

Marty, Martin. "The Comet That Fizzled." *Christian Century*, 27 February 1974, 247.

———. *Under God, Indivisible, 1941–1960*. Vol. 3 of *Modern American Religion*. Chicago: University of Chicago Press, 1996.

Martz, Larry, with Ginny Carroll. *Ministry of Greed: The Inside Story of the Televangelists and Their Holy Wars*. New York: Weidenfeld and Nicolson, 1988.

Massaquoi, Hans J. "The Mystery of Malcolm X." *Ebony*, September 1964.

Mathison, Richard R. *Faiths, Cults, and Sects of America: From Atheism to Zen*. Indianapolis: Bobbs-Merrill, 1960.

May, Elaine Tyler. *Homeward Bound: America Families in the Cold War Era*. New York: Basic Books, 1988.

May, Larry, ed. *Recasting America: Culture and Politics in the Age of the Cold War*. Chicago: University of Chicago Press, 1989.

McCombs, Maxwell E., and Donald L. Shaw. "The Agenda-Setting Function of Mass Media." *Public Opinion Quarterly*, Spring 1972, 176–87.

McCutcheon, Russell T. *Manufacturing Religion: The Discourse of Sui Generis Religion and the Politics of Nostalgia*. New York: Oxford University Press, 1997.

McDougall, Curtis D. *Superstition and the Press*. Buffalo: Prometheus, 1983.

McFerran, Douglass. "Christianity and the Religions of the Occult." *Christian Century*, 10 May 1972, 541–45.

———. "Religion and the Occult." *America*, 11 March 1972, 254–57.

McKerns, Joseph P., ed. *Biographical Dictionary of American Journalism*. New York: Greenwood, 1989.

McLaughlin, John. "The New Religion: II." *America*, 24 February 1968, 274–76.

McLoughlin, William G. *Revivals, Awakenings, and Reform*. Chicago: University of Chicago Press, 1978.

Meerloo, Joost A. M. *The Rape of the Mind: The Psychology of Thought Control, Menticide, and Brainwashing*. Cleveland: World, 1956.

Melton, J. Gordon. "Anti-Cultists in the United States: An Historical Perspective." In *New Religious Movements: Challenge and Response*, ed. Bryan Wilson and Jamie Cresswell, 213–33. New York: Routledge, 1999.

————. "The Other Spiritual Revival." *Christianity Today*, 8 December 1972, 19–22.

Melton, J. Gordon, and Robert L. Moore. *The Cult Experience: Responding to the New Religious Pluralism*. New York: Pilgrim, 1982.

"Merseysiders at the Ganges." *Time*, 1 March 1968, 25.

"Messiah from the Midwest." *Time*, 4 December 1978.

"Messiah of Waco, The." *Newsweek*, 15 March 1993, 56–8.

Miller, Donald, and Arpi Misha Miller. "Understanding Generation X: Values, Politics, and Religious Commitments." In *Gen X Religion*, ed. Richard W. Flory and Donald E. Miller, 1–12. New York: Routledge, 2000.

Miller, Douglas T. "Popular Religion in the 1950s: Norman Vincent Peale and Billy Graham." *Journal of Popular Culture*, Summer 1975, 66–76.

Miller, R. DeWitt. "The Southern California Riddle." *American Mercury*, May 1956, 99–102.

Miller, Timothy, ed. *America's Alternative Religions*. Albany: SUNY Press, 1995.

Mindich, David T. Z. *Just the Facts: How Objectivity Came to Define American Journalism*. New York: New York University Press, 1998.

"Mr. Van Dusen's Discovery." *Christian Century*, 21 September 1955, 1090.

Mitchell, Timothy. *Colonizing Egypt*. Berkeley: University of California Press, 1988.

————. "Orientalism and the Exhibitionary Order." In *Colonialism and Culture*, ed. Nicholas B. Dirks, 289–317. Ann Arbor: University of Michigan Press, 1992.

Mizruchi, Susan, ed. *Religion and Cultural Studies*. Princeton: Princeton University Press, 2001.

"Moon Landing in Manhattan." *Time*, 30 September 1974, 68–69.

"Moon's Credibility Game." *Christian Century*, 24 September 1975, 812.

Moore, R. Laurence. *Religious Outsiders and the Making of Americans*. New York: Oxford University Press, 1986.

Morgan, David. "The Image of Religion in American Life, 1936–51." In *Looking at Life Magazine*, ed. Erika Doss, 139–58. Washington: Smithsonian Press, 2001.

"Mormons and the Negro." *Newsweek*, 6 March 1967, 69.

Morrow, Lance. "In the Name of God." *Time*, 15 March 1993, 34–35.

———. "*Time* Essay: The Lure of Doomsday." *Time*, 4 December 1978, 30.

Muhammad, Elijah. *Message to the Blackman in America*. Chicago: Muhammad Mosque of Islam no. 2, 1965.

"Muslim Message, The: All White Men Devils, All Negroes Divine." *Newsweek*, 27 August 1962.

"Muslim Rally." *Christian Century*, 22 March 1961, 372.

"Muslims vs. Muslims." *Newsweek*, 5 February 1973, 61–62.

Mydans, Carl. "The Third Force in Christendom." *Life*, 9 June 1958, 112–21.

"Nation of Islam Mourns Elijah Muhammad, The." *Ebony*, May 1975, 74–81.

Needleman, Jacob. "Winds from the East." *Commonweal*, 30 April 1971, 188–90.

"Negroes Building Farm Empire." *U.S. News and World Report*, 21 September 1970, 83–84.

"Negro Racists, The." *Nation*, 6 April 1963, 278.

Neitz, Mary Jo, and Goldman, Marion S., eds. *Sex, Lies, and Sanctity: Religion and Deviance in Contemporary North America*. Greenwich, Conn.: JAI, 1995.

Neuman, W. Russell, Marion R. Just, and Ann N. Crigler. *Common Knowledge: News and Political Construction of Meaning*. Chicago: University of Chicago Press, 1992.

Newcomb, Horace. "On the Dialogic Aspects of Mass Communication." *Critical Studies in Mass Communication*, 1984, 34–50.

"New Move by the Black Muslims, A." *U.S. News and World Report*, 11 March 1963, 14.

"New Rebel Cry, The: Jesus Is Coming!" *Time*, 21 June 1971, 56–63.

"New 'Reformation?,' A." *Newsweek*, 22 August 1955, 82.

"Next Step: Button-Down Robes." *Time*, 1 May 1964, 23.

Nicholl, Donald. "Do We Need a New Religion?" *Catholic World*, March 1957, 429–33.

Niebuhr, H. Richard. *The Social Sources of Denominationalism*. Cleveland: World, 1962.

"Nightmare in Jonestown." *Time*, 4 December 1978, 16–21.

Nimmo, Dan, and James E. Combs. *Nightly Horrors: Crisis Coverage by Television Network News*. Knoxville: University of Tennessee Press, 1985.

Nourie, Alan and Barbara Nourie, eds. *American Mass-Market Magazines*. New York: Greenwood, 1990.

"Now Hear the Message to the Black Muslims from Their Leader, Elijah Muhammad." *Esquire*, April 1963, 97–101.

"Now It's Negroes vs. Negroes in America's Racial Violence." *U.S. News and World Report*, 8 March 1965.

O'Brien, John A. "Why Do Our Religions Fight Each Other? A Leading Catholic Author Warns That Religious Intolerance, Hatred, and Bigotry Imperil Our Democratic Way of Life." *Look*, 21 February 1956.

"Occult, The: A Substitute Faith." *Time*, 19 June 1972, 62–69.

"Of God and Greed." *Time*, 8 June 1987, 70–74.

O'Gara, James. "Muhammad Speaks." *Commonweal*, 26 April 1963, 130.

———. "Muslims, Black and White." *Commonweal*, 18 January 1963, 428.

Oliver, Revilo P. "The Black Muslims." *American Opinion*, January 1963, 23–39.

"On from Yankee Stadium." *Time*, 2 August 1963, 40.

"On Popular and Unpopular Religion." *Christian Century*, 17 June 1959, 715–16.

"On the Trail of High Weirdness," *U.S. News and World Report*, 14 November 1988, 67.

"Open Season on Sects." *Time*, 20 August 1973, 83–84.

"Ordeal in the Desert: Making Tougher Soldiers to Resist Brainwashing." *Newsweek*, 12 September 1955, 33–35.

"Original Black Capitalists, The." *Time*, 7 March 1969, 21.

Orsi, Robert A. "Beyond the Mainstream in the Study of American Religious History." *Journal of Ecclesiastical History*, April 1992, 287–92.

———. "Forum: The Decade Ahead in Scholarship." *Religion and American Culture*, Winter 1993, 1–8.

———. "Introduction: Crossing the City Line." In *Gods of the City: Religion and the American Urban Landscape*, ed. Robert A. Orsi, 1–40. Bloomington: Indiana University Press, 1999.

Osborne, Grant R. "Countering the Cultic Curse." *Christianity Today*, 29 June 1979, 22–25.

"Paranoia and Delusions." *Time*, 11 December 1978, 35.

"Parents v. Moonies." *Newsweek*, 25 April 1977, 83.

Parks, Gordon. "'What Their Cry Means to Me': A Negro's Own Evaluation." *Life*, 31 May 1963.

Pasley, Virginia. *21 Stayed: The Story of the American GIs Who Chose Communist China: Who They Are and Why They Stayed*. New York: Farrar, Straus, and Cudahy, 1955.

Patrick, Ted, with Tom Dulack. *Let Our Children Go!* New York: E. P. Dutton, 1976.

"Patrick: Deplugged." *Christianity Today*, 26 July 1974, 38.

Patterson, Floyd. "Cassius Clay Must Be Beaten." *Sports Illustrated*, 11 October 1965.

Peale, Norman Vincent. "'We *Need* Their Faith!'" *Reader's Digest*, December 1971, 138–41.

Peerman, Dean. "Korean Moonshine." *Christian Century*, 4 December 1974, 1139–41.

"Peoples Temple Cult of Death The,." *Newsweek*, 4 December 1978.

Pfeifer, Jeffrey E. "The Psychological Framing of Cults: Schematic Representations and Cult Evaluations." *Journal of Applied Social Psychology*, 1992, 531–44.

Pike, Sarah M. *Earthly Bodies, Magical Selves: Contemporary Pagans and the Search for Community*. Berkeley: University of California Press, 2001.

Plowman, Edward E. "Deprogamming: A Right to Rescue?" *Christianity Today*, 7 May 1976, 38–39.

———. "'Help Us Get Our Children Back.'" *Christianity Today*, 12 March 1976, 45–46.

———. "Ted Patrick Acquitted: Open Season for Deprogrammers." *Christianity Today*, 31 August 1973, 40–41.

"Power of Positive Chanting, The." *Time*, 17 January 1969, 51.

"Preacher-Bashing and the Public Life." *Christian Century*, 15 April 1987, 347.

"Priests and Abuse." *Newsweek*, 16 August 1993, 42–44.

Procter, William. "Moon Eclipse." *Christianity Today*, 11 October 1974, 49–50.

"Prosperity and Protest." *Time*, 14 April 1967, 104.

Prothero, Stephen. *The White Buddhist: The Asian Odyssey of Henry Steel Olcott*. Bloomington: Indiana University Press, 1996.

"Quandary of Cults, The." *Time*, 18 December 1978, 52.

"Quest for Spiritual Survival, The." *Life*, 9 January 1970.

"Questions Live On, The." *Newsweek*, 3 May 1993, 28–29.

Rachleff, Owen. *The Occult Conceit*. Chicago: Cowles, 1971.

Rasmussen, Mark. "How Sun Myung Moon Lures America's Children." *McCall's*, September 1976.

"Reactions to Youth's Reactions." *America*, 24–31 December 1966, 828–30.

"Recruits behind Bars." *Time*, 31 March 1961, 14.

"Reformation or Restoration?" *Newsweek*, 12 September 1955.

"Religions of the Future." *America,* 17 December 1966, 793.

"Religious Cults: Is the Wild Fling Over?" *U.S. News and World Report,* 27 March 1978, 44–45.

"Religious Cults: Newest Magnet for Youth." *U.S. News and World Report,* 14 June 1976, 52–54.

"Rescuing Cultists." *Newsweek,* 12 February 1979, 17–17A.

"Rev. Mr. Moon Waxes and Wanes." *America,* 5 October 1974, 162.

Rice, Berkeley. "Honor Thy Father Moon." *Psychology Today,* January 1976.

Richardson, James T. "Definitions of Cult: From Sociological-Technical to Popular-Negative." *Review of Religious Research,* June 1993, 348–56.

———. "Manufacturing Consent about Koresh: A Structural Analysis of the Role of Media in the Waco Tragedy." In *Armageddon in Waco: Critical Perspectives on the Branch Davidian Conflict,* ed. Stuart A. Wright, 153–76. Chicago: University of Chicago Press, 1995.

Richardson, James T., Joel Best, and David G. Bromley, eds. *The Satanism Scare.* New York: Aldine De Gruyter, 1991.

Richardson, James T., and Barend van Driel. "Journalists' Attitudes toward New Religious Movements." *Review of Religious Research,* December 1997, 116–36.

———. "Public Support for Anti-Cult Legislation." *Journal for the Scientific Study of Religion,* 1984, 412–18.

Rifkind, Lawrence J., and Loretta F. Harper. "The Branch Davidians and the Politics of Power and Intimidation." *Journal of American Culture,* Winter 1994, 65–72.

"Rise and Fall of 'Holy Joe,' The." *Time,* 3 August 1987, 54–55.

"Rising Clamor for Black Separatism." *U.S. News and World Report,* 21 September 1970, 82.

Robbins, Thomas. *Cults, Converts, and Charisma: The Sociology of New Religious Movements.* Beverly Hills: Sage, 1988.

Robins, Lottie. "Our Son's 'Heavenly Father.'" *Saturday Evening Post,* September 1976.

Robinson, Louie. "The Kingdom of King Narcisse." *Ebony,* July 1963.

Rochford, E. Burke, Jr. *Hare Krishna in America.* New Brunswick, N.J.: Rutgers University Press, 1985.

———. "Hare Krishna in America: Growth, Decline, and Accommodation." In *America's Alternative Religions,* ed. Timothy Miller, 215–22. Albany, SUNY Press, 1995.

Rodman, Gilbert. *Elvis after Elvis: The Posthumous Career of a Living Legend.* London: Routledge, 1996.

"Roman Catholics: A Priest's Protest." *Time,* 8 January 1965, 36.

Roof, Wade Clark. *A Generation of Seekers: The Spiritual Journeys of the Baby Boom Generation.* New York: Harper San Francisco, 1993.

Ross, A. S. "Blame It on the Devil." *Redbook,* June 1994.

Ross, Andrew. *No Respect: Intellectuals and Popular Culture.* New York: Routledge, 1989.

Rothstein, Mikael. *Belief Transformations: Some Aspects of the Relation between Science and Religion in Transcendental Meditation (TM) and the International Society for Krishna Consciousness (ISKCON).* Oakville, Calif.: Aarhus University Press, 1996.

Rovere, Richard H. "The American Establishment." *Esquire,* May 1962.

Rowley, Peter. *New Gods in America: An Informal Investigation into the New Religions of American Youth Today.* New York: David McKay, 1971.

Rozak, Theodore. "Politics of the Nervous System." *Nation,* 1 April 1968, 439–43.

Said, Edward. *Covering Islam.* New York: Vintage, 1997.

———. *Orientalism.* New York: Vintage, 1979.

Saliba, John A. *Understanding New Religious Movements.* Grand Rapids: Eerdmans, 1995.

———. "Vatican Response to the New Religious Movements." *Theological Studies,* March 1992, 3–39.

Sanders, J. Oswald, and J. Stafford Wright. *Some Modern Religions.* London: Tyndale House, 1956.

Sarna, Jonathan, ed. *Minority Faiths and the Protestant Mainstream.* Urbana: University of Illinois Press, 1998.

Schachtman, Tom. *Decade of Shocks: Dallas to Watergate, 1963-74.* New York: Poseidon, 1983.

Schantz, Mark S. *Piety in Providence: Class Dimensions of Religious Experience in Antebellum Rhode Island.* Ithaca: Cornell University Press, 2000.

Schein, Edgar H., Inge Schneier, and Curtis H. Barker. *Coercive Persuasion: A Socio-Psychological Analysis of the "Brainwashing" of American Civilian Prisoners by the Chinese Communists.* New York: W. W. Norton, 1961.

Schiller, Herbert I. *Culture Inc.: The Corporate Takeover of Public Expression.* New York: Oxford University Press, 1989.

Schmalzbauer, Jon. "Between Professional and Religious Worlds:

Catholics and Evangelicals In American Journalism." *Sociology of Religion*, 1999, 363–86.

Sconce, Jeffrey. "Brains from Space: Mapping the Mind in 1950s Science and Cinema." *Science as Culture*, 1995, 277–302.

"Sect Leader: Fake Miracles and Secondhand Suits." *U.S. News and World Report*, 4 December 1978, 27.

"Sects: Run for Your Life." *Time*, 13 September 1968, 58.

"Sects: The Slaves of Leonard Freeney." *Time*, 1 January 1965, 45.

Sewell, William H., Jr. "A Theory of Structure: Duality, Agency, and Transformation." *American Journal of Sociology*, July 1992, 1–29.

Sherin, John B. "The New Religion." *Catholic World*, March 1971, 283–84.

Shinn, Larry D. *The Dark Lord: Cult Images and the Hare Krishnas in America*. Philadelphia: Westminster, 1987.

Shupe, Anson. "Constructing Evil as a Social Process: The Unification Church and the Media." In *Uncivil Religion: Interreligious Hostility in America*, ed. Robert N. Bellah and Frederick E. Greenspahn, 205–18. New York: Crossroad, 1987.

Shupe, Anson, and David G. Bromley. "The Modern North American Anti-Cult Movement, 1971–91: A Twenty-Year Retrospective." In *Anti-Cult Movements in Cross-Cultural Perspective*, ed. Anson Shupe and David G. Bromley, 3–31. New York: Garland, 1994.

Shupe, Anson, and Jeffrey K. Hadden. "Cops, News, and Public Opinion: Legitimacy and the Social Construction of Evil in Waco." In *Armageddon in Waco: Critical Perspectives on the Branch Davidian Conflict*, ed. Stuart Wright, 177–202. Chicago: University of Chicago Press, 1995.

Silk, Mark. "Journalists with Attitude: A Response to Richardson and van Driel." *Review of Religious Research*, December 1997, 137–43.

———. *Unsecular Media: Making News of Religion in America*. Urbana: University of Illinois Press, 1995.

Singer, Margaret Thaler. "Coming Out of the Cults." *Psychology Today*, January 1979.

"Sins of the Fathers." *Newsweek*, 12 July 1993, 57.

Slaughter, Cynthia. "To Another Planet—and Back." *Time*, 14 June 1976, 50.

Smith, Christian. *American Evangelicalism: Embattled and Thriving*. Chicago: University of Chicago Press, 1998.

———. *Christian America?: What Evangelicals Really Want*. Berkeley: University of California Press, 2000.

Smith, Jonathan Z. "Religion, Religions, Religious." In *Critical Terms for*

Religious Studies, ed. Mark C. Taylor, 269-84. Chicago: University of Chicago Press, 1998.

"Snake Power." *Time*, 1 November 1968, 86.

Snow, David A. "Organization, Ideology, and Mobilization: The Case of Nichiren Shoshu in America." In *The Future of New Religious Movements*, ed. David G. Bromley and Anson Shupe, 153-72. Macon: Mercer University Press, 1987.

Sobel, Mechal. *The World They Made Together: Black and White Values in Eighteenth Century Virginia*. Princeton: Princeton University Press, 1987.

"Sociologist Bellah Criticizes Jesus Movement." *Christian Century*, 10 May 1972, 540.

"Soothsayer for Everyman." *Time*, 20 October 1967, 86.

"Sorcery: A Prevalence of Witches." *Time*, 27 December 1963, 53.

Southwick, Albert B. "Malcolm X: Charismatic Demagogue." *Christian Century*, 5 June 1963, 740-41.

"Spectacular Rise of the Mormon Church, The." *Reader's Digest*, February 1967, 78-82.

Spittler, Russell P. *Cults and Isms: Twenty Alternatives to Evangelical Christianity*. Grand Rapids: Baker Book House, 1962.

Stark, Rodney, and William Sims Bainbridge. *The Future of Religion: Secularization, Revival, and Cult Formation*. Berkeley: University of California Press, 1985.

Steigerwald, David. *The Sixties and the End of Modern America*. New York: St. Martin's, 1995.

Stein, Stephen J. "History, Historians, and the Historiography of Indigenous Sectarian Religious Movements in America." In *Religious Diversity and American Religious History: Studies in Traditions and Cultures*, ed. Walter H. Conser Jr. and Sumner B. Twiss, 128-56. Athens: University of Georgia Press, 1997.

Stellway, Richard J. "The Four Steps to Cultic Conversion." *Christianity Today*, 29 June 1979, 24-26.

"'Straights' Meet 'Streets.'" *Christianity Today*, 29 January 1971, 35.

"Strangers among Us, The." *People*, 19 April 1993, 34-39.

Sugarman, Daniel, and Hochstein, Rollie. "Searching for a New Faith." *Seventeen*, September 1971.

"Super Missionary, The." *Time*, 13 January 1975, 26.

Swartz, David. "Bridging the Study of Culture and Religion: Pierre Bourdieu's Political Economy of Symbolic Power." *Sociology of Religion*, 1996, 71-85.

————. *Culture and Power: The Sociology of Pierre Bourdieu*. Chicago: University of Chicago Press, 1997.

Sweeney, Gael. "The King of White Trash Culture: Elvis Presley and the Aesthetics of Excess." In *White Trash: Race and Class in America*, ed. Matt Wray and Annalee Newitz, 249–66. New York: Routledge, 1997.

Taft, William. *Encyclopedia of Twentieth Century Journalists*. New York: Garland, 1986.

Talese, Gay. "Charlie Manson's Home on the Range." *Esquire*, March 1970.

Taves, Ann. *Fits, Trances, and Visions: Experiencing Religion and Explaining Experience from Wesley to James*. Princeton: Princeton University Press, 1999.

Taylor, Thomas F. *Christianity Today*, 25 October 1993, 25–27.

"Teens Explore New Frontiers of Faith." *Seventeen*, December 1969.

"Teens Talk about Religion." *Seventeen*, April 1967.

"That New Black Magic." *Time*, 27 September 1968, 42.

"Theology: Good Grief Charles Schulz!" *Time*, 1 January 1965, 44–45.

"Theosophy: Cult of the Occult." *Time*, 19 July 1968, 61.

Thompson, Era Bell. "Meditation Can Solve the Race Problem." *Ebony*, May 1968.

"Those Negro Muslims" *Reporter*, 29 September 1960, 10.

Thursby, Gene R. "Hindu Movements since Mid-Century: Yogis in the States." In *America's Alternative Religions*, ed. Timothy Miller, 191–214. Albany: SUNY Press, 1995.

"Thy Kingdom Come." *Newsweek*, 15 March 1993, 52–5.

"To a Greater Christian Church: Steady Ecumenical Progress Is Spurred by a Fresh Idea." *Life*, 19 December 1960, 24.

"Today's Rebellious Generation." *America*, 17 September 1966, 271–72.

Tolkien, J. R. R. *The Hobbit*. New York: Ballantine, 1966.

"Toward a Hidden God." *Time*, 8 April 1966, 82–87.

"Tracking the Children of God." *Time*, 22 August 1977, 48.

"TV's Unholy Row." *Time*, 6 April 1987, 60–65.

Tweed, Thomas A. Introduction. In *Retelling U.S. Religious History*, ed. Thomas A. Tweed, 1–23. Berkeley: University of California Press, 1997.

Tweed, Thomas A., and Stephen Prothero, eds. *Asian Religions in America: A Documentary History*. New York: Oxford University Press, 1999.

Udom, E. U. Essien. *Black Nationalism: A Search for an Identity in America*. Chicago: University of Chicago Press, 1962.

Unger, Merrill F. *Demons in the World Today: A Study of Occultism in the Light of God's Word*. Wheaton, Ill.: Tyndale House, 1971.

Vachon, Brian. "The Jesus Movement Is upon Us." *Look*, 9 February 1971, 15–21.

Van Baalen, Jan Karel. *The Chaos of the Cults: A Study in Present-Day Isms*. 4th ed. Grand Rapids: Eerdmans, 1962.

Van Driel, Barend, and James T. Richardson. "Print Media Coverage of New Religious Movements: A Longitudinal Study." *Journal of Communication*, Summer 1988, 37–61.

———. "Research Note: Categorization of New Religious Movements in American Print Media." *Journal of Communication*, 1988, 171–83.

Van Dusen, Henry P. "Caribbean Holiday." *Christian Century*, 17 August 1955, 946–48.

———. "Force's Lesson for Others." *Life*, 9 June 1958.

Vaneigem, Raoul. *The Revolution of Everyday Life*. London: Aldgate, 1983.

Van Zuilen, A. J. *The Life Cycle of Magazines: A Historical Study of the Decline and Fall of the General Interest Mass Audience Magazine in the United States during the Period 1946-1972*. Uithoorn, Netherlands: Graduate Press, 1977.

"Victims in the Company of Cults." *U.S. News and World Report*, 15 March 1993, 4–5.

Victor, Jeffrey. *Satanic Panic: The Creation of a Contemporary Legend*. Chicago: Open Court, 1993.

Vidal, Gore. *Messiah*. New York: Penguin, 1998. Orig. pubd. 1954.

"Waco Madman Is Still Alive!" *Weekly World News*, 18 May 1993, 44–45.

Wainwright, Loudon. "Invitation to Instant Bliss." *Life*, 10 November 1967.

Wall, James. "Eager for the End." *Christian Century*, 5 May 1993, 475–76.

———. "The Heart of Darkness." *Christian Century*, 13 December 1978, 1195–96.

Wallace, Mike, with Gary Paul Gates. *Close Encounters*. New York: William Morrow, 1984.

Walsh, Richard A. "'Moonies': Religious Converts or Psychic Victims?" *America*, 14 May 1977, 438–40.

Warnke, Michael, with Dave Balsinger and Les Jones. *The Satan-Seller*. Plainfield, N.J.: Logos International, 1972.

"Was She Brainwashed?" *Time*, 6 October 1975, 33.

"Way of the Cults, The." *Newsweek*, 7 May 1956.

Weaver, David H., and G. Cleveland Wilhoit. *The American Journalist: A Portrait of U.S. News People and Their Work*. 2d ed. Bloomington: Indiana University Press, 1991.

"What Is Brainwashing?" *Newsweek*, 1 March 1976, 31.

"What Price Syncretism?" *Time*, 6 May 1957, 88.

"Where Have All the Children Gone?" *Christianity Today*, 5 November 1971, 38–40.

"Whispered Faith, The." *Time*, 11 October 1971, 25.

"'White Devil's Day Is Almost Over, The.'" *Life*, 31 May 1963.

"White Muslims?" *Time*, 30 June 1975, 52.

"Whose Children?" *Time*, 24 January 1972.

"Why Black Muslims Are Focusing on the Nation's Capital Now." *U.S. News and World Report*, 27 May 1963, 24.

"Why Cults Turn to Violence." *U.S. News and World Report*, 4 December 1978, 28–29.

"'Why I Quit the Moon Cult.'" *Seventeen*, July 1976.

"Why People Join." *Time*, 4 December 1978, 27.

Williams, Carson. "How Cults Bilk All of Us." *Reader's Digest*, November 1979, 237–44.

Williams, Donald. "Close-up of the Jesus People." *Christianity Today*, 27 August 1971, 5–7.

Willoughby, William F. "'Deprogramming' Jesus Freaks and Others: Can America Tolerate Private Inquisitions?" *Christian Century*, 2 May 1973, 510–11.

"Witnesses, The." *Time*, 30 June 1961, 47.

"Witnessing the End." *Time*, 18 July 1969, 62–63.

"Woe Outsiders Brought to Waco, The." *U.S. News and World Report*, 4 October 1993.

Wolseley, Roland E. *The Black Press, U.S.A.* 2d ed. Ames: Iowa State University Press, 1989.

Woods, Richard J. "Jesus Freaks, Gurus, and Dissent." *Progressive*, June 1974, 27–30.

Woodward, Kenneth L. "Mixed Blessings." *Newsweek*, 16 August 1993, 38–41.

Woodward, Kenneth L., and Mark Miller, "What Profits a Preacher? Revealing the Lifestyles of the Rich and Pious," *Newsweek*, 4 May 1987, 68.

"World of Cults, The." *Newsweek*, 4 December 1978.

Worthy, William. "The Angriest Negroes." *Esquire*, February 1961, 102–5.

Wright, Lawrence. *Remembering Satan: A Case of Recovered Memory and the Shattering of an American Family*. New York: Alfred A. Knopf, 1994.

Wright, Stuart. "Media Coverage of Unconventional Religion: Any 'Good

News' for Minority Faiths?" *Review of Religious Research*, December
1997, 101–15.

———, ed. *Armageddon in Waco: Critical Perspectives on the Branch
Davidian Conflict*. Chicago: University of Chicago Press, 1995.

Wuthnow, Robert. *The Consciousness Reformation*. Berkeley: University of
California Press, 1976.

"Yes, It's Big—but Is It Beautiful?" *Time*, 23 October 1972, 87.

"'Yesterday's Message.'" *Newsweek*, 30 June 1975, 71.

"YMCA for Jews." *Time*, 1 January 1965, 44–45.

"Yogi on the Beach." *Newsweek*, 13 May 1968, 111–12.

Zablocki, Benjamin. "The Blacklisting of a Concept: The Strange History
of the Brainwashing Conjecture in the Sociology of Religion." *Nova
Religio*, October 1997, 97–122.

"Zealot of God." *People*, 15 March 1993, 38–43.

Zimmerman, Thomas F. "Where Is the 'Third Force' Going?" *Christianity
Today*, 1 August 1960, 15–18.

INDEX

and reductionist, 11; on media influence, 19; on prophets, 52

Brainwashing, 4, 20, 53, 98, 127–37; and David Koresh, 180–83; and Korean War, 130–31; and Vietnam War, 131–32; views of in religious studies, 134–35

Branch Davidians, 4, 13, 177–88

Breault, Marc, 180, 183–84

Bromley, David, 15, 176–77; on apostate tales, 89; on brainwashing, 135

Brownson, Orestes, 32

Buckley, William F., 70, 158

Buddha, 97

Budrys, A. J., 131

Bureau of Alcohol, Tobacco and Firearms (ATF), 4, 177

California cults, 2, 10, 25–26, 33–37; as zealous, 43

Carson, Robert, 34

Carter, Richard, 41

Cary, Diana Serra, 50

Catholic priest sex abuse, 164–65, 193

Catholic World, 13, 46; on California cults, 50–51; on generation gap, 121

Center and periphery: boundaries drawn between, 32; Evangelical boundaries between, 47, 48; language of, 12, 189–90

Challenge of the Sects, 102

Chaos of the Cults, 48

Chidester, David, 186

Children of God, 122–25, 148, 173

Christian Century, 13, 18; on Branch Davidians, 180, 182, 185, 187–88;

on deprogramming, 139–40; on Nation of Islam, 68, 71–72, 80; on PTL Club media coverage, 168–69; on Third Force, 25, 49; on Unification Church, 142

Christianity and Crisis, 30

Christianity Today, 5, 13, 46; on Children of God, 123–24; on cults, 49; on deprogramming, 140; on Jonestown, 157; on Third Force, 46–47; on Unification Church, 141–42

Christian Science, 102; as cult, 47

Church of Jesus Christ of Latter Day Saints, 31, 32; Evangelical view of, 47

Church of Satan, 111–12

Church of Scientology, 128

Church of the Nazarene, 25

Class, 7, 10; and cult explosion, 102; and stereotypes in Nation of Islam reporting, 67–68, 73; and televangelism scandal reporting, 169–71

Clegg, Claude Andrew, 59

Coercive Persuasion, 134

Cogley, John, 51–52

Cold War: articulation of exotic and zealous during, 27, 37–39; consensus ideology of, 3, 6; containment, 38–39

Collins, Jane, 17

Combating Cult Mind-Control, 177

Commentary, 14; on Nation of Islam, 77

Commonweal, 46, 100; on Nation of Islam, 74; on sects, 51

Communism, 55; containment of, 38–39

Kammen, Michael, 40
Kennan, George, 38
King, Martin, 183–84
King, Martin Luther, Jr., 58, 84–85
Kingdom of the Cults, 44; brain-
washing mentioned in, 53
Kobler, John, 103–4
Koresh, David, 19, 175, 180–87. *See
also* Branch Davidians
Kozol, Wendy, 17, 18, 53, 60
Krosney, Herbert, 65
Ku Klux Klan, 65, 90, 92

Ladies Home Journal, 14
Lafarge, John, 63, 64
LaVey, Anton, 111, 112
LeMoult, John, 138–39
Lennon, John, 109
Leppard, David, 183–84
Let Our Children Go!, 137
Levine, Lawrence, 40
Lewis, Gordon, 48
Lichter, Robert, 16, 164, 186
Liebman, Rabbi Joshua, 29
Life, 2, 5, 6, 7, 8, 49, 99, 188; on
increasing religious pluralism
in 1960s, 100; on Nation of
Islam, 78; on Transcendental
Meditation, 108
Life is Worth Living, 29
Lifton, Robert Jay, 133, 134
Lincoln, Bruce, 70
Lincoln, C. Eric, 56, 61, 65–68
Lindecker, Clifford L., 183
Lindsell, Harold, 49
Linn, Edward, 87
Lomax, Louis, 61
Look, 2, 6, 31, 136; on Jesus move-
ment, 117; on Judaism, 30; on

Transcendental Meditation,
108; on WKFL, 33–34
Los Angeles Herald Dispatch, 60
Lowbrow, 39–40
Luce, Henry, 8, 26, 164; and cul-
tural consensus, 36, 60; and
Time, Inc., 8, 17; use of "low-
brow," 40; and Vietnam, 8–9, 99
Lutz, Catherine, 17, 130
Lynes, Russell, 40

Maaga, Mary, 144, 148–49
MacLean's, 1
Mad Man in Waco, 183
Magazines: general-interest and
special-interest, 14, 16. *See also*
Newsmagazines; *and the names
of individual magazines*
Maharishi, Mahesh Yogi, 101,
107–10
Mainstream, 7, 189; boundaries
of, 36, 45; and brainwashing,
4, 20, 53–54, 98, 127–37; cover-
age of, 17–18; left undefined in
coverage, 26; marginalization
of, 162–66; as normative, 28; as
Protestant establishment, 28; as
triple melting pot, 30
Malcolm X, 66; assassination of,
81–84; on brainwashing, 53
The Manchurian Candidate, 53
Manson, Charles, 175. *See also*
Manson family
Manson family, 112–13, 157, 160
Marcus, Greil, 74
Marshall, Thurgood, 62
Martin, Joel, 190–91
Martin, Walter, 44, 47; on brain-
washing, 53

Marty, Martin, 91, 187–88, 189

Massacre at Waco, Texas, 183

Massaquoi, Hans, 70

Mass media: multiple authorship in, 17; and social control, 60; stories as polysemic, 18

Mass movements, 2, 54, 64, 80, 92. See also *The True Believer*

Mathison, Richard, 44, 102

May, Elaine Tyler, 38

McCall's, 4, 144, 151–52, 160

McLoughlin, William, 100

McPherson, Aimee Semple, 172

The Media Elite, 164

Messiah, 53

Miller, Samuel, 37

Mitchell, Timothy, 173

Mizruchi, Susan, 12

Montgomery, Martin, 72–73

Moon, Sun Myung, 127, 157. *See also* Unification Church

Moonies. *See* Unification Church

Morgan, David, 29

Mormons. *See* The Church of Jesus Christ of Latter Day Saints

Morse, Samuel, 32

Ms., 175–77

Muhammad, Elijah, 57–58, 66, 70

Muhammad Speaks, 74

My Lai massacre, 99, 132

The Nation, 14; on Nation of Islam, 65

National Association of Evangelicals, 30, 46

The National Review, 14; on cults, 158; on Nation of Islam, 70

Nation of Islam, 2, 5, 14, 32, 188; and communism, 59–63, 66; dem-ographics of, 65–66; FBI monitoring of, 58–59; and foreign connections, 62–63; history and theology of, 57–59; as religious fraud, 69–73; as social mirror, 73–81; as subversive mass movement, 59–68; as successful capitalists, 93–94; television reports on, 16, 61; and violence, 65

Nativism, 32

Needleman, Jacob, 100

Neopaganism, 103, 111

New Amsterdam News, 60

Newsbeat, 61

Newsmagazines, 13, 16. *See also* Magazines; *and the names of individual newsmagazines*

Newsweek, 1, 5, 7, 49, 188; on brainwashing, 133, 136, 155–57; on Branch Davidians, 179, 180–83; on California cults, 25–26, 49; on Catholic priest sex abuse, 164–65; on Children of God, 125; on cults, 173; on deprogramming, 137–38, 143; on Jonestown, 155–57; on Ku Klux Klan, 92; on Nation of Islam, 65, 69, 71, 81, 87; and "Negro in America" poll, 86–87; on occult, 113, 116–17; on PTL Club, 166–68, 170–72; on Transcendental Meditation, 107–8; on Unification Church, 136

The New Yorker, 1–2, 13; James Baldwin essay in, 78

Nichiren Shoshu Sokkagakkai International of America (NSA), 104, 110

Niebuhr, H. Richard, 102

O'Brien, John, 31, 38
Occult, 3, 97–98, 111–17; definition of, 101
Occult America, 111
The Occult Conceit, 111
O'Gara, James, 74
Orientalism, 173
Orsi, Robert, 11, 189–90
Ostling, Richard, 164

Parent's Magazine, 128, 151–53
Parks, Gordon, 78
Pasley, Virginia, 130–31
Patrick, Ted, 137, 138, 140–41, 160
Peace of Mind, 29
Peale, Norman Vincent, 29; on Jesus movement, 118
Pentecostalism, 25, 38, 42, 138
People, 182
Peoples Temple, 14, 153–57. See also Jonestown
Perspectives, 182
Pfeifer, Jeffrey, 135–36
Pittsburgh Courier, 60
Plowman, Edward, 123–24, 140
The Power of Positive Thinking, 29
Prabhupada, C. Bhaktivedanta Swami, 101, 158
Praise the Lord (PTL) Club, 166–72
Preacher of Death, 183
Protestant Catholic Jew, 29. See also Herberg, Will
Prothero, Stephen, 101
Psychology Today, 150–51

Race, 7, 10; and Nation of Islam stories, 73
Rachleff, Owen, 111
Raelians, 192–93

Raising the Devil, 174
Rasmussen, Mark, 151–52
Reader's Digest, 4, 144; on cults, 128; on Jesus movement, 118, 120; on Nation of Islam, 68, 80–81; on Unification Church, 145
The Reader's Guide to Periodical Literature, 13, 14, 82, 84, 150, 163
Redbook, 177
Religion in the Age of Aquarius, 115
Religious periodicals, 14, 16
Remembering Satan, 175
Reno, Janet, 179
Reporter, 70
Representation, 12–13
Rice, Berkeley, 150–51
Richardson, James, 128, 136, 163
Riots, 84–85
The Rise of the Cults, 47
Ritual abuse. See Satanic cult legends
Rivera, Geraldo, 113, 174
Robbins, Lottie, 146–47
Robinson, Louie, 33
Rodman, Gilbert, 20
Rolling Stone, 109
Roman Catholics, 32; reporting by, 49–52; reporting on, 25, 49; reversing mainstream/fringe classifications, 52–53, 188. See also Catholic priest sex abuse
Roof, Wade Clark, 190
Rose, Elizabeth, 175–77
Rosemary's Baby, 111
Ross, A. S., 177
Ross, Andrew, 39, 44–45

Said, Edward, 173
Samson and Goliath, 192

Tweed, Thomas, 11, 15, 101
Twenty-One Stayed, 130–31

U.S. News and World Report, 2, 5;
    on Branch Davidians, 182–83;
    on cults, 128, 155, 161; on Jesus
    movement, 118; on Jonestown,
    155; on Nation of Islam, 55,
    82–84, 93
Unification Church, 98, 127–28,
    145–51, 160, 173. *See also* Moon,
    Sun Myung
Upanishads, 107

Vachon, Brian, 118
Van Baalen, Jan Karel, 48
Van Driel, Barend, 128, 136, 163
Van Dusen, Henry, 20, 49; on
    Third Force, 25, 38, 41
Vanity Fair, 174–75
Van Zuilen, A. J., 6
Vatican II. *See* Second Vatican
    Council

Vedanta Society, 26
Venta, Krishna, 34, 148
Victor, Jeffrey, 113, 174
Vidal, Gore, 53
Vietnam: coverage of, 84

Wainright, Loudon, 108
Wall, James, 180, 187–88
"White trash," 170–71
Will, George, 168
Willoughby, William, 139–40
Wisdom, Knowledge, Faith, and
    Love Fountain of the World
    (WKFL), 33–36, 53, 148
Woodward, Kenneth, 164, 167, 173
Worthy, William, 67–69
Wright, Lawrence, 175
Wuthnow, Robert, 100

Zablocki, Benjamin, 135
Zimmerman, Thomas, 46–47